SELF-RESTRAINT

V.

SELF-INDULGENCE

SELF-RESTRAINT

V.

SELF-INDULGENCE

M. K. GANDHI

GYAN

Published by

Gyan Publishing House
5, Ansari Road
Daryaganj, New Delhi-110002
Phone: 011-47034999, 9811692060
E-mail: books@gyanbooks.com

Distribution Network
gyanbooks.com
India, USA, Canada, UK, Australia

ISBN: 978-93-7014-464-4 (HB)

First Published, 1947

2nd Impression 2025

Printed at: Gyan Press, Delhi.

SELF-RESTRAINT V. SELF-INDULGENCE

Author: M. K. Gandhi

SELF-RESTRAINT

v.

SELF-INDULGENCE

BY

M. K. GANDHI

1947

PUBLISHER'S NOTI

Till now this book was issued in two separate volumes; the reader will find in this new edition both of them issued in one. The collection has been revised and brought up-to-date. Thus, the reader will find, collected under one cover, all the writings of Gandhiji on this important subject.

September, 1947

PREFACE TO THE THIRD EDITION

It is gratifying to note that the third edition of this volume is required by the public. I wish that I had time to add one or more chapters to the volume, but I cannot delay publication so that I might add the chapters. I would have done so if I could be sure of finding the time needed for it.

From what, however, I have discovered from the letters that regularly come to me from inquirers, I would like to issue this definite warning : Those who believe in self-restraint must not become hypochondriacs. The letters that come to me show that many correspondents brood over their ill-success in the exercise of self-restraint. Like everything else that is good, self-restraint too requires an inexhaustible store of patience. There is absolutely no reason to despond, and there must be no brooding. There should be no conscious effort to drive away evil thoughts. That process is itself a kind of indulgence.

The best prescription perhaps is non-resistance, i. e , ignoring the existence of evil thoughts and a continuous pre-occupation with duties that lie in front of one. This presupposes the existence of some kind of all-absorbing service requiring the concentration of mind, soul and body upon it. "Idle hands some mischief still will ever find to do", is never so applicable as in this case. Evil thoughts, much more evil deeds are impossible when we are thus pre-occupied. Strenuous labour in accordance with one's physical capacity is, therefore, absolutely necessary for those who will obey the law of self-restraint which is indispensable for individual as well as universal progress.

Satyagraha Ashram,
Sabarmati,
3rd August, 1928

M. K. GANDHI

PREFACE TO THE SECOND EDITION

That the first edition was sold out practically within a week of its publication, is a matter of joy to me. The correspondence that the series of articles collected in this volume has given rise to, shows the need of such a publication. May those who have not made self-indulgence a religion, but who are struggling to regain lost self-control which should under normal conditions be our natural state, find some help from a perusal of these pages. For their guidance the following instructions may prove needful :

1. Remember if you are married that your wife is your friend, companion and co-worker, not an instrument of sexual enjoyment.

2. Self-control is the law of your being. Therefore, the sexual act can be performed only when both desire it, and that too subject to rules which in their lucidity both may have agreed upon.

3. If you are unmarried you owe it to yourself, to society and to your future partner to keep yourself pure. If you cultivate this sense of loyalty, you will find it as an infallible protection against all temptation.

4. Think always of that Unseen Power which, though we may never see, we all feel within us as watching and noting every impure thought, and you will find that Power ever helping you.

5. Laws governing a life of self-restraint must be necessarily different from a life of self-indulgence. Therefore you will regulate your society, your reading, your haunts of recreation and your food.

You will seek the society of the good and the pure.

You will resolutely refrain from reading passion-breeding novels and magazines and read the works that sustain humanity. You will make one book your constant companion for reference and guidance.

You will avoid theatres and cinemas. Recreation is where you may not dissipate yourself but recreate yourself. You will, therefore, attend *bhajan-mandalis* where the word and the tune uplift the soul.

You will eat not to satisfy your palate but your hunger. A self-indulgent man lives to eat; a self-restrained man eats to live Therefore, you will abstain from all irritating condiments, alcohol which excites the nerves, and narcotics which deaden the sense of right and wrong. You will regulate the quantity and time of your meals.

6. When your passions threaten to get the better of you. go down on your knees and cry out to God for help. *Ramanama* is my infallible help As extraneous aid take a hip-bath, i. e., sit in a tub full of cold water with your legs out of it, and you will find your passions have immediately cooled. Sit in it for a few minutes unless you are weak and there is danger of a chill.

7. Take brisk walking exercise in the open air early in the morning and at night before going to bed.

8. 'Early to bed and early to rise, makes a man healthy, wealthy and wise,' is a sound proverb. 9 o'clock to bed and 4 o'clock to rise is a good rule. Go to bed on an empty stomach. Therefore, your last meal must not be after 6 p. m.

9. Remember that man is a representative of God to serve all that lives and thus to express God's dignity and love. Let service be your sole joy, and you will need no other enjoyment in life.

M. K. GANDHI

CONTENTS

PART I

Gandhiji's Writings

PART II

Extracts from Mahadev Desai's Weekly Letters

Appendices

1

'TOWARDS MORAL BANKRUPTCY'

I

Kind friends continue to send me cuttings from Indian newspapers approvingly dealing with the question of birth control by the use of contraceptives. My correspondence with young men on their private conduct is increasing. I am able to discuss in these pages only an infinitesimal portion of the questions raised by my correspondents. American friends send me literature on the subject, and some are even angry with me for having expressed an opinion against the use of contraceptives. They deplore that as an advanced reformer in many ways I should be mediaeval in my views about birth control. I find too that the advocates of the use of contraceptives number among them some of the soberest of men and women of all lands.

I therefore thought that there must be something very decisive in favour of the methods advocated, and felt too that I should say on the subject more than I have done. Whilst I was thinking of the problem and of the question of reading the literature on the subject, a book called *Towards Moral Bankruptcy* was placed in my hands for reading. It deals with this very subject and, as it appears to me, in a perfectly scientific manner. The original is in French by M. Paul Bureau and is entitled '*D' Indiscipline des moeurs* which literally means 'the indiscipline of morals'. The translation is published by Constable and Company and has an introduction by Dr. Mary Scharlieb, C. B. E., M. D., M. S. (Lond.). It covers 538 pages in 15 chapters.

Having read the book I felt that, before I summarized the author's views, I must in justice to the cause read the standard literature in favour of the methods advocated.

I consequently borrowed from the Servants of India Society such literature as they had on the subject. They have very kindly lent me some of the books in their possession. Kaka Kalelkar, who is studying the subject, has given me Havelock Ellis' volumes specially bearing on the subject, and a friend has sent me the special number of *The Practitioner* in which is collected some valuable medical opinion from well-known practitioners.

My purpose in collecting literature on the subject was to test the accuracy, so far as a layman could, of M. Bureau's conclusions. One often finds that there are two sides to questions even when scientists discuss them and that there is much to be said for either side. I was anxious, therefore, to know the viewpoints of the advocates of contraceptives before I introduced to the reader M. Bureau's volume. I have come to the deliberate conclusion that, so far at least as India is concerned, there is no case for the use of contraceptives. Those who advocate their use for Indian conditions either do not know them or choose to ignore them. But if it can be proved that the methods advocated are harmful even in the West, it would be unnecessary to examine the special Indian conditions.

Let us therefore see what M. Bureau has to say. His studies are confined to France. But France means much. It is considered to be one of the most advanced countries in the world, and if the methods have failed in France, they are not likely to succeed elsewhere.

Opinions may differ as to the meaning of the word 'failure'. I must therefore define the word as it is here meant. The methods must be proved to have failed, if it can be shown that moral bonds have loosened, that licentiousness has increased, and that instead of the check having been exercised by men and women for purposes of health and economic limitation of families only it has been used principally for feeding animal passions. This is the moderate position. The extreme moral position condemns the use of contraceptives in every conceivable circumstance, it being contended that it is not necessary for man or woman to satisfy the sexual instinct except when the act is meant for race reproduction, even as it is not necessary for man or woman to eat except for sustaining the body. There is also the third position. There is a class of men who contend that there is no such thing as morality, or that, if there is, it consists not in exercising restraint but in indulgence of every form of animal appetite, so long as it does not so impair the constitution as to render it unfit for the very indulgence which is its object. For this extreme position I do not suppose M. Bureau has written his volume. For M. Bureau concludes his book by quoting Tom Mann's saying, "The future is for the nations who are chaste".

In the first part of his book M. Bureau has collected facts which make most dismal reading. It shows how vast organizations have sprung up in France which merely pander to man's basest tastes. Even the one claim of the advocates of contraceptives that abortions must disappear with the use of these methods cannot be sustained. "It is certain," says M. Bureau, "that during the twentyfive years that have especially seen the increase in France of anti-conceptionist methods, the number of criminal abortions has not become less". M. Bureau is of opinion that abortions are on the increase. He puts down the figure at anything between 275,000 and 325,000 per year. Public opinion does not look upon them with the horror that it did years ago.

II

"In the wake of abortion," says M. Bureau, "come infanticide, incest, and crimes that outrage nature. There is nothing special to say about the first, except that the crime has become more frequent in spite of all the facilities offered to unmarried mothers and of the extension of anti-conceptionist practices and abortion. It no longer arouses the same reprobation among so-called respectable people, and juries usually return a verdict of 'not guilty'."

M. Bureau devotes a full section to the growth of pornographic literature. He defines it as "the exploitation, with an erotic or obscene intention, of the resources which literature, the drama, and pictures place at men's disposal for their mental refreshment and repose." And he adds, "In every branch of its business it has secured markets, the extent of which may be gauged by the ingenuity and excellent commercial organization of the directors, the enormous amount of capital, the unexampled perfection of the methods employed." "The impression experienced has been so strong and so unique that the whole psychological life of the individual is affected by it," and "a sort of secondary sexual life, which exists wholly in the imagination, is created."

M. Bureau then quotes this pathetic paragraph from M. Ruyssen :

"All pornographic and sadic literature secures in this psychological law the most powerful enticement which it exerts over an innumerable number of readers, and the flourishing circulation of this literature shows beyond dispute that those who live a secondary sexual life through their imagination are legion, not to mention those in lunatic asylums — especially in a period like our own, when the abuse of newspapers and books creates around all consciences what W. James calls 'a plurality of under-universes', in which each can lose himself, and forget, along with himself, the duties of the present hour."

These disastrous consequences, it should never be forgotten, are a direct result of one single fundamental error, namely that sexual indulgence for its own sake is a human necessity, and that without it neither man nor woman reaches his or her full growth. Immediately a person becomes possessed of such an idea and begins to look upon what in his estimation was at one time a vice as a virtue, there is no end to the multiplication of devices that would excite animal passions and help him to indulge in them.

M. Bureau then gives chapter and verse to show how the daily press, the magazine, the pamphlet, the novel, the photograph and the theatre increasingly pander to and provide for this debasing taste.

But the reference hitherto has been to the decay of morals amongst unmarried people. M. Bureau next proceeds to show the measure of moral indiscipline in the married state. He says: "Among the aristocracy, the middle class, and the peasants, vanity and avarice are responsible for a vast number of marriages." "Marriage is entered upon also to obtain an advantageous post, to join two properties, especially two landed estates, to regularize a former connection or to legitimatize a natural child; to provide unfailing and devoted attentions for a man's rheumatics and old age, to be able to choose the place of his garrison at the time of conscription," also "to put an end to a life of vice of which they are beginning to be weary and to substitute another form of sexual life."

M. Bureau then cites facts and figures to show that these marriages, instead of reducing licentiousness, actually promote it. This degradation has been immensely helped by the so-called scientific or mechanical inventions designed to restrict the effect of the sexual act without interfering with the act itself. I must pass by the painful paragraphs regarding the increase in adultery and startling figures regarding judicial separations and divorces which during the last twenty years have more than doubled themselves. I can also make only a passing reference to the extension of unrestricted freedom for indulgence to the female sex on the principle of 'the same moral standard for the two sexes'. The perfection of the anti-conceptional practices and the methods of bringing about abortion has led to the emancipation of either sex from all moral restraint. No wonder marriage itself is laughed at. Here is a passage M. Bureau quotes from a popular author: "Marriage is always according to my judgment one of the most barbarous institutions ever imagined. I have no doubt that it will be abolished if the human race makes any progress towards justice and reason. . . . But men are too gross and women too cowardly to demand a nobler law than that which rules them."

The results of the practices referred to by M. Bureau and of the theories by which the practices are justified are minutely examined. He exclaims: "We are, then, being carried away by the movement of moral indiscipline towards new destinies. What are they? Is the future that opens before us one of progress and light, of beauty and growing spirituality, or of retrogression and darkness, of deformity and animalism that is ever demanding more? Is the indiscipline, which has been established, one of those fruitful revolts against antiquated rules, one of those beneficent rebellions which posterity remembers with gratitude because they were at certain epochs the necessary preliminary to its progress and its rise, or is it not rather the old Adam which rises up within us against the rules whose very strictness is indispensable if we are to withstand the thrust of its bestial appeal? Are we face to face with an evil revolt against the discipline of safety and life?" Then M. Bureau cites overwhelming testimony to show that hitherto the results have been disastrous in every respect. They threaten life itself.

III

It is one thing when married people regulate, so far as it is humanly possible, the number of their progeny by moral restraint, and totally another when they do so in spite of sexual indulgence and by means adopted to obviate the result of such indulgence. In the one case the people gain in every respect. In the other there is nothing but harm. M. Bureau has produced figures and diagrams to show that the increasing use of contraceptives for the purpose of giving free play to animal passion and yet obviating the natural results of such indulgence has resulted in the birth rate being much lower than the death rate, not in Paris only but in the whole of France. Out of 87 areas into which France is divided, in 68 the birth rate is lower than the death rate. In one case, i. e. Lot, deaths were 162 against 100 births. Next comes Tarnet-Garonne with 156 deaths against 100 births. Even out of 19 areas where the birth rate is higher than the death rate, the difference is negligible in several cases. In ten areas alone is there an effective difference. The lowest death rate, i. e. 72 against 100 births, occurs in Morbihan and Pas-de-Calais. M. Bureau shows that this process of depopulation, which he calls 'voluntary death', has not yet been arrested.

M. Bureau then examines the condition of French provinces in detail, and he quotes the following paragraph from M. Gide written in 1914 about Normandy: "Normandy has lost in the course of 50 years more than 300,000 inhabitants, that is to say, a population equal to that of the whole department of the Orne. Every 20 years she now loses the equivalent of a department, and as she includes but five, a century will be enough to see her fat meadows empty of Frenchmen — I say advisedly of Frenchmen, for assuredly others will come to occupy them, and it would be a pity were it otherwise. Germans work the iron mines round Caen and for the first time, only yesterday, a vanguard of Chinese labourers landed where William the Conqueror set sail for England." And M. Bureau adds by way of comment on the paragraph, "How many other provinces are in no better condition!"

He then goes on to show that this deterioration in population has inevitably led to the deterioration in the military strength of the nation. He believes that the cessation of emigration from France is also due to the same cause. He then traces to the same cause the decay of French colonial expansion, the decay of French commerce and the French language and culture.

M. Bureau then asks, "Are the French people who have rejected the ancient sexual discipline more advanced in securing happiness, material prosperity, physical health, and in intellectual culture?" He answers, "With regard to the improvement in health, a few words will suffice. However strong our wish to answer all objections methodically, it is all the same very difficult to take seriously the assertion that sexual 'emancipation' would tend to strengthen one's body and improve one's health. On every side one hears of the diminished vigour of both young people and adults. Before the war the military authorities had to lower time after time the physical standard of the recruits, and power of endurance has seriously diminished throughout the whole nation. Doubtless it would be unjust to maintain that lack of moral discipline is alone responsible for this decline, but it has a large share in it, together with alcoholism, insanitary housing, etc.; and if we look closely, we shall easily discover that this indiscipline and the sentiments which perpetuate it are the strongest allies of these other scourges. . . . The frightful extension of venereal diseases has done incalculable injury to the public health."

M. Bureau even disputes the theory advanced by Neo-Malthusians that wealth of individuals in a society which regulates its births increases in proportion to the restriction it imposes upon them, and fortifies his answer by comparing the favourable German birth rate and her increasing material prosperity with the decreasing birth rate of France side by side with its decreasing wealth. Nor has the phenomenal expansion of trade in Germany, M. Bureau contends, been attained at the cost of the workmen more than elsewhere. He quotes M. Rossignol: "People died of hunger in Germany when she had but 41,000,000 inhabitants: they have become richer and richer since she numbered 68,000,000," and adds, "These people, who are by no means ascetics, found it possible to place annually in the savings banks sums which in 1911 amounted to 22,000 million francs; while in 1895 the deposits only reached 8,000 millions; an increase of 850 millions a year."

The following paragraph which M. Bureau writes about the general culture of Germany after describing its technical progress will be read with much interest:

"Without being initiated into the depths of sociology one can have no doubt of it, for it is quite evident that such technical progress would have been impossible, had not workmen of a more refined type, foremen more highly educated, perfectly trained engineers been found. . . . The industrial schools are of three kinds: professional, numbering over 500, with 70,000 pupils; technical, still more numerous, and some of them with over 1,000 pupils; lastly, the colleges devoted to higher instruction with their 15,000 pupils, which confer like the Universities the envied title of doctor. . . . 365 commercial schools attract 31,000 pupils and in innumerable schools courses of agriculture give instruction to over 90,000. What, compared with these 400,000 pupils in the different lines of the production of wealth, are the 35,000 pupils of our professional courses, and why, since 1,770,000 of our people, of whom 779,798 are below eighteen years of age, live by the cultivation of the soil, are there but 3,255 pupils in our special schools of agriculture?" M. Bureau is careful enough to note that all this phenomenal rise of Germany is not entirely due to the surplus of births over deaths, but he does contend with justice that given other favourable conditions a preponderating birth rate is an indispensable condition of national growth. Indeed, the proposition he has set forth to prove is that a growing birth rate is in no way inconsistent with great material prosperity and moral progress. We in India are not in the position of France so far as our birth rate is concerned. But it may be said that the preponderating birth rate in India, unlike as in Germany, is no advantage to our national growth. But I must not anticipate the chapter that will have to be set apart for a consideration of Indian conditions in the light of M. Bureau's facts and figures and conclusions.

After dealing with an examination of German conditions where the birth rate preponderates over the death rate, M. Bureau says, "Are we not aware that France occupies the fourth place — and that a very long way below the third — in regard to the total sum of national wealth? France has an annual revenue from her investments of 25,000 million francs, while the Germans are drawing from their investments a revenue estimated at 50,000 million francs. . . . Our national soil has suffered, in thirtyfive years from 1879 to 1914, a depreciation of 40,000 million francs, and is worth only 52,000, instead of 92,000, millions! Whole departments of the country lack men to work the soil, and there are districts where one sees scarcely any but old men." He adds that "moral indiscipline and systematic sterility means the diminution of natural abilities in the community, and the undisputed predominance of the old men in social life. . . . In France, there are but 170 children and young people to every 1,000 inhabitants, while in Germany there are 220, in England 210. . . The proportion of the old is greater than it should be, and the others who are prematurely aged through moral indiscipline and voluntary sterility share in all the senile fears of a debilitated race."

The author then observes, "We know that the immense majority of French people are indifferent to this domestic position (slack morals) of their rulers thanks to the convenient theory of the 'wall round private life'." And he quotes with sorrow the following observation of M. Leopold Monod:

"It is a fine thing to go to war in order to cast down infamous abuses, and to break the chains of those who suffer from them. But how about men whose fears have not known how to guard their consciences from enticements; men whose courage is at the mercy of a caress or a fit of sulks; . . . men who, with no shame perhaps glorying in the exploit, repudiate the vow which in a joyous and solemn hour they made to the wife of their youth; men who burden their home with the tyranny of an exaggerated and selfish egotism — how can such men be liberators?"

The author then sums up:

"Thus, whichever way we turn, we always find that the various forms of our moral indiscipline have caused serious hurt to the individual, the family, and society at large, and have inflicted on us suffering which is literally inexpressible. The licentious conduct of our young people, prostitution, pornography, and marriages for money, vanity or luxury, adultery and divorce, voluntary sterility and abortion, have debilitated the nation and stopped its increase; the individual has been unable to conserve his energies, and the quality of the new growth has diminished simultaneously with its quantity. 'Fewer births and more fine men' was the watchword, which had something enticing about it for those who, shut up in their materialistic conception of individual and social life, thought they could assimilate the breeding of men to that of sheep or horses. As Auguste Comte said with stinging force, these pretended physicians of our social ills would have done better to become veterinary surgeons, incapable as they always were of comprehending the infinite complexity of the psychology both of the individual and of the society.

"The truth is that of all the attitudes which a man adopts, of all the decisions at which he arrives, of all the habits which he contracts, there is none which exerts over his personal and social life an influence comparable to that exerted by his attitudes, his decisions, and his habits with regard to the appeals of the sexual appetite. Whether he resists and controls them, or whether he yields and allows himself to be controlled by them, the most remote regions of social life will experience the echo of his action, since nature has ordained that the most hidden and intimate action should produce infinite repercussions.

"Thanks to this very mystery, we like to persuade ourselves, when we violate in any way the moral discipline, that our misdeed will have no grievous consequence. As to ourselves, in the first place, we are satisfied, since our own interest or pleasure has been the motive of our action; as to society at large, we think it is so high above our modest selves that it will not even notice our misdeeds; and above all, we secretly hope that 'the others' will have the sense to remain devout and virtuous. The worst of it is that this cowardly calculation almost succeeds while our conduct is as yet an abnormal and exceptional act; then, proud of our success, we persevere in our attitude, and when there is occasion we come—and this is our supreme punishment—to believe it lawful.

"But a day comes when the example given by this conduct involves other defections; each of our evil deeds has the result of making more difficult and more heroic that attachment to virtue which we have counted on in 'the others', and our neighbour, tired of being duped, is now in a hurry to imitate us. That day the downfall begins, and each can estimate at once the consequences of his misdeeds and the extent of his responsibilities. . . .

"The secret act has come out of the hiding place in which we thought it was confined. Endowed in its own way with a kind of immaterial radio-activity, it has run through all sections; all suffer from the fault of each, because the influence of our actions, like the wavelets spreading from an eddy, makes itself felt in the most remote regions of the general social life. . . . .

"Moral indiscipline at once dries up the fountains of the race, and hastens the wear and tear of the adults whom it debilitates both morally and physically."

IV

Having dealt with the indiscipline of morals and its aggravation by the use of contraceptives and its terrible results the author proceeds to examine the remedies. I must pass over the portions that deal with legislative measures, their necessity and yet utter inefficiency. He then discusses the necessity, by a careful education of public opinion, of the duty of chastity for the unmarried, the duty of marriage for that vast mass of mankind that cannot for ever restrain their animal passions, the duty, having once married, of conjugal fidelity, and the duty of continence in marriage. He examines the argument against chastity that its "precept is against the physiological nature of man and woman and injurious to the happy equilibrium of their health", and that it is "an intolerable attack on the freedom and autonomy of the individual, his right to happiness and to live his life in his own way."

The author contests the doctrine that "the organ of generation is like the rest" requiring satisfaction. "If it were," he says, "an organ like the others, how could we explain the absolute inhibitory power which the will possesses over it, or the fact that the awakening of sensuality, which pharisaism calls the sexual necessity, is the result of the innumerable excitements which our civilisation provides for young boys and girls several years before normal adult age?"

I cannot resist the temptation of copying the following valuable medical testimony collected in the book in support of the proposition that self-restraint is not only not harmful but necessary for the promotion of the health and perfectly possible:

"The sexual instinct," says Oesterlen, Professor at Tubingen University, "is not so blindly all-powerful that it cannot be controlled, and even subjugated entirely, by moral strength and reason. The young man, like the young woman, should learn to control himself until the proper time. He must know that robust health and ever-renewed vigour will be the reward of this voluntary sacrifice.

"One cannot repeat too often that abstinence and the most absolute purity are perfectly compatible with the laws of physiology and morality, and that sexual indulgence is no more justified by physiology and psychology than by morality and religion."

"The example of the best and noblest among men," says Sir Lionel Beale, Professor at the Royal College in London, "has at all times proved that the most imperious of instincts can be effectively resisted by a strong and serious will, and by sufficient care as to manner of life and occupation. Sexual abstinence has never yet hurt any man when it has been observed, not only through exterior restrictive causes, but as a voluntary rule of conduct. Virginity, in fine, is not too hard to observe, provided that it is the physical expression of a certain state of mind....... Chastity implies, not only continence, but also purity of sentiments, the energy which is the result of deep convictions."

"Every kind of nervous activity," says the Swiss psychologist Forel, who discusses sexual anomalies with a moderation equal to his knowledge, "is increased and strengthened by exercise. On the other hand, inactivity in a particular region reduces the effects of the exciting causes which correspond to it.

"All causes of sexual disturbance increase the intensity of desire. By avoiding these provocations it becomes less sensitive, and the desire gradually diminishes. The idea is current among young people that continence is something abnormal and impossible, and yet the many who observe it prove that chastity can be practised without prejudice to the health."

"I know," says Ribbing, "a number of men of 25, 30 and older than that, who have observed perfect continence, or who when they married had done so up to that time. Such cases are not rare; only they don't advertise themselves.

"I have received many confidences from students, healthy both in body and mind, who have remonstrated with me for not having sufficiently insisted on the ease with which sensual desires can be ruled."

"Before marriage, absolute continence can and ought to be observed by young men," says Dr. Acton. "Chastity no more injures the body than the soul," declares Sir James Paget, physician to the English Court. "Discipline is better than any other line of conduct."

"It is a singularly false notion," writes Dr. E. Perier, "and one which must be fought against, since it besets not only the children's mind, but that of the fathers as well: the notion of imaginary dangers in absolute continence. Virginity is a physical, moral, and intellectual safeguard to young men."

"Continence," says Sir Andrew Clarke, "does not harm, it does not hinder development, it increases energy and enlivens perception. Incontinence weakens self-control, creates habits of slackness, dulls and degrades the whole being, and lays it open to diseases which can be transmitted to several generations. To say that incontinence is necessary to the health of young men is not only an error, but a cruelty. It is at once false and hurtful."

"The evils of incontinence are well-known and undisputed," writes Dr. Surbled, "those produced by continence are imaginary; what proves this is the fact of the many learned and voluminous works devoted to the explanation of the former, while the latter still await their historian. As to these latter there are but vague assertions, which hide themselves, for very shame, in mere talk, but which will not endure the daylight."

"I have never seen," writes Dr. Montegazza in *La Physiologie de l'amour*, "a disease produced by chastity. . . . All men, and especially young men, can experience the immediate benefits of chastity."

Dr. Dubois, the famous professor of neuropathology at Berne, affirms that "there are more victims of neurasthenia among those who give free rein to their sensuality than among those who know how to escape from the yoke of mere animalism;" and his testimony is fully confirmed by that of Dr. Fere, physician at the Bicetre Hospital, who testifies that those who are capable of psychic chastity can maintain their continence without any fear for their health, which does not depend on the satisfaction of the sexual instinct.

"There has been unfitting and light talk," writes Professor Alfred Fournier, "about 'the dangers of continence for the young man'. I can assure you that if these dangers exist I know nothing about them, and that as a physician I am still without proof of their existence, though I have had every opportunity in the way of subjects under my professional observation.

"Besides this, as a physiologist I will add that true virility is not attained before the age of twentyone, or thereabouts, and the sexual necessity does not obtrude itself before that period, especially if unhealthy excitements have not aroused it prematurely. Sexual precocity is merely artificial, and is most often the result of ill-directed upbringing.

"In any case, be sure that danger of this kind lies far less in restraining than in anticipating the natural tendency; you know what I mean."

Lastly, after these most authoritative testimonies, to which it would be easy to add many others, M. Bureau quotes the resolution unanimously voted at Brussels in 1902 by the 102 members present at the Second General Congress of the International Conference of Sanitary and and Moral Prophylaxis, a Congress which assembled together the most competent authorities on the subject throughout the world: "Young men must above all be taught that chastity and continence are not only not harmful, but also that these virtues are among those to be most earnestly recommended from the purely medical and hygienic standpoint."

M. Bureau then proceeds:

"There was also a unanimous declaration issued by the professors of the Medical Faculty of Christiania University, a few years ago: 'The assertion that a chaste life will be prejudicial to the health rests, according to our unanimous experience, on no foundation. We have no knowledge of any harm resulting from a pure and moral life.'

"The case has therefore been heard, and sociologists and moralists can repeat with M. Ruyssen this elémentary and physiological truth 'that the sexual appetite does not need, like the requirements of aliment and exercise, a minimum of necessary satisfaction. It is a fact that man or woman can lead a chaste life without experiencing, except in the case of a few abnormal subjects, serious disturbance or even painful inconvenience. It has been said — and cannot be too often repeated, since such an elementary truth can be so widely disregarded — that no disease ever comes through continence to normal subjects, who form the immense majority, while many diseases, very well known and very serious, are the results of incontinence. Nature has provided in the most simple and infallible way for the excess of nutrition which is represented by the seminal fluid and the menstrual flux.'

"Dr. Viry is therefore right in denying that the question is one of a true instinct or a real need. 'Everyone knows what it would cost him not to satisfy the need of nourishment or to suppress respiration, but no one quotes any pathological consequences, either acute or chronic, as having followed either temporary or absolute continence. . . . In normal life we see the example of chaste men who are neither less virile in character, nor less energetic in will, nor less robust than others, nor less fitted to become fathers if they marry. . . . A need which can be subject to such variations, an instinct which accommodates itself so well to lack of satisfaction, is neither a need nor an instinct.'

"Sexual relationship is far from answering to any physiological need of the growing boy; quite the contrary, it is perfect chastity which is sternly required by the exigencies of his normal growth and development, and those who violate it cause irreparable injury to their health. 'The attainment of puberty is accompanied by great changes, a veritable disturbance of various functions, and a general development. The adolescent boy needs all his vital strength, for during this period there is often a weakening of the resistance to sicknsss: disease and mortality are higher than in the earlier period. . . . The long work of general growth, of organic evolution, that whole series of physical and psychic changes, at the end of which the child becomes a man, involves a toilsome effort of nature. At that moment, all overdriving is dangerous, but especially the premature exercise of the sexual function.'"

V

After dealing with the physiological benefits of chastity M. Bureau' quotes the following passage from Professor Montegazza on its moral and intellectual advantages:

"All men, and young men in particular, can experience the immediate benefit of chastity. The memory is quiet and tenacious, the brain lively and fertile, the will energetic, the whole character gains a strength of which libertines have no conception; no prism shows us our surroundings under such heavenly colours as that of chastity, which lights up with its rays the least objects in the universe, and transports us into the purest joys of an abiding happiness that knows neither shadow nor decline." And the author adds: "The joy, the cordial merriment, the sunny confidence of vigorous young men who have remained chaste . . . are an eloquent contrast to the restless obsessions and feverish excitement of their companions who are slaves to the demands of sensuality." He then compares the benefits of chastity with the 'miserable consequences of lust and debauchery.' "No disease," the author states, "could ever be quoted as the result of continence; who is not aware of the frightful diseases of which moral indiscipline is the source? . . . The body . . . finds itself converted into an indescribable state of rottenness. . . . Nor can we forget the worse defilement of imagination, heart and understanding. On every side we hear complaint of the lowering of character, the unbridled lust of youth, the overflowing of selfishness."

So much for the so-called necessity of sexual indulgence and the consequent liberty taken by the youth before marriage. The protagonists of the doctrine of such indulgence further contend that restraint of the sexual passion is a restraint upon 'the freedom to dispose of one's own body'. The author shows by elaborate argument that restraint on individual freedom in the matter of sexual indulgence is a necessity from the standpoint of sociology and social psychology.

"In the eyes of sociologists," the author says, "social life is nothing but a network of multiform relations, nothing but an interlacing of actions and reactions, in the midst of which an activity, isolated and really separated from the rest, is unthinkable. On whatever step we resolve, whatever action we attempt, solidarity unites our resolution and our action to those of our brothers; and not even our most secret thought or most fugitive wish fails of an echo so distant that the mind is for ever incapable of measuring the distance. The social quality is not, in man, an adventitious or merely accessory quality: it is immanent, part of his humanity itself; he is a social being because he is a man. There is no other field of activity so truly our own: physiology and morality, economics and politics, the intellectual and aesthetic domains, the religious and the social, are all conditioned by a universal system of mysterious bonds and undefined relations. The bond is so firm, the net so closely meshed that sometimes the sociologist stands in real trouble before this immensity which unfolds itself before him, across all time and space; he measures in one glance how great, under certain circumstances, is the responsibility of the individual, and how he risks becoming petty by liberty which some social circles might be tempted to grant him."

"If," the author further says, "we can say that under certain circumstances I am not at liberty to spit in the street, . . . how can I claim the much more important right of disposing of my sexual energy as I like? Does that energy by a unique privilege escape the universal law of solidarity? Who does not see, on the contrary, that the sovereign importance of the function only increases the social reaction of the individual acts? Look at this young man and this girl who have just established that false union of which the reader knows the character; they are persuaded that the agreement concerns nobody but themselves. They shut themselves up in their independence, and pretend to believe that their intimate and secret action has no interest for society and is altogether beyond its control. A childish illusion! The social solidarity which unites the people of one nation, and, beyond the individual nations, all humanity, finds no difficulty in passing through all walls, even those of the secret chambers, and a terrible interrelation joins that supposed private action to the most distant series of actions in that social life which it helps to disorganize. Whether he wills it or not, every individual, who asserts his right to temporary or sterile sexual relations, who claims the liberty to use the reproductive energy with which he is endowed merely for his own enjoyment, spreads in society the germs of division and disorder. All deformed as they are by our selfishness and our disloyalties, our social institutions still take for granted that the individual will accept with goodwill the obligations inherent in the satisfaction of the reproductive appetite. It is by discounting this acceptance that society has built up its countless mechanisms of labour and property, of wages and inheritance, of taxation and military service, of the right of parliamentary suffrage and civil liberties. By his refusal to take his share the individual disorganizes everything at one stroke, he violates the social pact in its very essence, and while he makes the burden heavier on others' shoulder, he is no better than an exploiter and a parasite, a thief and a swindler. We are responsible in the face of society for our physiological energy, as for all our energies, and, it might be said, even more than for all the others, since a society unarmed and almost wholly without external pressure is obliged to remit to our goodwill the care to use that energy judiciously and conformably to the social good."

The author is equally strong on the psychological ground: "It was said long ago that liberty is in appearance an alleviation, in reality a burden. That is precisely its grandeur. Liberty binds and compels; it increases the sum of the efforts which each is bound to make. The individual desires to be free, he is all inflamed with the longing to realise himself in the expansion of his autonomy. The programme seems simple enough, and yet his first experiences are enough to show him its painful complexity. It is in vain that unity is the dominating characteristic of our nature and our moral life; we feel within us various and contradictory impulses; in each of them we are conscious of ourselves, and yet everything proves to us that we must choose between them. You say, young man, that you wish to live your own life, to realize yourself; but what part of yourself do you wish to realize, we ask with the great pedagogue, Foerster? Which is the better part, that which has its seat in the centre of your intellectual force, or that which occupies the lowest, the sensual, part of your nature? If it is true that progress in the individual and in society consists in a growing spiritualization and in the ever more complete mastery of spirit over matter, the choice cannot be doubtful, but there must still be energy to act, and the undertaking is not an easy one. Perhaps you will reply: But I do not choose, I wish to realize my being in one harmonious and organized whole. Very well; but take care, this very resolution is a choice, for harmony is only established at the cost of strife. *Sterb und Werde*, die and become, said Goethe, and the words are but the echo of others spoken nineteen centuries ago by Christ, 'Amen, I say to you, unless the grain of wheat falling into the ground die, it remaineth alone; but if it die, it bringeth forth much fruit.'

" 'We wish to be men — an easy thing to say,' writes M. Gabriel Seailles, 'but the right turns into duty, stern duty, in which no one does not fail more or less; we wish to be free, we announce it with a menacing air; if we call liberty doing as we like, the slavery of instinct, we need not be so proud of it; if we are speaking of the true liberty, let us gird up our loins and prepare ourselves for the unending fight. We talk about our unity, our identity, our liberty, and proudly conclude that we are immortal sons of God. Alas! if we only try to seize this *Self*, it escapes our grasp, it resolves itself into a multitude of incoherent beings which deny each other, it is rent by contradictory desires which in turn constitute itself; it is wholly (its own essential being excepted) the prejudice to which it submits, the objects which tempt it; its pretended liberty is nothing but a slavery which it does not feel, so does not resist.'

"Says Ruyssen :

"'While continence is a virtue full of repose, incontinence opens the door to an unknown guest who may become formidable. The revelation of passion, which is troublesome at any age, may become in youth the signal of a radical perversion, we would say of an irreparable disturbance, of the balance of the will and the senses. The boy who has contact for the first time with any woman whatsoever, as a passing encounter, is really playing with his physical, intellectual, and moral life; he does not know but it will be the same tomorrow in the family, at work, in social life; he does not know how the sensual revelation will come back to haunt him, what servitude without hope may represent the too exact term of 'mastery'; and we know of more than one life ruined after a beginning of richest promise, the first disappointments of which dated from the first moral fall.'

"The celebrated verses of the poet echo these remarks of the philosopher :

> "'Man's virgin soul is as a vessel deep,
> If the first drops inpoured should tainted be,
> Across the soul all ocean's waves may sweep,
> Yet fail that vast abyss from stain to free.'

"And, not less, this advice of the great British physiologist, John G. M. Kendrick, professor of physiology at Glasgow University :

"'The illicit satisfaction of nascent passion is not only a moral fault, it is a terrible injury to the body. The new need becomes a tyrant if yielded to; a guilty complacency will listen to it, and make it more imperious; every fresh act will forge a new link in the chain of habit.

"'Many have no longer strength to break it, and helplessly end in physical and intellectual ruin, slaves of a habit contracted often through ignorance rather than perversity. The best safeguard consists in cultivating within oneself purity of thought and discipline of one's whole being.' "

M. Bureau adds to the foregoing the following from Dr. Escande :

" As to sexual desire, we assert, the intelligence and the will have absolute control over it. It is necessary to employ the term sexual *desire*, not *need*, for there is no question of a function, the non-accomplishment of which is incompatible with existence. Really it is not a need at all; but many men are persuaded that it is. The interpretation they give to the desire makes them look on cohabitation as absolutely necessary. Now we cannot look on the sexual act as resulting from senile and passive obedience to natural laws. We are, on the contrary, concerned with a voluntary act, following on a determination or an acquiescence, often premeditated and prepared for."

VI

After having insisted on chastity before and during marriage and shown by overwhelming proof that not only is self-restraint not impossible, not harmful, but perfectly possible and wholly beneficial both to the mind and the body, M. Bureau devotes a chapter to the value and possibility of perpetual continence. The following opening paragraph is worth reproducing:

" In the first rank of these liberators, these heroes of the true sexual emancipation, it is only right to name the young men and women who, the better to devote themselves to the service of a great cause, choose to remain all their life in chastity, and renounce the joys of marriage. The reasons for their resolve vary according to circumstances; one feels it a duty to remain with an infirm father or mother; another takes the place, to orphaned brothers and sisters, of the departed parents; another desires to devote himself or herself entirely to the service of science or of art, of the poor or the sick, or to a work of moral education or of prayer. Similarly the merit of the voluntary sacrifice may be greater or less; some, thanks to the benefits of a wise protective education and the practice of a good moral hygiene, are almost without sensual temptations; others, more advanced in the path of virtue, have succeeded, it may be at the cost of sharp conflicts, of which they alone know the hardness, in mastering the beast and taming the flesh. On any supposition, the final resolve is the same: these men and women have been led to think that the best way for them to serve is not to marry; and they have entered into an engagement, it may be with themselves, it may be with God, to remain in the perfect chastity of the celibate life. However definite and undoubted may be the duty of marriage, as we shall see, under certain circumstances, all these resolutions are legitimate, because they are inspired by a noble and generous purpose. 'Painting is a jealous mistress who suffers no rival,' replied Michael Angelo when marriage was suggested to him; and how many after him have had a like experience!"

I can corroborate this testimony from the experience of European friends of almost every description given by M. Bureau, friends who exercised perpetual restraint. It is only in India that from childhood we must hear of marriages. Parents have no other thought, no other ambition, save that of seeing their children well married and provided for. The one thing brings premature decay of mind and body, and the other induces idleness and often makes of one a parasite. We exaggerate the difficulty of chastity and voluntary poverty and impute extraordinary merit to them, reserve them for *mahatmas* and *yogis* and rule the latter out of ordinary life, forgetting that real *mahatmya* and *yoga* are unthinkable in a society where the ordinary level is brought down to the mudbank. On the principle that evil like the hare travels faster than good which like the tortoise though steady goes slow, voluptuousness of the West comes to us with lightning speed, and with all its variegated enchantment dazzles and blinds us to the realities of life. We are almost ashamed of chastity, and are in danger of looking upon self-imposed poverty as a crime in the face of the Western splendour that descends upon us from minute to minute through the cable and day to day through the steamers that discharge their cargo on our shores. But the West is not wholly what we see in India. Even as the South African Whites ill-judge us when they judge us through the Indian settlers, so shall we ill-judge the West through the human and the other Western cargo that delivers itself to us every day. There is in the West a small but inexhaustible reservoir of purity and strength which those who have eyes of penetration may see beneath the deceptive surface. Throughout the European desert there are oases from which those who will may drink the purest water of life. Chastity and voluntary poverty are adopted without brag, without bluster, and in all humility by hundreds of men and women, often for no other than the all-sufficing cause of service of some dear one or of the country. We often prate about spirituality as if it had nothing to do with the ordinary affairs of life and had been reserved for anchorites lost in the Himalayan forests or concealed in some inaccessible Himalayan cave. Spirituality that has no bearing on and produces no effect on everyday life is 'an airy nothing'. Let young men and women for whose sake *Young India* is written from week to week know that it is their duty, if they would purify the atmosphere about them and shed their weakness, to be and remain chaste and know too that it is not so difficult as they have been taught to imagine.

Let us further listen to M. Bureau: "In proportion as it (modern sociology) follows the evolution of our manners, and as methodical study digs more deeply the soil of social realities, the better is the value perceived of the help which the practice of perpetual chastity brings to the great work of the discipline of the senses." "If marriage is the normal state of life for the immense majority of people, it cannot be that all can, or ought to, marry. Even putting aside the exceptional vocations of which we have just spoken, there are at least three classes of celibates who cannot be blamed for not being married : the young people of both sexes who for professional or economic reasons think it a duty to defer their marriage; the people who are involuntarily condemned to celibacy because they cannot find a suitable partner; finally those who ought to abstain from marriage in consequence of their physiological defects that could be transmitted, and who are in some cases strictly bound to renouce all idea of it. Is it not evident, then, that the renunciation made by these people, doubly necessary both for their own happiness and the interest of society, will be rendered so much the less painful and so much the more cheerful, because they will find beside them others who, in full possession of their physical and intellectual vigour and sometimes with abundant means, have declared their firm resolution to remain celibate all their lives ? These voluntary and choice celibates, who have willed to consecrate themselves to God without reserve, to prayer and to the training of the souls, declare that in their eyes celibacy, far from being a reduced condition of life, is on the contrary a superior state, in which man asserts, in its plenitude, the mastery of will over instinct."

"To young people of both the sexes," says the author, "who are still too young to marry, perpetual celibacy shows that it is possible to pass one's youth chastely; to the married it recalls the duty which lies upon them to maintain exact discipline in their conjugal relations and never to allow a consideration of self-interest, however legitimate it may be in itself, to prevail over the higher demands of moral generosity and loyalty."

"The vow of the voluntary celibate," says Foerster, "far from degrading marriage, is on the contrary the best support of the sanctity of the conjugal bond, since it represents in a concrete form man's freedom in the face of the pressure of his nature. It acts like a conscience with regard to passing whims and sensual assaults. Celibacy is also a protection to marriage in the sense that its existence prevents married people from looking upon themselves in their mutual relations as mere slaves to obscure natural forces, and it leads them to take openly, in the face of nature, the position of free beings who are capable of mastery. Those who scoff at perpetual celibacy as unnatural or impossible do not know really what they are doing. They fail to see that the line of thought which makes them talk as they do must necessarily lead, by strict logic, to prostitution and polygamy. If the demand of nature is irresistible, how can a chaste life be required of married people ? And lastly, they forget the great number of marriages in which, it may be for several months or years, or even for life, one of the spouses is condemned to a real celibacy by the sickness or other disability of the partner. For this reason alone, true monogamy rises or falls with the esteem that is paid to celibacy."

VII

The chapter on perpetual continence is followed by chapters on the duty and indissolubility of marriage. Whilst the author contends that perpetual continence is the highest state, it is not possible for the multitude for whom marriage must be regarded as a duty. He shows that, if the function and limitations of marriage are rightly understood, there never can be any advocacy of contraceptives. It is the wrong moral training that has brought about the prevalent moral indiscipline. Having dealt with the opinion of 'advanced' writers ridiculing marriage the author says :

"Happily for future generations, this opinion of pseudo-moralists and of writers who are often utterly lacking in moral sense, and equally so sometimes in the real literary spirit, is very far from being that of the true psychologists and sociologists of our time; and in nothing is the rupture more complete between the noisy world of the press, the novel and the stage, and that other world where thought is cultivated, and the mysterious elements of our psychological and social life are studied in detail."

M. Bureau rejects the argument of free love. He holds with Modestin that "marriage is the union of man and woman, the association of all life, the communication of divine and human rights of law." Marriage is not a "mere civil contract" but a "sacrament, a moral obligation". It has succeeded in "making the gorilla stand erect". "It is a great mistake to imagine that everything is permissible to those lawfully married, and even supposing that husband and wife ordinarily respect the moral law as to transmission of life, it is untrue that it is lawful to *add* other modes of sexual intercourse which please them. This prohibition is as much in their interest as in that of the society of which their marriage ought to be the maintenance and development." The author holds that the ever-renewed opportunities of deviation from strict discipline which marriage affords to the sexual instinct are a constant menace to pure love. This peril can only be exorcised by watchfulness to keep the satisfaction of the sexual appetite within the limits defined by the very ends of marriage. "It is always dangerous," says St. Francis of Sales, "to take to violent medicines, since if one takes more than should be taken, or if they are not well made up, much harm is done; marriage has been blessed and ordained partly as a remedy for concupiscence, and it is undoubtedly a very good remedy, but all the same a violent one, and consequently very dangerous if not discreetly used."

The author then combats the theory of individual liberty to contract or break the marriage bond at will or to live frankly a life of indulgence without its consequent obligation. He insists on monogamy and says:

"It is untrue that the individual is at liberty to contract marriage or to remain in selfish celibacy, as he pleases; still less are duly married people free to agree together to the rupture of their union. Their freedom is shown when they choose each other, and each is bound to choose only with full knowledge, after careful thought, the one with whom he believes he can assume the responsibilities of the new life he is entering. But as soon as the marriage has been accomplished and consummated, the act performed involves, far away and in all directions, incalculable consequences which extend infinitely beyond the two persons who have brought them about. These consequences may be unperceived, in a time of anarchic individualism such as ours, by the spouses themselves, but their importance is certified by the grave sufferings which come upon the whole body social as soon as the stability of the home is shaken, as soon as the variable caprice of the sensual appetite takes the place of the beneficent discipline of the positive monogamic union. To one who is conscious of these indefinitely extended repercussions and these subtle connections, it matters little to know that, since all human institutions are subject to the universal law of evolution, that of marriage must certainly, like all the rest, undergo in its turn necessary transformations, since there can be no doubt that progress in this direction can only take the form of eventually drawing more closely the marriage bond. The attacks now made on the rule of the indissolubility of marriage, when divorce is asked for by mutual consent, will only bring into more prominent relief the social value of a rule against which protest is made, and as the years roll by, this rule, which for some centuries, when its social value could not yet be appreciated, was simply a prescription of religious discipline, will appear more and more as a principle as beneficial to the individual as it is salutary for society at large.

"The rule of indissolubility is not an arbitrary adornment; on the contrary, it is bound up with the most delicate mechanism of the individual and collective social life; and since people talk about evolution, they should ask on what condition this indefinite progress of the race, which all agree to desire, is possible. Writes Foerster : 'The deepening of the sense of responsibility, the training of the individual towards autonomous discipline willingly consented to, the growth of patience and charity, the control of selfishness, the maintenance of the emotional life against the elements that make for dissolution and the impulse of passing caprice — all these are elements in man's interior life which we are entitled to consider the absolute and permanent conditions of all higher social culture, and on this account exempt from all such disorder as might result from a serious change in economic conditions. To tell the truth, economic progress is itself closely bound up with general social progress, for economic security and success depends in the long run on the sincerity and loyalty of our social cooperation. Every economic modification which ignores these fundamental conditions is self-condemned. If we wish, therefore, to take up the study, at once both moral and social, of the absolute value of the various methods of sexual relations, the following question is decisive : What method is the best adapted to the deepening and strengthening of our whole social life ? Which is the most capable, at the different periods of life, of developing to the utmost the sense of responsibility, self-abnegation and sacrifice, of most effectively restraining undisciplined selfishness and capricious frivolity ? When the matter is viewed from this standpoint, there is not the slightest doubt that monogamy, because of its social and educative value, must form part of the permanent heritage of all more advanced civilization; and true progress will draw more closely, rather than relax, the marriage bond. . . . The family is the centre of all human preparation for the social life, that is to say, all preparation for responsibility, sympathy, self-control, mutual tolerance, and reciprocal training. And the family only fills this central place because it lasts all through life and is indissoluble, and because, thanks to this permanence, the common family life becomes deeper, more stable, more adapted to men's mutual intercourse, than any other. It may be said that monogamic marriage is the conscience of all human social life.' "

He quotes Auguste Comte : "Our hearts are so changeable that society must intervene to hold in check the vacillation and caprices which would otherwise drag down human existence to be nothing but a series of unworthy and pointless experiences."

"A fiction," writes Dr. Toulouse, "which often hinders the happiness of married people, is that the instinct of love is a tyrant and must be satisfied at any price. . . . Now the very characteristic quality of man, and the apparent end of his evolution, is an ever-growing independence of his appetites. The child learns to master his coarser needs, and the adult to overcome his passions. This scheme of all good upbringing is not chimerical, nor something outside practical life. For the end of our nature is precisely to be subject, in great degree, to the personal tendencies which constitute our will. What one shelters behind as 'temperament' is usually nothing but weakness. The man who is really strong knows how to use his powers at the right time."

VIII

It is now time to conclude this series of articles. It is not necessary to pursue M. Bureau in his examination of the doctrine of Malthus who startled his generation by his theory of overpopulation and his advocacy of birth control if the human species was not to be extinct. Malthus, however, advocated continence, whereas Neo-Malthusianism advocates not restraint but the use of chemical and mechanical means to avoid the consequences of animal indulgence. M. Bureau heartily accepts the doctrine of birth control by moral means, *i. e.*, self-restraint, and, as we have seen, rejects and vigorously condemns the use of chemical or mechanical means. The author then examines the condition of the working classes and the proportion of births among them, and finally closes the book by examining the means of checking the practice of grossest immoralities under the name of individual freedom and even humanity. He suggests organized attempt to guide and regulate the public opinion and advocates state interference but finally relies upon quickening of the religious life. Moral bankruptcy cannot be met or arrested by ordinary methods, most certainly not when immorality is claimed as a virtue and morality condemned as a weakness, superstition or even immorality. For many advocates of contraceptives do indeed condemn continence as unnecessary and even harmful. In this state of things religious aid is the only effective check upon licensed vice. Religion here may not be taken in its narrow, parochial sense. True religion is the greatest disturbing factor in life whether individual or collective. A religious awakening constitutes a revolution, a transformation, a regeneration. And nothing but some such dynamic force can positively prevent the moral catastrophe towards which, in M. Bureau's estimation, France seems to be moving.

* * * *

But we must here leave the author and his book. French conditions are not Indian conditions. Ours is a somewhat different problem. Contraceptives are not universal in India. Their use has hardly touched the educated classes. The use of contraceptives in India is, in my opinion, unwarranted by any single condition that can be named. Do middle class parents suffer from too many children? Individual instances will not suffice to make out a case for excessive birth-rate among the middle classes. The cases in India where I have observed the advocacy of these methods are those of widows and young wives. Thus in the one case it is illegitimate birth that is to be avoided, not the secret intercourse. In the other it is again pregnancy that is to be feared, and not the rape, of a girl of tender age. Then there remains the class of diseased, weak, effeminate young men who would indulge in excesses with their own wives or others' wives and would avoid the consequences of acts which they know to be sinful. The cases of men or women in full vigour of life desiring intercourse and yet wishing to avoid the burden of children are, I make bold to say, rare in this ocean of Indian humanity. Let them not parade their cases to justify and advocate a practice that in India, if it became general, is bound to ruin the youth of the country. A highly artificial education has robbed the nation's youth of physical and mental vigour. We are offspring in many cases of child marriages. Our disregard of the laws of health and sanitation has undermined our bodies. Our wrong and deficient dietary composed of corroding spices has produced a collapse of the digestive apparatus. We need, not lessons in the use of contraceptives and helps to our being able to satisfy our animal appetite, but continuous lessons to restrain that appetite, in many cases even to the extent of absolute continence. We need to be taught by precept and example that continence is perfectly possible and imperatively necessary if we are not to remain mentally and physically weak. We need to be told from the housetop that if we will not be a nation of manikins, we must conserve and add to the limited vital energy we are daily dissipating. Our young widows need to be told not to sin secretly but come out boldly and openly to demand marriage which is their right as much as that of young widowers. We need to cultivate public opinion that shall make child marriages impossible. The vacillation, and the disinclination to do hard and sustained work, the physical inability to perform strenuous labours, collapses of enterprises brilliantly begun, the want of originality, one notices so often, are due largely to excessive indulgence. I hope young men do not deceive themselves into the belief that when there is no procreation the mere indulgence does not matter, does not weaken. Indeed the sexual act, with the unnatural safeguard against procreation, is likely to be far more exhausting than such act performed with a full sense of the responsibility attached to it.

"The mind is its own place, and in itself
Can make a heaven of hell, a hell of heaven."

If we begin to believe that indulgence in animal passion is necessary, harmless and sinless, we shall want to give reins to it and shall be powerless to resist it. Whereas if we educate ourselves to believe that such indulgence is harmful, sinful, unnecessary, and can be controlled, we shall discover that self-restraint is perfectly possible. Let us beware of the strong wine of libertinism that the intoxicated West sends us under the guise of new truth and so-called human freedom. Let us, on the contrary, listen to the sober voice from the West, that through the rich experience of its wise men at times percolates to us, if indeed we have outgrown the ancient wisdom of our forefathers.

Charlie Andrews has sent me an informing article* on *Generation and Regeneration* written by William Loftus Hare and published in *The Open Court* (March 1926). It is a closely reasoned scientific essay. He shows that all bodies perform two functions : '*viz.*, internal reproduction for the building up of the body, and external reproduction for the continuance of the species. ' These processes he names regeneration and generation respectively. "The regenerative process – internal reproduction – is fundamental for the individual and therefore necessary and primary, the generative process is due to a superfluity of cells and is therefore secondary. . . . The law of life, then, at this level is to feed the germ cells firstly for regeneration and secondly for generation. In case of deficiency, regeneration must take the first place and generation be suspended. Thus we may learn the origin of the suspension of reproduction and follow it to its later phases of human continence and asceticism generally. Inner reproduction can never be suspended except at the cost of death, the normal origin of which is thus also discerned." After describing the biological process of regeneration the writer states: "Among civilized human beings sexual intercourse is practised vastly more than is necessary for the production of the

* See Appendix I.

next generation and is carried on at the expense of internal reproduction, bringing disease, death and more in its train."

No one who knows anything of Hindu philosophy can have difficulty in following this paragraph from Mr. Hare's essay :

"The process of regeneration is not and cannot be mechanistic in character, but like the primitive fission is vitalistic. That is to say, it exhibits intelligence and will. To suppose that life separates, differentiates and segregates by a process that is purely mechanistic is inconceivable. True, these fundamental processes are so far removed from our present consciousness as to seem to be uncontrolled by the human or animal will. But a moment's reflection will show, that just as the will of the fully developed human being directs his external movements and actions in accordance with the guidance of the intellect, — this, indeed being its function, — so the earlier processes of the gradual organization of the body must, within the limits provided by environment, be allowed to be directed by a kind of will guided by a kind intelligence. This is now known to psychologists as 'the unconscious'. It is a part of our self, disconnected from our normal daily thinking, but intensely awake and alert in regard to its own functions — so much so that it never for a moment subsides into sleep as the consciousness does."

Who can measure the almost irreparable harm done to the unconscious and more permanent part of our being by the sexual act indulged in for its own sake? 'The nemesis of reproduction is death. The sexual act is essentially katabolic (or a movement towards death) in the male, and in parturition of the offspring it is katabolic for the female.' Hence the writer contends: "Virility, vitality and immunity from disease are the normal lot of nearly or quite continent persons." "Withdrawal of germ cells from their upward regenerative course for generative or merely indulgent purposes deprives the organs of their replenishing stock of life, to their cost slowly and ultimately." "It is these physical facts which constitute the basis of a personal sexual ethic, counselling moderation, if not restraint—at any rate, explaining the origin of restraint." The author, as can be easily imagined, is opposed to birth control by chemical and mechanical means. He says: "It removes all prudential motives for self-restraint, and makes it possible for sexual indulgence in marriage to be limited only by the diminution of desire or the advance of old age. Apart from this, however, it inevitably has an influence outside the marriage relation. It opens the door for irregular, promiscuous and unfruitful unions, which, from the point of view of modern industry, sociology and politics, are full of danger. I cannot go into these here. It is sufficient to say that by contraception, inordinate sexual indulgence both in and out of marriage is facilitated, and, if I am right in my foregoing physiological arguments, evil must come to both individuals and the race."

Let the Indian youth treasure in their hearts the quotation with which M. Bureau's book ends:

"The future is for the nations who are chaste."

2

BIRTH CONTROL*

It is not without the greatest hesitation and reluctance that I approach this subject. The question of using artificial methods for birth control has been referred to me by correspondents ever since my return to India. Though I have answered them personally, I have never hitherto dealt with the subject publicly. My attention was drawn to the subject, now thirtyfive years ago, when I was a student in England. There was then a hot controversy raging between a purist who would not countenance anything but natural means and a doctor who advocated artificial means. It was at that early time in my life that I became, after leanings for a brief period towards artificial means, a convinced opponent of them. I now observe that in some Hindi papers the methods are described in a revoltingly open manner which shocks one's sense of decency. I observe, too, that one writer does not hesitate to cite my name as among the supporters of artificial methods of birth control. I cannot recall a single occasion when I spoke or wrote in favour of such methods. I have seen also two distinguished names having been used in support. I hesitate to publish them without reference to their owners.

There can be no two opinions about the necessity of birth control. But the only method handed down from ages past is self-control or *brahmacharya*. It is an infallible sovereign remedy doing good to those who practise it. And medical men will earn the gratitude of mankind, if instead of devising artificial means of birth control they will find out the means of self-control. The union is meant not for pleasure but for bringing forth progeny. And union is a crime when the desire for progeny is absent.

Artificial methods are like putting a premium upon vice. They make man and woman reckless. And

*Reprinted from *Young India*, March 12, 1925

respectability that is being given to the methods must hasten the dissolution of the restraints that public opinion puts upon one. Adoption of artificial methods must result in imbecility and nervous prostration. The remedy will be found to be worse than the disease. It is wrong and immoral to seek to escape the consequences of one's acts. It is good for a person who over-eats to have an ache and a fast. It is bad for him to indulge his appetite and then escape the consequences by taking tonics or other medicines. It is still worse for a person to indulge his animal passions and escape the consequences of his acts. Nature is relentless and will have full revenge for any such violation of her laws. Moral results can only be produced by moral restraints. All other restraints defeat the very purpose for which they are intended. The reasoning underlying the use of artificial methods is that indulgence is a necessity of life. Nothing can be more fallacious. Let those who are eager to see the births regulated explore the lawful means devised by the ancients, and try to find out how they can be revived. An enormous amount of spade work lies in front of them. Early marriages are a fruitful source of adding to the population. The present mode of life has also a great deal to do with the evil of unchecked procreation. If those causes are investigated and dealt with, society will be morally elevated. If they are ignored by impatient zealots, and if artificial methods become the order of the day, nothing but moral degradation can be the result.

A society that has already become enervated through a variety of causes will become still further enervated by the adoption of artificial methods. Those men therefore who are light-heartedly advocating artificial methods cannot do better than study the subject afresh, stay their injurious activity and popularize *brahmacharya* both for the married and the unmarried. That is the only noble and straight method of birth control.

3

SOME ARGUMENTS CONSIDERED*

My article on birth control has, as was to be expected, given rise to energetic correspondence in favour of artificial methods. I select three typical letters. There is a fourth letter which is largely theological. I therefore omit it. Here is one of the three letters:

"I have read your article on 'birth control' with great interest. The subject is, at present, exercising the minds of many educated men. Last year, we had long and heated debates. They proved at least this much, that young men are acutely interested in this problem, that there is a great deal of prudery and prejudice about it, that in a free and open discussion one's sense of 'decency' is rarely shocked. Your article has set me thinking afresh, and I appeal to you for some more light, to dispel many doubts that arise in my mind.

"I agree that 'there can be no two opinions about the necessity of birth control'. I further agree that '*brahmacharya* is an infallible sovereign remedy doing good to those who practise it' But I ask whether the problem is not one of 'birth control' than of 'self-control'. If so, let us see if self-control is a feasible method of birth control for the average person.

"I believe that this problem can be examined from two different points of view, that of the individual and that of society It is the duty of each individual to restrain his carnal passions, and thus evolve his spiritual strength At all times, there are a few such persons, of great moral fibre, who set up this noble standard before themselves, and will follow no other But I wonder whether they have any perception of the problem of birth control, which we are intent on solving. A *sannyasi* is out for salvation, but not for birth control

"But can this method solve an economic, social, and political question of the greatest importance to the vast majority of people within a reasonable period of time? It presses for solution on every thinking and prudent *grihastha* even now. How many children can one feed, clothe, educate, and settle in life is a question which brooks no delay. Knowing human nature as you do, can you reasonably expect large numbers completely to abstain from sexual pleasure, after the need for progeny has been satisfied? But I believe you would permit a rational and temperate exercise of the sexual instinct, as is recommended by our *smritikaras*. The vast majority may be asked neither to indulge the

*Reprinted from *Young India*, April 2, 1925

passion nor to repress it, but only to regulate it. But even if this were possible, would this method control birth? I believe that we shall then have better people, but not fewer people. In fact, the problem of population would become more acute, as an efficient population grows faster than an inefficient one. The art of cattle-breeding does not give us fewer cattle, but more and better cattle

"I agree that 'union is meant not for pleasure, but for bringing forth progeny'. But you must grant that pleasure is the chief, if not the only, inducement to it. It is Nature's lure to fulfil its purpose. How many would fulfil it, and do fulfil it, where pleasure is lacking? How many go for pleasure and get progeny, and how many go for progeny and also find pleasure? You say that 'union is a crime, when the desire for progeny is absent.' It beautifully suits a *sannyasi* like you to say so. For have you not also said that he who owns more than he needs is a 'thief' and 'robber', that he who loves not others more loves himself less? But why be so hard on poor and weak mortals? To them, a little pleasure, without desire for progeny would soothe and meet natural changes in body and mind The fear of progeny would in several cases agitate nerves, and in some cases delay marriage. The desire for progeny, in normal cases, would cease after a few years of marriage Would union after that be a crime? Do you think that a man afraid of committing that 'crime' would be morally superior by sitting tight over the safety valve of his restless passions? After all, why do you tolerate 'thieves' who hold more than they need, but not the 'criminals' who unite after the desire for progeny is satisfied? Is it because 'thieves' are too numerous and powerful to reform?

"Lastly, you allege that 'artificial methods are like putting a premium upon vice. They make man and woman reckless' This is a heavy charge, if true. I ask whether 'public opinion' has ever been strong enough to restrain sexual excess. I am aware of drunkards being restrained by fear of such opinion. But I am also aware of the sayings that 'God never sends mouths but He sends meat also,' and 'children are born because of God's will,' as well as of the prejudice that a large progeny is a proof of manliness. I know cases where such opinion gives a licence to husbands over wives, and considers the exercise of the sex instinct as the main bond of marriage. Besides, is it certain that 'adoption of artificial methods *must* result in imbecility and nervous prostration?' There are methods, and methods, and I believe that science has discovered, or will soon discover, innocuous methods. This is not beyond the wit of man.

"But it seems that you would not allow their use in any case, for 'it is wrong and immoral to seek to escape the consequences of one's acts.' This is unexceptionable, only you assume that even a moderate exercise of one's appetite, without desire for progeny, is immoral. Moreover I ask if any one is ever restrained by the fear of progeny, the consequences of one's acts. In any case, many are impelled to seek the advice of quacks, reckless of their health and happiness. How many abortions have not been caused while 'seeking to escape the consequences of one's acts'? But, even if 'fear proved an effective restraint, the 'moral' results would be poor indeed. Besides, by what system of justice should the sins of parents be visited upon the heads of their progeny and the imprudence of individuals hurt society? It is true that 'Nature is relentless, and will have full revenge for any such violation of her laws.' But why assume that the use of artificial methods is *such a violation*? None calls the use of artificial teeth, eyes and limbs as 'unnatural'. That alone is unnatural which does not secure our well-being. I do not believe that mankind is by nature vicious, and that the use of these methods will make it worse. There is enough of licence even now, not even India excepted It is as easy to prove that this new power will be properly used as that it may be abused. But let us recognize that man is on the point of winning this tremendous power over Nature, and that we can ignore it only at our cost. Wisdom lies in controling it, not in shunning it. Some of the noblest workers seek the propagation of these methods, not for indulgence, but to help men to self-control

"Let us also not forget that woman and her needs have been ignored too long She means to have her say in this matter, for she refuses to allow man to treat her body as 'tilth for offspring'. The strain of modern civilization is too great to permit her to rear a large family with all the drudgery and worry it means. Dr. Marie Stopes and Miss Ellen Key would never seek the 'nervous prostration' of woman The methods they suggest can be made effective chiefly by women, and are more likely to evolve wise motherhood than reckless indulgence In any case there are circumstances when a lesser evil may avoid a greater. There are dangerous diseases which must be avoided even at the cost of 'nervous prostration'. There are natural periods of lactation when union is unavoidable but injurious if fruitful. There are women, otherwise healthy, who can bear children only at a serious risk to their lives

"I neither wish nor expect you to turn into a propagandist of birth control You are at your best in keeping the light of Truth and Chastity burning in its purity and holding it before mortals who seek it. But a prudent parent will seek that light more than an imprudent one. He who realizes the need of birth control may easily evolve self control. The present licence, thoughtlessness and ignorance are so great that even you cry as if in a wilderness. There is great need for more enlightened discussion than your apologetic and 'reluctant' article permits. If you cannot join in it you must at least recognize it, and if need be, guide it betimes, for there are breakers ahead; and it will serve no purpose to blink your eyes at the danger, and 'hesitate on approaching this subject.'"

Let me clear the ground by saying that I have not written for *sannyasis* or as a *sannyasi*. I do not claim to be one in the accepted sense of the term. My observations are based upon unbroken personal practice with a slight aberration for a period of twentyfive years and that of those who have joined me in the experiment for a long enough period to warrant certain conclusions. In the experiment both young and old men and women are included. I claim a certain degree of scientific accuracy for the experiment. It has undoubtedly a strictly moral basis, but it originated in the desire for birth control. My own case was peculiarly for that purpose. Tremendous moral consequences developed as an afterthought though in a perfectly natural sequence. I venture to claim that by judicious treatment it is possible to observe self-control without much difficulty. Indeed it is a claim put forth not merely by me but German and other Nature Cure practitioners. The latter teach that water treatment or earth compresses and a non-heating and chiefly fruitarian diet soothe the nervous system and bring animal passions under easy subjection whilst they at the same time invigorate the system. The same result is claimed by *rajayogis* for scientifically regulated *pranayama* without reference to the higher practices. Neither the western nor the ancient Indian treatment is intended for the *sannyasi* but essentially for the householder. If it is contended that birth control is necessary for the nation because of over-population, I dispute the proposition. It has never been proved. In my opinion, by a proper land system, better agriculture and a supplementary industry, this country is capable of supporting twice as many people as there are in it today. But I have joined hands with the advocates of birth control in India from the standpoint of the present political condition of the country.

I do suggest that men must cease to indulge their animal passions after the need for progeny has ceased. The remedy of self-control can be made popular and effective. It has never had a trial with the educated class. That class has not yet, thanks to the joint-family system, felt the pressure. Those that have, have not given a thought to the moral issues involved in the question. Save for stray lectures on *Brahmacharya* no systematic propaganda has been carried on for advocating self-control for the definite purpose of limiting progeny. On the contrary the superstition of a larger family being an auspicious thing and therefore desirable still persists. Religious teachers do not generally teach that restriction of progeny in given circumstances is as much a religious obligation as procreation may be under certain other circumstances.

I am afraid that advocates of birth control take it for granted that indulgence in animal passion is a necessity of life and in itself a desirable thing. The solicitude shown for the fair sex is most pathetic. In my opinion it is an insult to the fair sex to put up her case in support of birth control by artificial methods. As it is, man has sufficiently degraded her for his lust, and artificial methods, no matter how well-meaning the advocates may be, will still further degrade her. I know that there are modern women who advocate these methods. But I have little doubt that the vast majority of women will reject them as inconsistent with their dignity. If man means well by her, let him exercise control over himself. It is not she who tempts. In reality man being the aggressor is the real culprit and the tempter.

I urge the advocates of artificial methods to consider the consequences. Any large use of the methods is likely to result in the dissolution of the marriage bond and in free love. If a man may indulge in animal passion for the sake of it, what is he to do whilst he is, say, away from his home for any length of time, or when he is engaged as a soldier in a protracted war, or when he is widowed, or when his wife is too ill to permit him the indulgence without injury to her health notwithstanding the use of artificial method?

But says another correspondent:

"With respect to your article on birth control in a recent issue, may I respectfully point out that you start by begging the whole question when you assert that artificial methods are injurious? In the Contraceptive Section of the last International Birth Control Conference (London, 1922) attended by members of the medical profession only, the following resolution was passed with 3 dissentients out of 164 present: 'That this meeting of the medical members of the fifth International Birth Control Conference wishes to point out that birth control by hygienic contraceptive devices is absolutely distinct from abortion in its physiological, legal and moral aspects. It further records its opinion, that *there is no evidence that the best contraceptive methods are injurious to health or conducive to sterility*'

"Now it seems to me that the opinion of such a large body of medical men and women including some of the most eminent names in the profession can hardly be set aside with a stroke of the pen. You say: 'Adoption of artificial method must lead to imbecility and nervous prostration.' Why 'must'? I venture to submit that modern scientific methods do not lead to anything of the kind, though the use of harmful methods through ignorance may. This is only one more argument why proper methods should be taught to all who are likely to need them, *i e*, to all adults capable of reproduction. You blame these methods for being artificial, and still want medical men to find out 'means of self-control'. I do not quite understand what you mean, but as you refer to medical men, would not any 'means of self-control' devised by them be equally artificial? You say: 'Union is meant not for pleasure, but for bringing forth progeny'. Meant by whom? By God? In that case, what did he create the sexual instinct for? You further say: 'Nature is relentless and will have full revenge for any such violation of her laws.' But nature at any rate is not a person as God is supposed to be, and does not issue orders to anybody. It is not possible to violate Nature's laws. The consequences of actions are inevitable in Nature. Good and bad are words that we apply to them The people who use artificial methods do take the consequences of their acts like those who don't. Your argument, therefore, does not mean anything unless you can prove that artificial methods are injurious. I assert from observation and experiment that they are not, provided proper methods are used. Actions must be judged moral or immoral according to their results and not by *a priori* assumptions as to their morality.

"The method you propose was also advised by Malthus, but is absolutely impracticable except for a few selected individuals like you. What is the use of advocating methods which cannot be practised? The benefits of *Brahmacharaya* have been greatly exaggerated. Modern medical authorities (I mean those who have no religious prejudices) think that it is positively harmful beyond the age of 22 or so. It is religious prejudice which makes you think that sexual union is a sin except for procreation As nobody can guarantee the result beforehand, you condemn everybody either to complete abstinence or to take the chance of sinning. Physiology does not teach this, and it is now too late in the day to ask people to ignore science in favour of dogma"

This writer has taken up an uncompromising attitude. I hope I have given enough illustrations to show that self-restraint and not indulgence must be regarded as the law of life, if we are to accept and retain the sanctity of the marriage tie. I have not begged the question, for I do contend that artificial methods, however proper they may be, are harmful. They are harmful not perhaps in themselves but because they increase the appetite which grows with every feed. The mind that is so tuned as to regard indulgence not only lawful but even desirable will simply feed itself on the indulgence, and will at last become so weak as to lose all strength of will. I do maintain that every act of indulgence means loss of precious vitality so needful to keep a man or woman strong in body, mind and soul. Though I have now mentioned the soul, I have purposely eliminated it from the discussion which is intended merely to combat the arguments advanced by my correspondents who seem to disregard its existence. The tuition that is needed for much married and enervated India is not that of indulgence with artificial means but complete restraint, if only for the sake of regaining lost vitality. Let the immoral medicines whose advertisements disfigure our press be a warning to the advocates of birth control. It is not prudery or false modesty which restrains me from discussing the subject. The restraining force is the certain knowledge that the devitalized and enervated youth of the country fall an easy prey to the specious arguments advanced in favour of indulgence.

It is perhaps now hardly necessary for me to combat the medical certificate produced by the second correspondent. It is wholly irrelevant to my case. I neither affirm nor deny that proper artificial methods injure the organs or produce sterility. No array, however brilliant, of medical men can disprove the ruin which I have witnessed of hundreds of youths who have indulged their passions even though it may be with their own wives.

The analogy drawn by the first writer from false teeth seems to me to be inapplicable. False teeth are indeed artificial and unnatural, but they may serve a necessary purpose; whereas artificial methods are like antidotes taken by a man who wants to eat not for satisfying hunger but for pleasing the palate. Eating for the sake of pleasure is a sin like animal indulgence for the sake of it.

The last letter is interesting for the information it gives:

> "The question is now vexing the Governments of the world. I refer to your article on birth control'. You doubtless know the antipathy of the American Government towards its propagation. You have no doubt also heard about the free sanction given to it by an Eastern Power—I mean the Empire of Japan. The one rules out birth control altogether,—whether as a result of artificial means or natural ones,—for reasons best known to every one. The other sponsors it for reasons also universally known. In my opinion, there is nothing to admire in the action of the first. Is there much, however, to despise in the step of the second? Don't you think that the Japanese Government should be given credit at least for facing facts? They must stop procreation, they must also take human nature at its *present worth*. Is not birth control, as at present understood in the West, the only way out for them? You will say 'An emphatic No'. But may I ask if the course you suggest is practicable? It *may be very ideal, but is it practicable?* Can humanity be expected to forego sexual pleasure to any very appreciable degree? It may be easy to find a glorious few who practise self-control or *Brahmacharya*. Can this method be however depended upon for a mass movement in this direction? And nothing less than a mass movement is necessary in India to meet the situation."

I must confess my ignorance of the facts about America and Japan. Why Japan is advocating birth control I do not know. If the writer's facts are correct and if birth control by artificial methods is at all general in Japan, I make bold to say that this fine nation is rushing headlong to its moral ruin.

I may be wholly wrong. My conclusions may be based on false data. But the advocates of artificial methods have need to be patient. They have no data at all except the modern examples. Surely it is too early to predict anything with any degree of certainty of a system of control which on the face of it seems to be repugnant to the moral sense of mankind. It is easy enough to trifle with youthful nature. It will be difficult to undo the evil effects of such trifling.

4

ON THE NECESSITY OF CONTINENCE*

I would request those who have carefully read through the book so far to peruse this chapter with even greater care, and ponder well over its subject matter. There are still several more chapters to be written, and they will, of course, be found useful in their own way. But no other chapter is nearly as important as this. As I have already said, there is not a single matter mentioned in this book which is not based on my personal experience, or which I do not believe to be strictly true.

Many are the keys to health, and they are all quite essential; but one thing needful, above all others, is *Brahmacharya*. Pure air, pure water, and wholesome food certainly contribute to health. But how can we be healthy if we expend all the health that we acquire? How can we help being paupers if we spend all the money that we earn? There can be no doubt that men and women can never be virile or strong unless they observe true *Brahmacharya*.

* Translation of a chapter in the author's Gujarati book on health (Part I, chapter IX).

What, then, is *Brahmacharya*? It means that men and women should refrain from carnal knowledge of each other. That is to say, they should not touch each other with a carnal thought, they should not think of it even in their dreams. Their mutual glances should be free from all suggestion of carnality. The hidden strength that God has given us should be conserved by rigid self-discipline, and transmitted into energy and power, — not merely of body, but also of mind and soul.

But what is the spectacle that we actually see around us? Men and women, old and young, without exception, are caught in the meshes of sensuality. Blinded for the most part by lust, they lose all sense of right and wrong. I have myself seen even boys and girls behaving as if they were mad under its fatal influence. I too have behaved likewise under similar influences, and it could not well be otherwise. For the sake of a momentary pleasure, we sacrifice in an instant all the stock of vital energy that we have laboriously accumulated. The infatuation over, we find ourselves in a miserable condition. The next morning we feel hopelessly weak and tired, and the mind refuses to do its work. Then in order to remedy the mischief, we consume large quantities of milk, *bhasmas*, *yakutis* and what not. We take all sorts of 'nervine tonics' and place ourselves at the doctor's mercy for repairing the waste, and for recovering the capacity for enjoyment. So the days pass and years, until at length old age comes upon us, and finds us utterly emasculated in body and in mind.

But the law of Nature is just the reverse of this. The older we grow, the keener should our intellect be; the longer we live, the greater should be our capacity to communicate the benefit of our accumulated experience to our fellow-men. And such is indeed the case with those who have been true *Brahmacharis*. They know no fear of death, and they do not forget God even in the hour of death; nor do they indulge in vain desires. They die with a smile on their lips, and boldly face the day of judgment. They are true men and women; and of them alone can it be said that they have conserved their health.

We hardly realize the fact that incontinence is the root cause of most of the vanity, anger, fear, and jealousy in the world. If our mind is not under our control, if we behave once or oftener every day more foolishly than even little children, what sins may we not commit consciously or unconsciously? How can we pause to think of the consequences of our actions, however vile or sinful they may be?

But you may ask, 'Who has ever seen a true *Brahmachari* in this sense? If all men should turn *Brahmacharis*, would not humanity be extinct and the whole world go to rack and ruin?' We will leave aside the religious aspect of this question and discuss it simply from the secular point of view. To my mind, these questions only betray our timidity and worse. We have not the strength of will to observe *Brahmacharya*, and therefore set about finding pretexts for evading our duty. The race of true *Brahmacharis* is by no means extinct; but if they were commonly to be met with, of what value would *Brahmacharya* be? Thousands of hardy labourers have to go and dig deep into the bowels of the earth in search of diamonds, and at length they get perhaps merely a handful of them out of heaps and heaps of rock. How much greater, then, should be the labour involved in the discovery of the infinitely more precious diamond of a *Brahmachari*? If the observance of *Brahmacharya* should mean the end of the world, that is none of our business. Are we God that we should be so anxious about its future? He who created it will surely see to its preservation. We need not trouble to enquire whether other people practise *Brahmacharya* or not. When we enter a trade or profession, do we ever pause to consider what the fate of the world would be if all men were to do likewise? The true *Brahmachari* will, in the long run, discover for himself answers to such questions.

But how can men engrossed in the cares of the material world put these ideas into practice? What about those who are married? What shall they do who have children ? And what shall be done by those people who cannot control themselves ? We have already seen what is the highest state for us to attain. We should keep this ideal constantly before us, and try to approach it to the utmost of our capacity. When little children are taught to write the letters of the alphabet, we show them the perfect shapes of the letters, and they try to reproduce them as best they can. In the same way, if we steadily work up to the ideal of *Brahmacharya* we may ultimately succeed in realizing it. What if we have married already ? The law of Nature is that *Brahmacharya* may be broken only when the husband and wife feel a desire for progeny. Those, who, remembering this law, violate *Brahmacharya* once in four or five years, will not become slaves to lust, nor lose much of their stock of vital energy. But, alas ! how rare are those men and women who yield to the sexual craving merely for the sake of offspring ! The vast majority turn to sexual enjoyment merely to satisfy their carnal passion, with the result that children are born to them quite against their will. In the madness of sexual passion, they give no thought to the consequences of their acts. In this respect, men are even more to blame than women. The man is blinded so much by his lust that he never cares to remember that his wife is weak and unable to bear or rear up a child. In the West, indeed, people have transgressed all bounds. They indulge in sexual pleasures, and devise measures in order to evade the responsibilities of parenthood. Many books have been written on this subject, and a regular trade is being carried on in contraceptives. We are as yet free from this sin, but we do not shrink from imposing the heavy burden of maternity on our women, and we are not concerned even to find that our children are weak, impotent and imbecile. Every time we get a child, we offer thanksgiving prayers to God and so seek to hide from ourselves the wickedness of our acts. Should we not rather deem it a sign of the wrath of God to have children who are feeble, sensual, crippled and timid ?

Is it a matter for joy that mere boys and girls should have children? Is it not rather a curse? We all know that the premature fruit of a too young plant weakens the parent, and so we try all means of delaying the appearance of fruit. But we sing hymns of praise and thanksgiving to God when a child is born of a boy father and a girl mother! Could anything be more dreadful? Do we think that the world is going to be saved by the countless swarms of such impotent children endlessly multiplying in India or elsewhere? Verily, we are, in this respect, far worse than even the lower animals; for in their case the male and the female are brought together solely with the object of breeding from them. Man and woman should regard it a sacred duty to keep apart from the moment of conception up to the time when the child is weaned. But we go on with our fatal merry-making blissfully forgetful of that sacred obligation. This almost incurable disease enfeebles our mind and leads us to an early grave, after making us drag a miserable existence for a short while. Married people should understand the true function of marriage, and should not violate *Brahmacharya* except with a view to progeny.

But this is so difficult under our present conditions of life. Our diet, our ways of life, our common talk, and our environments are all equally calculated to rouse animal passions; and sensuality is like a poison eating into our vitals. Some people may doubt the possibility of our being able to free ourselves from this bondage. This book is written not for those who go about with such doubting of heart, but only for those who are really in earnest, and who have the courage to take active steps for self-improvement. Those who are quite content with their present abject condition will find this tedious even to read; but I hope it will be of some service to those who have realized and are disgusted with their own miserable plight.

From all that has been said, it follows that those who are still unmarried should try to remain so; but if they cannot help marrying, they should defer it as long as possible. Young men, for instance, should take a vow to remain unmarried till the age of twentyfive or thirty. We cannot consider here all the advantages other than physical which they will reap and which are as it were added unto the rest.

My request to those parents who read this chapter is that they should not tie a mill-stone round the necks of their children by marrying them young. They should look to the welfare of the rising generation, and not merely seek to pamper their own vanity. They should cast aside all silly notions of family pride or respectability, and cease to indulge in such heartless practices. Let them rather, if they are true well-wishers of their children, look to their physical, mental and moral improvement. What greater disservice can they do to their progeny than compel them to enter upon married life, with all its tremendous responsibilities and cares, while they are mere children ?

Then again the true laws of health demand that the man who loses his wife, as well as the woman that loses her husband, should remain single ever after. There is a difference of opinion among medical men as to whether young men and women need ever let their vital energy escape, some answering the question in the affirmative, others in the negative. But while doctors thus disagree we must not give way to over-indulgence from an idea that we are supported by medical authority. I can affirm, without the slightest hesitation, from my own experience as well as that of others, that sexual enjoyment is not only not necessary for, but is positively injurious to health. All the strength of body and mind that has taken long to acquire is lost all at once by a single dissipation of the vital energy. It takes a long time to regain this lost vitality, and even then there is no saying that it can be thoroughly recovered. A broken mirror may be mended and made to do its work, but it can never be anything but a broken mirror.

As has already been pointed out, the preservation of our vitality is impossible without pure air, pure water, pure and wholesome food, as well as pure thoughts. So vital indeed is the relation between health and morals that we can never be perfectly healthy unless we lead a clean life. The earnest man, who, forgetting the errors of the past, begins to live a life of purity, will be able to reap the fruit of it straightaway. Those who practise true *Brahmacharya* even for a short period will see how their body and mind improve steadily in strength and power, and they will not at any cost be willing to part with this treasure. I have myself been guilty of lapses even after having fully understood the value of *Brahmacharya*, and have of course paid dearly for it. I am filled with shame and remorse when I think of the terrible contrast between my condition before and after these lapses. But from the errors of the past I have now learnt to preserve this treasure intact, and I fully hope, with God's grace, to continue to preserve it in the future; for I have, in my own person, experienced the inestimable benefits of *Brahmacharya*. I was married early, and had become the father of children as a mere youth. When, at length, I awoke to the reality of my situation, I found that I was steeped in ignorance about the fundamental laws of our being. I shall consider myself amply rewarded for writing this chapter if at least a single reader takes a warning from my failings and experiences, and profits thereby. Many people have told me — and I also believe it — that I am full of energy and enthusiasm, and that I am by no means weak in mind; some even accuse me of strength bordering on obstinacy. Nevertheless there is still bodily and mental ill health as a legacy of the past. And yet, when compared with my friends, I may call myself healthy and strong. If even after twenty years of sensual enjoyment, I have been able to reach this state, how much better off should I have been if I had kept myself pure during those twenty years as well? It is my full conviction, that if only I had lived a life of unbroken

Brahmacharya all through, my energy and enthusiasm would have been a thousandfold greater and I should have been able to devote them all to the furtherance of my country's cause as my own. If an imperfect *Brahmachari* like myself can reap such benefit, how much more wonderful must be the gain in power, — physical, mental, as well as moral, — that unbroken *Brahmacharya* can bring to us!

When so strict is the law of *Brahmacharya* what shall we say of those guilty of the unpardonable sin of illegitimate sexual enjoyment? The evil arising from adultery and prostitution is a vital question of religion and morality and cannot be fully dealt with in a treatise on health. Here we are only concerned to point out how thousands who are guilty of these sins are afflicted by venereal diseases. God is merciful in this that the punishment swiftly overtakes sinners. Their short span of life is spent in abject bondage to quacks in a futile quest after a remedy for their ills. If adultery and prostitution disappeared, at least half the present number of doctors would find their occupation gone. So inextricably indeed has venereal disease caught mankind in its clutches that thoughtful medical men have been forced to admit, that so long as adultery and prostitution continue, there is no hope for the human race, all the discoveries of curative medicine notwithstanding. The medicines for these diseases are so poisonous that although they may appear to have done some good for the time being, they give rise to other and still more terrible diseases which are transmitted from generation to generation.

In concluding this chapter which has grown longer than I expected, let me briefly point out how married people can observe *Brahmacharya*. It is not enough to observe the laws of health as regards air, water and food. The husband should avoid privacy with his wife. Little reflection is needed to show that the only possible motive for privacy between husband and wife is the desire for sexual enjoyment. They should occupy separate rooms at night, and be constantly engaged in good work during the day. They should read such books as fill them with noble thoughts and meditate over the lives of great men, and live in the constant realization of the fact that sensual enjoyment is the root of much misery. Whenever they feel a craving for sexual indulgence, they should bathe in cold water, so that the heat of passion may be cooled down, and be refined into the energy of virtuous activity. This is a difficult thing to do, but we have been born to wrestle with difficulties and conquer them; and he who has not the will to do so can never enjoy the supreme blessing of true health.

5

SELF-CONTROL*

I have been asked to say a few words about *Brahmacharya*. There are some subjects which I occasionally discuss in the pages of *Navajivan*, but which I rarely deal with in my speeches. *Brahmacharya* is one of these. I hardly ever speak about it, as I know that it cannot be explained by words and is a very difficult subject. You wish me to speak about *Brahmacharya* in the general restricted acceptance of the term, not about *Brahmacharya* with the wider significance of control of all the senses. Even the observance of *Brahmacharya* as ordinarily understood is described in the *Shastras* as a hard task. This is true in the main, but I may be permitted to make a few observations which point the other way. *Brahmacharya* appears to be difficult because we do not control the other senses. Take for example the organ of taste which leads the rest. *Brahmacharya* will come easy to anyone who controls his palate. Zoologists tell us that *Brahmacharya* is observed by the lower animals, as for instance cattle, to a greater extent than by human beings, and this is a fact. The reason is that cattle have perfect control over the palate,

* Translation by V. G. Desai of a Gujarati speech before the Seva Samaj, Bhadran, reported in *Navajivan*, 26th February, 1925.

not by will but by instinct. They subsist on mere fodder, and of this too, they take a quantity just sufficient for nutrition. They eat to live, do not live to eat, while our case is just the reverse. The mother pampers her child with all kinds of delicacies. She believes that she can evince her love only by feeding the child to the utmost. By doing this she does not enhance the child's enjoyment of his food, but on the other hand makes everything insipid and disgusting for him. The taste depends upon hunger. Even sweets will not be as tasteful to one who is not hungry as a slice of dry bread is to another who is really so. We prepare food in various ways with a variety of spices in order to be able to load the stomach, and wonder when we find *Brahmacharya* difficult to observe.

We misuse and corrupt the eyes which God has given us and do not direct them to the right things. Why should not the mother learn *Gayatri* and teach it to the child? She need not trouble with the inner and deeper meaning of the *mantra*. It is enough for her to understand and explain to the child that it inculcates reverence for the sun. This is but a rough interpretation of the *mantra* which I am placing before you. How shall we revere the sun? By looking up to the sun and performing an ablution as it were of the eyes. The author of the *Gayatri* was a *Rishi*, a seer. He taught us that nowhere else can we see such a beautiful drama as is daily staged before our eyes at the time of sunrise. There is no stage-manager greater than God or more sublime, and there is no more magnificent stage than the sky. But where is the mother who washes her child's eyes and then asks him to have a look at the sky? Mothers in our country are unfortunately concerned with quite other things. The boy may perhaps turn out to be a big official, thanks to his education at school, but we are apt to ignore the very large part which the home atmosphere plays in his education. Parents wrap their children up in heavy clothing and smother them while they fondly imagine that they are adding to their beauty. Clothes are meant just to cover the body, protect it against heat and cold, not to beautify it. If a child is trembling with cold, we must send him to the fireside to warm himself or out into the street for a run, or into the field for work. It is only thus that we can help him to build a splendid constitution. By keeping the child confined in the house we impart a false warmth to his body. By pampering his body we only succeed in destroying it.

So much for the clothes. Then again, the light conversation carried on in the house creates a very harmful impression on the child's mind. Elders talk of getting him married. The things which he sees around him also tend to corrupt him. The wonder is that we have not sunk to the lowest depths of barbarism. Restraint is observed in spite of conditions which render it well-nigh impossible. A gracious Providence has so arranged things that man is saved in spite of himself. If we remove all these obstacles in the way of *Brahmacharya*, it not only becomes possible but also easy to observe.

We are thus weak and yet we have to compete with a world of men physically stronger than ourselves. There are two ways of doing this: the one godly, and the other satanic. The satanic way is to adopt all measures right or wrong for developing the body, such as beef-eating etc. A friend of my childhood used to say that we must take meat, and that otherwise we could not develop our physique so as to meet the English on equal terms. Beef-eating became the vogue in Japan when the time came for her to face other nations. We must follow in her wake if we wish to build our bodies in the satanic way.

But if we build up our bodies in the godly way, the only means at our disposal is *Brahmacharya*. I pity myself when people call me a *naishthika Brahmachari*. How could such description apply to one who, like me, is married and has children? A *naishthika Brahmachari* would never suffer from fever, headache, cough or appendicitis, as I have suffered. Medical men say that appendicitis is caused even by an orange-seed remaining in the intestines. But an orange-seed cannot find permanent lodgment in a clean healthy body. When the intestines get weakened they are unable to expel such foreign matter. My intestines too must have weakened and hence the inception of appendicitis in me. Children eat all manner of things and the mother can never watch them all the time. Yet they do not suffer as their intestines are functioning vigorously. Let no one therefore mistake me for a *naishthika Brahmachari*, who should be made of infinitely sterner stuff. I am not an ideal *Brahmachari* although I aspire to be one.

Brahmacharya does not mean that one may not touch a woman, even one's sister, in any circumstance whatsoever. But it does mean that one's state of mind should be as calm and unruffled during such contact as when one touches, say, a piece of paper. A man's *Brahmacharya* avails for nothing if he must hesitate in nursing his sister who is ill. He has to be as free from excitement in case of contact with the fairest damsel on earth as in contact with a dead body. If you wish your children to attain such *Brahmacharya*, the framing of their curriculum must not rest with you but with a *Brahmachari* like myself, imperfect as I am.

A *Brahmachari* is a *Sannyasi* by nature. *Brahmacharyashram* is superior to *Sannyasa*, but we have thoroughly degraded it, and hence the degradation of *Grihasthashram* as well as *Vanaprasthashram*, and the disappearance of *Sannyasa* Such is our sorry plight.

If we take to the satanic way I have described, we will not be able to face the Pathans even after five hundred years. But if we take to the godly way we can meet them this very day. For, the change of mental attitude necessary in following the latter can take place in a moment, while building up the body to the required standard would take ages. The nation, God willing, can follow the godly way if only the parents prepare an atmosphere favourable to the observance of *Brahmacharya* on the part of the rising generation.

6

*BRAHMACHARYA**

It is not easy to write on this subject. But my own experience being fairly extensive I am always desirous of placing some of its results before the reader. Some letters which I have received have reinforced this desire.

A correspondent asks:

> "What is *Brahmacharya*? Is it possible to observe it in its perfection? If yes, have you attained that state?"

"*Brahmacharya* properly and fully understood means search after Brahma. As Brahma is present in every one of us, we must seek for it within with the help of meditation and consequent realization. Realization is impossible without complete control of all the senses. Therefore *Brahmacharya* signifies control of all the senses at all times and at all places in thought, word and deed.

Perfect *Brahmacharis*, men or women, are perfectly sinless. They are therefore near to God. They are like God.

I have no doubt that such perfect observance of *Brahmacharya* is possible. I regret to say that I have not attained such perfection, although my effort in that direction is ceaseless and I have not given up hope of attaining it in this very life.

I am on my guard when awake. I have acquired control over the body. I am also fairly restrained in speech. But as regards thoughts there still remains much for me to do. When I wish to concentrate my thoughts upon a particular subject, I am disturbed by other thoughts too and thus there is a conflict between them. Yet during waking hours I am able to prevent their collision. I may be said to have reached a state where I am free from unclean thoughts. But I cannot exercise an equal control over my thoughts in sleep. In sleep all manner of thoughts enter my mind, and I

*Translation by Valji Govindji Desai of an article in *Navajivan*, 25th May, 1924.

also dream unexpected dreams. Sometimes there arises a craving for pleasures previously enjoyed. When these cravings are impure there are bad dreams. This condition implies sinful life.

My thoughts of sin are scotched but not killed. If I had acquired perfect mastery over my thoughts, I should not have suffered from pleurisy, dysentery and appendicitis as I have during the last ten years. I believe that when the soul is sinless, the body which she inhabits is healthy too. That is to say, as the soul progresses towards freedom from sin, the body also tends to become immune from disease. But a healthy body in this case does not mean a strong body. A powerful soul lives only in a weak body. As the soul advances in strength the body languishes. A perfectly healthy body might yet be quite emaciated. A strong body is often diseased. Even if there be no disease, such a body catches infection soon, while a perfectly healthy body enjoys complete immunity from it. Pure blood has the power of expelling all obnoxious germs.

This wonderful state is indeed difficult to reach. Or else I should have reached it already, for I am confident that I have not been indifferent in adopting every single measure conducing to that end. There is no external thing which can keep me from my goal, but it is not given us easily to wipe out the impressions left by past actions. I am not at all despondent in spite of this delay, for I can conceive the state of perfect freedom from sin, I can even catch a faint glimpse of it. And the progress I have made gives ground for hope, not for despair. Even if I die without realizing my aspiration, I shall not believe that I am defeated. For I believe in a future life as strongly as I do in the present. And so I know that the least possible effort is not wasted.

I have entered into these autobiographical details in order that my correspondents and others in a like condition might feel encouraged and cultivate self-confidence. *Atma* is the same in every one of us. All souls possess equal potentialities; only some have developed their powers while others have them in a dormant condition. These latter too will have a like experience, if only they try.

Thus far I have dealt with *Brahmacharya* in its wider significance. *Brahmacharya* in the popular or current acceptance of the term means control of animal passion in thought, word and deed. This meaning is also correct as the control of passion has been held to be very difficult. The same stress has not been laid upon the control of the palate, and hence the control of passion has grown more difficult and almost impossible. Medical men believe that passion is stronger in a body worn out by disease, and therefore *Brahmacharya* appears hard to our enervated people.

I have spoken above of a weak but healthy body. Let no one therefore run away with the idea that we should neglect physical culture. I have expounded the highest form of *Brahmacharya* in my broken language which may perhaps be misunderstood. One who wishes to attain perfect control of all the senses must be prepared in the end to welcome weakness of body. All desire for bodily strength vanishes when there is no longer any attachment for the body.

But the body of a *Brahmachari* who has conquered animal passion must be very strong and full of lustre. Even this restricted *Brahmacharya* is a wonderful thing. One who is free from carnal thoughts even in his dreams is worthy of the world's adoration. It is clear that control of the other senses is an easy thing for him.

Another friend writes:

> "My condition is pitiable. The same vicious thoughts disturb me day and night, in the office, on the road, when I am reading or working or even praying. How am I to control my thoughts? How can I look upon womankind as upon my own mother? How can nothing but the purest affection emanate from the eyes? How can I eradicate wicked thoughts? I have your article on *Brahmacharya* before me, but it seems I cannot profit by it at all."

This is indeed heart-rending. Many of us are in a like predicament. But so long as the mind is up against wicked thoughts there is no reason to get disheartened. The eyes should be closed and the ears stopped with cotton, if they are sinning. It is a good practice to walk with the eyes cast downwards so that there is no occasion for them to wander in other directions. One should flee from the place where unclean talk is going on or where unclean music is being sung.

Control should be acquired over the organ of taste. My experience is that one who has not mastered taste cannot control animal passion either. It is no easy task to conquer the palate. But conquest of passion is bound up with the conquest of the palate. One of the means of controlling taste is to give up spices and condiments altogether or as far as possible. Another and a more effective means is always to cultivate a feeling that we eat just in order to sustain the body and never for taste. We take in air not for taste but for life. Just as we take water to quench our thirst, in the same way should we take food only to satisfy hunger. Unfortunately parents make us contract a contrary habit from very childhood. They corrupt us by giving us all manner of delicacies not for our sustenance but out of mistaken affection. We have got to fight against this unfavourable home atmosphere.

But our most powerful ally in conquering animal passion is *Ramanama* or some similar *mantra*. The *Dwadasha mantra* will also serve the same purpose. One may repeat any *mantra* one pleases. I have suggested *Ramanama* as I have been familiar with it since childhood and as it is my constant support in my struggles. One must be completely absorbed in whatever *mantra* one selects. One should not mind if other thoughts disturb one during the *japa*. I am confident that one who still goes on with the *japa* in faith will conquer in the end. The *mantra* becomes one's staff of life and carries one through every ordeal. One should not seek worldly profit from such sacred *mantras*. The characteristic power of these *mantras* lies in their standing guard over personal purity, and every diligent seeker will realize this at once. It should, however, be remembered that the *mantra* is not to be repeated parrotlike. One should pour one's soul into it. The parrot repeats such *mantras* mechanically; we must repeat them intelligently in the hope of driving out undesirable thoughts and with full faith in the power of the *mantras* to assist us to do so.

7

TRUTH *v.* BRAHMACHARYA*

A friend writes to Mahadev Desai :

"You will remember that in an article on *Brahmacharya* published in *Navajivan* some time ago, translated in *Young India* by you, Gandhiji admitted that he still had bad dreams. The moment I read it I felt that such admissions could have no wholesome effect, and I came to know later that my fear was justified.

"During our sojourn in England my friends and I kept our character unscathed in spite of temptations. We remained absolutely free from wine, woman and meat. But on reading Gandhiji's article one of the friends exclaimed to me in despair: 'If such is the case with Gandhiji even after his herculean efforts, where are we? It is useless to attempt to observe *Brahmacharya*. Gandhiji's confession has entirely changed my point of view. Take me to be lost from today.' Not without some hesitation I tried to reason with him, 'If the way is so difficult for men like Gandhiji, it is much more so for us, and we should therefore redouble our effort;' — the way Gandhiji or you would argue. But it was all in vain. A character that had been spotless so long was thus bespattered with mire. What would Gandhiji or you say, if someone were to hold Gandhiji responsible for this fall?

"As long as I had only one such instance in mind, I did not write to you. You would possibly have put me off by saying that it was an exceptional case. But there were more such instances, and my fear has been more than justified.

I know that there are certain things which are quite easy for Gandhiji to achieve, and which are impossible for me. But by the grace of God, I can say that something which may be impossible for even Gandhiji may be possible for me. It is this consciousness or pride that has saved me from a fall, though the admission above-mentioned has completely disturbed my sense of security.

*Reprinted from *Young India*, February 25, 1926.

"Will you please invite Gandhiji's attention to this fact, especially when he is just in the midst of his autobiography? It is certainly brave to say the truth and the naked truth, but the world and the readers of *Navajivan* and *Young India* will misunderstand him. I fear that one man's food may be another man's poison."

The complaint does not come to me as a surprise. When non-cooperation was in full swing, and when during the course of the struggle I confessed to an error of judgment, a friend innocently wrote to me: "Even if it was an error, you ought not to have confessed it. People ought to be encouraged to believe that there is at least one man who is infallible. You used to be looked upon as such. Your confession will now dishearten them." This made me smile and also made me sad. I smiled at the correspondent's simpleness. But the very thought of encouraging people to believe a fallible man to be infallible was more than I could bear. A knowledge of one as one is, can always do good to the people, never any harm. I firmly believe that my prompt confessions of my errors have been all to the good for them. For me at any rate they have been a blessing.

And I may say the same thing of my admission about the bad dreams. It would do the world a great deal of harm, if I claimed to be a perfect *Brahmachari* without being one. For it would sully *Brahmacharya* and dim the lustre of truth. How dare I undervalue *Brahmacharya* by false pretences? I can see today that the means I suggest for the observance of *Brahmacharya* are not adequate, are not found to be invariably efficacious, because I am not a perfect *Brahmachari*. It would be an awful thing for the world to be allowed to believe that I was a perfect *Brahmachari* whilst I could not show the royal road to *Brahmacharya*.

Why should it not be sufficient for the world to know that I am a genuine seeker, that I am wide awake, and that my striving is ceaseless and unbending? Why should not this knowledge be sufficient encouragement to others? It is wrong to deduce conclusions from false premises. It is wisest to draw them from things achieved.

Why argue that, because a man like me could not escape unclean thoughts, there is no hope for the rest? Why not rather argue that, if a Gandhi, who was once given to lust, can today live as friend and brother to his wife and can look upon the fairest damsel as his sister or daughter, there is hope for the lowliest and the lost? If God was merciful to one who was so full of lust, certainly all the rest would have His mercy too.

The friends of the correspondent who were put back because of a knowledge of my imperfections had never gone forward at all. It was a false virtue that fell at the first blast. The truth and observance of *Brahmacharya* and similar eternal principles do not depend on persons imperfect as myself. They rest on the sure foundations of the penance of the many who strove for them and live them in their fulness. When I have the fitness to stand alongside those perfect beings, there will be much more determination and force in my language than today. He whose thoughts do not wander and think evil, whose sleep knows no dreams and who can be wide awake even whilst asleep, is truly healthy. He does not need to take quinine. His incorruptible blood will have the inherent virtue of resisting all infection. It is for such a perfectly healthy state of body, mind and spirit that I am striving. This knows no defeat or failure. I invite the correspondent, his friends of little faith, and others to join me in that striving, and I wish that they may go forward even like the correspondent quicker than I. Let my example inspire those who are behind me with more confidence. All that I have achieved has been in spite of my weakness, in spite of my liability to passion, and because of my ceaseless striving and infinite faith in God's grace.

No one need therefore despair. My Mahatmaship is worthless. It is due to my outward activities, due to my politics which is the least part of me and is therefore evanescent. What is of abiding worth is my insistence on truth, non-violence and *Brahmacharya*, which is the real part of me. That permanent part of me, however small, is not to be despised. It is my all. I prize even the failures and disillusionments which are but steps towards success.

8

PURITY*

I am being inundated with letters on *Brahmacharya* and means to its attainment. Let me repeat in different language what I have already said or written on previous occasions. *Brahmacharya* is not mere mechanical celibacy, it means complete control over all the senses, and freedom from lust in thought, word and deed. As such it is the royal road to self-realization or attainment of *Brahma*.

The ideal *Brahmachari* has not to struggle with sensual desire or desire for procreation; it never troubles him at all. The whole world will be to him one vast family, he will centre all his ambition in relieving the misery of mankind, and the desire for procreation will be to him as gall and wormwood. He who has realized the misery of mankind in all its magnitude will never be stirred by passion. He will instinctively know the fountain of strength in him, and he will ever persevere to keep it undefiled. His humble strength will command respect of the world, and he will wield an influence greater than that of the sceptred monarch.

But I am told that this is an impossible ideal, that I do not take count of the natural attraction between man and woman. I refuse to believe that the sensual affinity, referred to here, can be at all regarded as natural; in that case the deluge would soon be over us. The natural affinity between man and woman is the attraction between brother and sister, mother and son, or father and daughter. It is this natural attraction that sustains the world. I should find it impossible to live, much less carry

* Reprinted from *Young India*, April 29, 1926. It then appeared under the caption 'On Brahmacharya'.

on my work, if I did not regard the whole of womankind as sisters, daughters or mothers. If I looked at them with lustful eyes, it would be the surest way to perdition.

Procreation is a natural phenomenon indeed, but within specific limits. A transgression of those limits imperils womankind, emasculates the race, induces disease, puts a premium on vice, and makes the world ungodly. A man in the grip of the sensual desire is a man without moorings. If such a one were to guide society, to flood it with his writings, and men were to be swayed by them, where would society be? And yet we have that very thing happening today. Supposing a moth whirling round a light were to record the moments of its fleeting joy and we were to imitate it, regarding it as an example, where would we be? No, I must declare with all the power I can command that sensual attraction even between husband and wife is unnatural. Marriage is meant to cleanse the hearts of the couple of sordid passion and take them nearer to God. Lustless love between husband and wife is not impossible. Man is not a brute. He had risen to a higher state after countless births in the brute creation. He is born to stand, not to walk on all fours or crawl. Bestiality is as far removed from manhood as matter from spirit.

In conclusion I shall summarize the means to its attainment.

The first step is the realization of its necessity.

The next is gradual control of the senses. A *Brahmachari* must needs control his palate. He must eat to live, and not for enjoyment. He must see only clean things and close his eyes before anything unclean. It is thus a sign of polite breeding to walk with one's eyes towards the ground and not wandering about from object to object. A *Brahmachari* will likewise hear nothing obscene or unclean, smell no strong, stimulating thing. The smell of clean earth is far sweeter than the fragrance of artificial scents and essences. Let the aspirant to *Brahmacharya* also keep his hands and feet engaged in all the waking hours in healthful activity. Let him also fast occasionally.

The third step is to have clean companions, clean friends and clean books.

The last and not the least is prayer. Let him repeat *Ramanama* with all his heart regularly every day, and ask for divine grace.

None of these things is difficult for an average man or woman. They are simplicity itself. But their very simplicity is embarrassing. Where there is a will, the way is simple enough. Men have not the will for it and hence vainly grope. The fact that the world rests on the observance, more or less, of *Brahmacharya* or restraint, means that it is necessary and practicable.

IN CONFIDENCE

(*By M. K. Gandhi*)

I receive so many letters questioning me regarding celibacy and I hold such strong views upon it, that I may no longer, especially at this the most critical period of national life, withhold my views and results of my experiences from the readers of *Young India*.

The word in Sanskrit corresponding to celibacy is *Brahmacharya* and the latter means much more than celibacy. *Brahmacharya* means perfect control over all the senses and organs. For a perfect *Brahmachari* nothing is impossible. But it is an ideal state which is rarely realised. It is almost like Euclid's line which exists only in imagination, never capable of being physically drawn. It is nevertheless an important definition in Geometry yielding great results. So may a perfect *Brahmachari* exist only in imagination. But if we did not keep him constantly before our mind's eye, we should be like a rudderless ship. The nearer the approach to the imaginary state, the greater the perfection.

But for the time being I propose to confine myself to *Brahmacharya* as in the sense of celibacy. I hold that a life of perfect continence in thought, speech and action is necessary for reaching spiritual-perfection. And a nation that does not possess such men is the poorer for the worst. But my purpose is to plead for *Brahmacharya* as a temporary necessity in the present stage of national evolution.

We have more than an ordinary share of disease, femines and pauperism—even starvation among millions. We are being ground down under slavery in such a subtle manner that many of us refuse even to recognise it as such, and mistake our state as one of progressive freedom in spite of the triple curse of economic, mental and moral drain. The evergrowing military expenditure, and the injurious fiscal policy purposely designed to benefit Lancashire and other British interests, and the extravagant manner of running the various departments of the state constitute a tax on India which has deepened her poverty and reduced her capacity for withstanding disease. The manner of administration has in Gokhale's words 'stunted' national growth so much that the tallest of us have to bend. India was even made to crawl on her belly in Amritsar. The studied insult of the Punjab, and the refusal to apologise for the insolent breach of the pledged word to Indian Musulmans are the most recent examples of the moral drain. They hurt the very soul within us. The process of emasculation would be complete if we submit to these two wrongs.

Is it right for us who know the situation to bring forth children in an atmosphere so debasing as I have described! We only multiply slaves and weaklings if we continue the process of procreation whilst we feel and remain helpless, diseased and famine stricken. Not till India has become a free nation, able to withstand avoidable starvation, well able to feed herself in times of famine, possessing the knowledge to deal with malaria, cholera, influenza and other epidemics, have we the right to bring forth progeny. I must not conceal from the reader the sorrow I feel when I hear of births in this land. I must express that for years I have contemplated with satisfaction the prospect of suspending procreation by voluntary self-denial: India is to-day ill-equipped for taking care even of her present population, not because she is over-populated but because she is forced to foreign domination whose creed is progressive exploitation of her resources.

How is the suspension of procreation to be brought about. Not by immoral and artificial checks that are resorted to in Europe but a life of discipline and self-control. Parents must teach their children the practice of Brahmacharya. According to the Hindu Shastras the lowest age at which boys may marry is 25. If the mothers of India could be inclined to believe that it is sinful to train boys and girls for a married life, half the marriages of India will automatically stop. Nor need we believe the fetish of early puberty among girls because of our hot climate. I have never known a grosser superstition than this of early puberty. I make bold to say that the climate has absolutely nothing to do with puberty. What does bring about untimely puberty is the mental and moral atmosphere surrounding our family life. Mothers and other relations make it a religious duty to teach innocent children that they are to be married when they reach a particular age. They are betrothed when they are infants or even babes in arms. The dress and the food of the children are also aids to stimulating passions. We dress our children like dolls not for their but for our pleasure and vanity. I have brought up children by the score. And they have without difficulty taken to and delighted in any dress given to them. We provide them with all kinds of heating and stimulating foods. Our blind love takes no note of their capacity. The result undoubtedly is an early adolescense, an unmature progeny and an early grave. Parents furnish an object lesson which the children easily grasp. By reckless indulgence in their passions they serve for their children as models of unrestrained licence. Every untimely addition to the famil is ushered in amid trumpets of joy, and feasting. The wonder is that we are not less restrained than we are, not-with-standing our surroundings. I have not a shadow of doubt that married people if they wish well to the country and want to see India become a nation of strong and handsome full-formed men and women they would practice perfect self-restraint and cease to procreate for the time being. I tender this advice even to the newly married. It is easier not to do a thing at all than to cease doing it, even as it is easier for a life abstainer to remain teetotaller than for a drunkard or even a temperate man to abstain. To remain erect is infinitely easier than to rise from a fall. It is wrong to say that continence can be safely preached only to the satiated. There is hardly any meaning, either, in preaching continence to an enfeebled person. And my point is that whether we are young or old, satiated or not, it is our duty at the present moment to suspend bringing forth heirs to our slavery.

May I point out to parents that they ought not to fall into the argumentative trap of the rights of partners. Consent is required for indulgence, never for restraint, this is an obvious truth.

When we are engaged in a death grip with a powerful government, we shall need all the strength physical, material and moral, and spiritual. We cannot gain it unless we husband the one thing which we must prize above everything else. Without this personal purity of life, we must remain a nation of slaves. Let us not deceive ourselves by imagining that because we consider the system of government to be corrupt, Englishmen are to be despised as competitors in a race for personal virtue. Without making any spiritual parade of the fundamental virtues, they practise them at least physically in an abundant measure. Among those who are engaged in the political life of the country there are more celibates and spinsters than among us. Spinsters, among us are practically unknown except the nuns who leave no impression on the political life of the country. Whereas in Europe thousands claim celibacy as a common virtue.

I now place before the reader a few simple rules which are based on the experience not only of myself but of many of my associates.

(1) Boys and girls should be brought up simply and naturally in the full belief that they are and can remain innocent.

(2) All should abstain from heating and stimulating foods, condiments such as chillies, fatty and concentrated foods such as fritters, sweets and fried substances.

(3) Husband and wife should occupy separate rooms and avoid privacy.

(4) Both body and mind should be constantly and healthily occupied.

(5) 'Early to bed and early to rise' should be strictly observed.

(6) All unclean literature should be avoided. The antidote for unclean thoughts is clean thoughts.

(7) Theatres, cinemas &c. which tend to stimulate passion should be shunned.

(8) Nocturnal dreams need not cause any anxiety. A cold bath every time for a fairly strong person is the finest preventive in such cases. It is wrong to say that an occasional indulgence is a safeguard against involuntary dreams.

(9) Above all one must not consider continence even as between husband and wife to be so difficult as to be practically impossible. On the contrary self-restraint must be considered to be the ordinary and natural practice of life.

(10) A heart-felt prayer every day for purity makes one progressively pure.

ENSLAVING THROUGH SLAVES.

In one of his recent speeches Mr. Mohamed Ali told of an Egyptian he met in London, who on being informed of the massacre at Jallianwalla, and the Punjab atrocities exclaimed in angry accents, 'Verily India deserves all that, for she is helping the British in imposing slavery on us.' We wonder if the Egyptian was quite entitled to reproach a whole nation in the way he did, when we remember that a slave nation as we are we have often been unknowing and unwilling agents in acts of humiliation and inhumanity. But now that the whole nation is awaking to a consciousness of its strength and we know of the bloody tragedy that is being enacted in Mesopotamia, it would stand to our lasting shame and humiliation if we continued for a moment longer to be party to that blood-guiltiness.

The *Nation* received by the last mail has an article the contents of which must make us hang down our heads in shame in as much as a number of our countrymen in Mesopotamia, taken there as Combatants or non-Combatants are helping in what the paper calls an act of 'perfidy', "for perfidy it is to promise a population its freedom and then to hang and shoot men for claiming it until you have the whole country in a state of war." In a few clear and direct statements supported by weighty authority, the *Nation* sums up the woeful tale of murder and humiliation, and of the enormous "sacrifice of life, fame and treasure" in Mesopotamia. In helping to organise the Arabs' political and economic life, the British officials "have been so successful in that task that seven times as large a force as the Turks kept in Mesopotamia is found to be too small to maintain order." "In cold figures we are spending on this war against three millions of Arabs more than we spend on the education of the British people. Thousands of lives British and Indian, will be sacrificed, and every death in Mesopotamia lies directly at the door of Mr. Lloyd George and his colleagues." These methods of Britain as a Mandatory Power are a crime both against the British and the Indian nations in as much as they have never been authorized by either of the two. But they are also a crime against humanity and civilisation. Says the *Nation*, "Colonel Lawrence, who knows the modern Arab of the Middle East better than any other living man, tells us that those methods have been worse than the methods of General Dyer." Quoting again from Col. Lawrence's article in the "Sunday Times", the *Nation* says, "Things have been far worse than we have been told, our administration more bloody and inefficient than the public knows. It is a disgrace to our imperial record and may soon be too inflamed for any ordinary cure." "There have been," the *Nation* goes on, "Heaven knows, impostures enough over mandates and the League of Nations, but even one-hardened world would be a little shocked to learn that Arabs were actually deported from Mesopotamia in order to secure a mandate for Great Britain."

The Congress rightly included in the Resolution on Non-co-operation, immediate stoppage of recruitment as soldiers, clerks and labourers in Mesopotamia. Circumstanced as we are it is impossible for us to withdraw the soldiers clerks and labourers that are already there helping in the impossible task of humiliating a proud and noble race. It is imperative that in atonement of that sin—involuntary sin—if for nothing else, we must stand as brother to brother with the Mussalmans in their fight for the honour of Islam which is a fight no less for the liberty of the Arabs than for the religious liberty of the whole Moslem world. And having sinned once we may not add to our store of sin by helping in or even countenancing the sending of recruits in that unfortunate land for any purpose whatsoever.

THE BRITISH GUIANA COLONISATION SCHEME.

(*By Mr. H. S. L. Polak.*)

So far, no public announcement has been made of the personnel of the Deputation, to be appointed by the Government of India in terms of the recommendation of the Select Committee of the Indian Legislative Council, to proceed to British Guiana with the object of investigating on the spot the conditions of Indians settled there. It would seem that there is considerable need of some such investigation, in view of certain facts that have appeared in the local press. It ought to be noted, in the first place, that Mr. J. A. Luckhoo, the principal Indian Member of the Colonization delegation to India, has resigned his Presidentship of the British Guiana Indian Association, whose headquarters are at Georgetown. It will be remembered that Mr Luckhoo and his Indian colleagues issued a pamphlet purporting to be published under the auspices of the British Guiana Indian Association, in which the Colonization Scheme was strongly recommended. Most serious exception was taken by the Association to the wrong use to which its name had been put. It passed a resolution, which was circulated in India, in which the pamphlet was disallowed as being unauthorised, and the Scheme itself was discredited as being not a genuine Scheme of colonization but one of Labour importation, which is quite a different matter altogether.

Upon Mr. Luckhoo's return to Georgetown, it would seem from newspaper reports that I have received that, he convened, in his capacity as President, a meeting of the Association w[illegible] he took severely to task for this resolution. He informed the meeting that unless the resolution was rescinded he would have no option but to resign his office as President. After an animated discussion, however, the Association decided that it would not withdraw the resolution, by which it was prepared to stand, and as a result, Mr. Luckhoo has been replaced in the Presidentship by Mr. J. Viapree, a well known local Solicitor, who was the Senior Vice President.

From this episode, it seems fairly clear that Indian opinion in British Guiana remains hostile to the Scheme so eloquently advocated by Mr. Luckhoo, and I may add that I have independent evidence, both from British Guiana and from this country, that the Association's view of the real character of the so called Colonization Scheme is well based.

From certain incidents that have occurred in the Colony of late, one is justified in drawing the deduction that everything is not so rosy there as it has been represented to be, and that the economic situation is far from being as bright as we have been led to believe. For example, on the 17th July, 900 Indian immigrants returned to India by one steamer. It seems a disproportionately large number. Then, too, writers to the "Daily Argosy" draw marked attention to the number of homeless and ill-clad beggars of Indian race seen about the streets of Georgetown, and local Indians have started a subscription list to erect a shelter for these destitute people. The "Daily Chronicle" of July 1, reports that the whole of the Indian Labourers on one estate went on strike for increased wages. They complained that they were coerced into working for a miserable weekly pittance of 1.92 Dol. (women 1.44 Dol.), and when they rebelled against this, their wives were assaulted by the overseer. It seems very improbable that Indians, coming to the Colony under the Colonization Scheme, will fare appreciably better than their countrymen and women already there, and having regard to the way in which the latter are apparently treated, it would seem very desirable that India should hesitate long before sending any more of her children to the Colony.

At any rate, it is not a very good advertisement for a Colonization Scheme.

At the present time, there is widespread labour unrest in British Guiana. The British Guiana Labour Union has been organizing strikes in order to demand increased wages owing to the higher cost of living, and it is a significant thing that Jamaican labourers are emigrating not to British Guiana, which is alleged by the promoters of the Colonization Scheme to be in great need of labour, but to Cuba, where wages are very much higher. It seems to me that there is ample scope for most cautious inquiry before India is committed to the so called Colonization Scheme. I do not think that one can compare average Indian emigrants with average British emigrants. The former have not any powerful economic organization for their protection, and, though theoretically there may be racial equality, practice and theory are, in these matters, very seldom in accord, especially when employers and workers are of different race, and the employers are of the same race as the officials. In the event of a conflict of interests, it is rarely the employers that suffer. I think, therefore, that Indians should hesitate very long before they commit themselves to this scheme, and that they should insist upon a most searching investigation of local conditions and the satisfactory answering of certain very obvious questions before even voluntary emigration to the Colony is promoted.

PANDIT MOTILAL ON LAW COURTS.

AN APPEAL TO LAWYERS.

[Last week we published, from the able pen of Babu Rajendra Prasad who till lately enjoyed leading position on the Patna Bar, a thoughtful article on the state of litigation and legal profession in India. Pandit Motilal Nehru, our respected President of the Amritsar Congress and one of the leading lawyers in the country—unquestionably the leading lawyer in his province—has now issued an appeal to the members of his profession wherein, besides exhorting them to make the boycott of law-courts a complete success and organise Panchyats for arbitration, he has described the evils of litigation, from his long experience of 37 years at the Bar. We publish the appeal in extenso from the *Independent*—Ed. Y. I.]

There can be no difference of opinion as to the desirability of avoiding litigation in courts and settling all disputes by mutual compromise or private arbitration. You may be in favour of or against the policy of Non-co-operation laid down by the Calcutta Special Congress, you may or may not belong to any of the current schools of political thought, you may not even be interested at all in politics, you cannot, whatever your position or occupation in life, deny that the nature of the litigation introduced by British laws and encouraged by the machinery of British Courts in this country is responsible for some of the greatest evils we suffer from.

I have had the honour of belonging to the legal profession for the last 37 years and whatever its detractors might say, I maintain that it is second to none in the world in its high traditions and its brilliant record of public service. At the same time I cannot conceal from myself the fact that the moral tone of the profession has steadily declined during my own experience and that from top to bottom. The leaders have in succeeding years yielded more and more to the prevailing commercial spirit of the age and have gone on raising their fees from time to time till they have now reached enormous figures out of all proportion to the nature, quality or quantity of the work required to be done. The employment of counsel at present partakes of the nature af a contract of hiring which it was never intended to be, and the good old principle that counsel's fees were mere honorariums can only excite laughter in these advanced days. A keen competition to break all various records in the matter of high fees is proceeding between eminent lawyers with annual income already running into six figures and it is impossible to say where it will lead to. The effect of this on the unfortunate litigants is thus crisply put in the popular saying: "*Adalat men jo jita so hara jo hara so mara.*" (Success in Court is defeat, defeat is death.)

I am free to confess that I have taken no small part in this competition and indeed was in the thick of it till some four weeks ago. What contribution I have made to the disastrous results so graphically described in the Hindi saying I cannot tell; but in the very nature of things the total output during the last 37 years could not have been insignificant. It is perhaps possible in view of modern conditions of life to defend high fees and cite precedents associated with honoured names but I am concerned here with the consequences to the country at large and these in all honesty can only be described as ruinous.

Much the greater evil of the present system however, is the creation of a class of lawyers and litigants who but for the excuse afforded by the existing machinery of the courts, would find no place in any decent society. Their methods are wellknown and their agents infest the precincts of almost every court. There can be no greater condemnation of the ordinary law court morality than what one often hears when litigants of this class approach each other for an amicable settlement, "We are not in the court why don't you tell the truth?" is not an uncommon form in which a fact alleged by one party is challenged by the other.

Coming to the courts themselves we all know what kind of justice is to be expected in criminal matters under the special procedure prescribed for the trial of Europeans. During the last 150 years, every Indian who has met with his death at the hands of a European has either had an enlarged spleen or his death has turned out to be the result of a pure accident. There has not been a single case, so far as I am aware of murder pure and simple. The climax was reached in the Punjab the other day. After the travesty of justice we have experienced in that unfortunate province, I feel that it is to drag the noble profession in the mire to practise it before courts which are the outcome of an unrighteous and oppressive system. The disreputable class of practioners I have just referred to are but the black sheep you find in every fold and under normal conditions it would be the business of the profession to drive them out. But when law courts are made subservient to the ends of the executive and such functions as they exercise can be suspended at the sweet will and pleasure of a legal or a provincial despot, when the enormities committed in the name of law and order are condemned by the British Parliament from which the courts derive their jurisdiction, it is time that we ceased to have anything to do with these effete creations of autocratic power.

We hold widely divergent views on certain public questions. It is idle to waste valuable time in trying to bring about a consensus of opinion on these. The best course is to agree to differ till

10

ABOLISH MARRIAGE !*

A correspondent, whom I know well, raises an issue. I take it for purely academic interest, because I know the views he has set forth are not his. "Is not our present-day morality unnatural?" he asks. "If it was natural, it should have been the same everywhere in all ages; but every race and community seem to have its own peculiar marriage laws, and in enforcing them men have made themselves worse than beasts. For diseases which are unknown amongst animals are quite common amongst men; infanticide, abortions, child-marriages, which are impossible in the brute creation, are the curse of the society that holds up marriage as a sacrament, and no end of evil results have sprung from what we uphold as laws of morality. And the miserable condition of Hindu widows — what is it due to, but to the existing marriage laws? Why not go back to nature, and take a leaf out of the book of the brute creation?"

I do not know whether the advocates of free love in the West resort to the argument summarized above or have any stronger reasons to put forth, but I am sure that the tendency to regard the marriage bond as barbarous is distinctly Western. If the argument is also borrowed from the West, there is no difficulty about meeting it.

It is a mistake to institute a comparison between man and the brute, and it is this comparison that vitiates the whole argument. For man is higher than the brute in his moral instincts and moral institutions. The law of nature as applied to the one is different from the law of nature as applied to the other. Man has reason, discrimination, and free will such as it is. The brute has no such thing. It is not a free agent, and knows no distinction between virtue and vice, good and evil. Man,

* A condensed translation from *Navajivan*, reprinted from *Young India*, June 3, 1926.

being a free agent, knows these distinctions, and when he follows his higher nature, shows himself far superior to the brute, but when he follows his baser nature, can show himself lower than the brute. Even the races regarded as the most uncivilized on earth accept some restriction on sexual relations. If it be said that the restriction is itself barbarous, then freedom from all restraints should be the law of man. If all men were to act according to this lawless law, there would be perfect chaos within twentyfour hours. Man being by nature more passionate than the brute, the moment all restraint was withdrawn, the lava of unbridled passion would overspread the whole earth and destroy mankind. Man is superior to the brute inasmuch as he is capable of self-restraint and sacrifice, of which the brute is incapable.

Some of the diseases that are so common at the present day are the result of infringement of marriage laws. I should like to know a single instance of a man strictly observing the restraint of the marriage bond having suffered from the diseases the correspondent has in mind. Infanticide, child marriages and the like are also the result of the breach of marriage laws. For the law lays down that a man or woman shall choose a mate only when he or she has come of age, is healthy, and capable of restraint, and desires to have progeny. Those who strictly obey this law and regard the marriage bond as a sacrament have never an occasion to be unhappy or miserable. Where marriage is a sacrament, the union is not the union of bodies but the union of souls indissoluble even by the death of either party. Where there is a true union of souls, the remarriage of a widow or widower is unthinkable, improper and wrong. Marriages, where the true law of marriage is ignored, do not deserve the name. If we have very few true marriages nowadays, it is not the institution of marriage that is to blame, but the prevailing form of it, which should be reformed.

The correspondent contends that marriage is no moral or religicus bond but a custom, and a custom which is opposed to religion and morality, and hence deserves to be abolished. I submit that marriage is a fence that protects religion. If the fence were to be destroyed, religion would go to pieces. The foundation of religion is restraint, and marriage is nothing but restraint. The man who knows no restraint has no hope of self-realization. I confess it may be difficult to prove the necessity of restraint to an atheist or a materialist. But he who knows the perishable nature of flesh from the imperishable nature of the spirit instinctively knows that self-realization is impossible without self-discipline and self-restraint. The body may either be a playground of passion, or a temple of self-realization. If it is the latter, there is no room there for libertinism. The spirit needs must curb the flesh every moment.

Woman will be the apple of discord where the marriage bond is loose, where there is no observance of the law of restraint. If men were as unrestricted as the brutes, they would straightway take the road to destruction. I am firmly of opinion that all the evils that the correspondent complains of can be eradicated not by abolishing marriage but by a systematic understanding and observance of the law of marriage.

I agree that, whereas amongst some communities marriage is permitted amongst very near relations, it is prohibited among other communities; that whereas some communities forbid polygamy, some permit it. Whilst one would wish that there was a uniform moral law accepted by all communities, the diversity does not point to the necessity of abolishing all restraint. As we grow wise in experience, our morality will gain uniformity. Even today the moral sense of the world holds up monogamy as the highest ideal, and no religion makes polygamy obligatory. The ideal remains unaffected by the relaxation of practice according to time and place.

I need not reiterate my views regarding remarriage of widows, as I consider remarriage of virgin widows not only desirable but the bounden duty of all parents who happen to have such widowed daughters.

11

CONSERVATION OF VITAL ENERGY*

Readers of *Young India* will excuse me for discussing in public delicate problems I would fain discuss only in private. But the literature I have felt compelled to glance through, and the copious correspondence my review of M. Bureau's book has given rise to, demand a public discussion of a question which is of paramount interest to society. A Malabar correspondent writes :

> "In your review of M. Bureau's book it is stated that there is no case on record of celibacy or long abstention producing any evil effects on us. In my own case, however, three weeks seem to be the utmost limit of beneficial abstention. At the end of that period I usually feel a heaviness of body, a restlessness both of body and mind, leading to bad temper. Relief is obtained either by normal coitus or nature herself coming to the rescue by an involuntary discharge. Far from feeling weak or nervous, I become the next morning calm and light, and am able to proceed to my work with added gusto.
>
> "A friend of mine, however, developed distinctly injurious symptoms by abstention. He is about 32 years of age, a strict vegetarian and a very religious person He is absolutely free from any vicious habits of body or mind. Yet he was having till two years ago, when he married, copious discharges at night followed by weakness of body and depression of spirits. Lately he developed excruciating pain in the abdominal region. On the advice of an *ayurvedic* doctor he married and is now cured.
>
> "I am intellectually convinced of the superiority of celibacy on which all our ancient *Shastras* agree. But the experiences I have quoted above make it clear that we are not able to absorb in our system the highly vital secretion of the testes, which consequently becomes a toxic product. I humbly request you, therefore, to publish in *Young India*, for the benefit of people like me who have no doubt as to the importance of chastity and abstention, any device, such as the *asanas* of *Hathayoga*, which will enable us to assimilate and absorb the vital product in our system."

The instances quoted by the correspondent are typical. In several such cases I have observed hasty generalizations from insufficient data. Ability to retain and assimilate the vital fluid is a matter of long training.

*Reprinted from *Young India*, September 2, 1926.

It must be so, as it gives a strength to body and mind such as no other process does with equal effect. Drugs and mechanical contrivances may keep the body in a tolerable condition, but they sap the mind and make it too weak to resist the play of a multitude of passions which like so many deadly foes surround every human being.

Too often do we expect results in spite of practices which are calculated to retard, if not to defeat, them. The common mode of life is shaped to minister to our passions. Our food, our literature, our amusements, our business hours are all regulated so as to excite and feed our animal passions. The vast majority of us want to marry, to have children and generally to enjoy ourselves, be it ever so moderately. It will be so more or less to the end of time.

But there are, as there always have been, exceptions to the general rule. Men have wanted to live a life wholly dedicated to the service of humanity, which is the same thing as saying to God. They will not divide their time between the rearing of a special family and the tending of the general human family. Necessarily such men and women cannot afford to live the general life which is designed to promote the special, individual interest. Those who will be celibates for the sake of God need to renounce the laxities of life, and find their enjoyment in its austere rigours. They may be 'in the world' but not 'of it'. Their food, their business, their hours of business, their recreations, their literature, their outlook upon life must, therefore, be different from the general.

It is now time to inquire whether the correspondent and his friend *desired* to live the life of complete abstention and whether they modelled it accordingly. If not, it is not difficult to understand the relief that the relaxation brought in the first case and the weakness that supervened in the second case. Marriage no doubt was the remedy in that second case, as in the vast majority of cases marriage is the most natural and desirable state when one finds oneself even against one's will living the married life in one's daily thought. The potency of thought unsuppressed but unembodied is far greater than that of thought embodied that is translated into action. And when the action is brought under due control, it reacts upon and regulates the thought itself. Thought thus translated into action becomes a prisoner and is brought under subjection. Thus considered, marriage too is a mode of restraint.

I must not undertake in the course of a newspaper article to give detailed instructions for the guidance of those who desire to live a life of ordered restraint. I must refer them to my booklet on health written years ago with that end in view. It does need revision in certain parts in the light of fresh experiences, but there is nothing in the book which I would withdraw. General directions, however, may be safely reiterated here:

1. Eat moderately, always leaving the dining room with a feeling of pleasant hunger.

2. Highly spiced and fatty vegetarian foods must be avoided. Separate fat is wholly unnecessary when an adequate supply of milk is available. A little food suffices when there is little vital waste.

3. Both the body and the mind must be constantly occupied in clean pursuits.

4. Early to bed and early to rise is a necessity.

5. Above all a life of restraint presupposes an intense living desire for reunion with God. When there is heart perception of this central fact, there will be continuously increasing reliance upon God to keep His instrument pure and in order. The Gita says: "Passions return again and again in spite of fasting, but even the desire ceases when the Divine is seen." This is literally true.

The correspondent refers to *asanas* and *pranayama*. I believe that they have an important place in the practice of restraint. But my own experiences in this direction, I am sorry to say, are not worth recording. There is, to my knowledge, little literature on the subject that is based on present experience. But it is a field worthy of exploration. I would, however, warn the inexperienced reader from trying it or accepting the directions of the next *hathayogi* he may meet with. Let him be sure that an abstemious and godly life is wholly sufficient to achieve the much to be desired restraint.

12

INFLUENCE OF ATTITUDES*

"I have been very interested in your articles in *Young India* on the subject of birth control. I expect you have read J. A. Hadfield's book *Psychology and Morals*. I want to draw your attention to this passage from it · 'We therefore speak of sexual pleasure when the expression of this instinct is alien to our moral sense, and we speak of sexual joy when the expression of this instinct is in conformity with the sentiment of love. Such expressions of sex feelings, far from destroying, actually deepen, the love of husband and wife, whereas free sexual indulgence on the one hand, and on the other hand *sexual abstinence practised under the false idea that the instinct is but a low pleasure, often produces irritability and the weakening of love.*' i. e. he holds that the act of sexual union has a sacramental value in deepening the love between a man and a woman, quite apart from the production of children. If he is right in this — and I am inclined to think he is, for, apart from the fact that he is an eminent psychologist, I have myself known of cases in which married life has been distorted and spoiled by attempts to repress the natural desire for physical expression of love — then I wonder how you would justify your doctrine that the only justifiable act of union is that intended for the production of children. For consider this case. A young man and a young woman love each other. It is beautiful and part of God's plan that they should do so. But they haven't enough money to support and educate a child. And I suppose you would agree that to bring a child into the world without being able to do these things is sinful; or if you like, say that it is bad for the woman's health to have one, or that she has had too may — anything like that. Now according to you a couple has two alternatives — either they must marry and yet live separately, in which case, if Hadfield is right, their love will tend to be spoiled, because of the irritability produced by repressed desires, or they must remain unmarried, in which case too their love will be spoiled, for nature gloriously ignores our human

*Reprinted from *Young India*, September 16, 1926.

institutions. They might, of course, go right away from each other: but even in separation their minds would be active, and so able to develop complexes. And even if you change society so that it is possible for all people to have as many children as come, there is still the danger to the race of overbreeding and to the individual woman of excessive childbirth. For a man might control himself tremendously and still have a child a year. You must either advocate chastity or birth control, for occasional indulgence may lead — as it has sometimes done amongst English clergymen — to the death of the mother bringing each year into the world the children her husband is pleased to say God sends her

What you call self-control is quite as much an interference with nature as contraceptives — more in fact. Men may overindulge their passions through birth control methods — but then they do this without them in all conscience — and at least if they don't produce children by their sin, they alone will suffer for it and not others. Remember the mine-owners will win this present fight because there are too many miners. The too profuse breeders punish not only the children they breed but also humanity in general."

So writes a correspondent. The letter to me is a study in mental attitudes and their influence. Mind takes a rope to be a snake, and the man with that mentality turns pale and runs away, or takes up a stick to belabour the fancied snake. Another mistakes a sister for wife and has animal passion rising in his breast. The passion subsides the moment he discovers his mistake. And so in the case quoted by the correspondent. No doubt, whilst 'abstinence is practised under the false idea that the instinct is but a low pleasure,' it is likely 'to produce irritability and the weakening of love.' But if abstinence is practised with the desire to strengthen the bond of love, to purify it, and to conserve the vital energy for a better purpose, instead of promoting irritability it will promote equanimity, and instead of loosening the bond of affection strengthen it. Love based upon indulgence is at best a selfish affair and likely to slightest strain. And why should the sacrament in the human species, if it is the lower animals? Why should we not it is in reality, i. e. a simple act of procreation to which we are helplessly drawn for the perpetuation of the species? Only man, having been gifted with a free will to a limited extent, exercises the human prerogative of self-denial for the sake of the nobler purpose to which he is born than his brother animals. It is the force of habit which makes us think the sexual act to be necessary and desirable for the promotion of love, apart from procreation, in spite of innumerable experiences to the contrary that it does not deepen love, that it is in no way necessary for its retention or enrichment. Indeed instances can be quoted in which that bond has grown stronger with abstinence. No doubt abstinence must be a voluntary act undertaken for mutual moral advancement.

Human society is a ceaseless growth, an unfoldment in terms of spirituality. If so, it must be based on ever-increasing restraint upon the demands of the flesh. Thus marriage must be considered to be a sacrament imposing discipline upon the partners, restricting them to the physical union only among themselves and for the purpose only of procreation when both the partners desire and are prepared for it. Then in either case supposed by the correspondent, there would be no question of sexual act outside the desire for procreation.

There is an end to all argument, if we start, as my correspondent has started, with the premise that sexual act is a necessity outside of the purpose of procreation. The premise is vitiated in the presence of authentic instances that can be cited of complete abstinence having been practised by some of the highest among mankind in all climes. It is no argument against the possibility or desirability of abstinence to say that it is difficult for the vast majority of mankind. What was not possible for the vast majority a hundred years ago has been found possible today. And what is a hundred years in the cycle of time open to us for making infinite progress? If scientists are right, it was but yesterday that we found ourselves endowed with the human body. Who knows, who dare prescribe, its limitation? Indeed every day we are discovering the infiniteness of its capacity for good as well as evil.

If the possibility and desirability of abstinence be admitted, we must find out and devise the means of attaining it. And as I have said in a previous article, life must be remodelled, if we are to live under restraint and discipline. We may not, as the vulgar saying goes, eat the cake and have it too. If we would impose restraint upon the organs of procreation, we must impose it upon all the others. If the eye and the ear and the nose and the tongue, the hands and the feet are let loose, it is impossible to keep the primary organ under check. Most cases of irritability, hysteria and even insanity, which are wrongly ascribed to attempts at continence, will in truth be found traceable to the incontinence of the other senses. No sin, no breach of nature's laws, goes unpunished.

I must not quarrel about words. If self-control be an interference with nature precisely in the same sense as contraceptives, be it so. I would still maintain that the one interference is lawful and desirable because it promotes the well-being of the individuals as well as society, whereas the other degrades both and is therefore unlawful. Self-control is the surest and the only method of regulating the birth-rate. Birth-control by contraceptives is race suicide.

Lastly, if the mine-owners are in the wrong and still win, they will do so not because the miners overbreed, but because the miners have not learnt the lesson of restraint all along the line. If miners had no children, they would have no incentive for any betterment and no provable cause for a rise in wages. Need they drink, gamble, smoke? Will it be any answer to say that mine-owners do all the things and yet have the upper hand? If the miners do not claim to be better than the capitalist, what right have they to ask for the world's sympathy? Is it to multiply capitalists and strengthen capitalism? We are called upon to pay homage to democracy under the promise of a better world when it reigns supreme. Let us not reproduce on a vast scale the evils we choose to ascribe to capitalist and capitalism.

I am painfully conscious of the fact that self-control is not easily attainable. But its slowness need not ruffle us. Haste is waste. Impatience will not end the evil of excessive birth-rate among the proletariat. Workers among the proletariat have a tremendous task before them. Let them not rule out of their lives the lessons of restraint that the greatest teachers among mankind have handed to us out of the rich stores of their experiences. The fundamental truths they have given us were tested by them in a better laboratory than any equipped under the most up-to-date conditions. The necessity of self-control is the common teaching of them all.

13

A MORAL STRUGGLE*

"I am a husband aged 30. My wife is about the same age. We have five children, of which two are fortunately dead I know the responsibility for the rest of our children But I find it difficult, if not impossible, to discharge that responsibility. You have advised self-restraint. Well, I have practised it for the last three years, but that is very much against my partner's wish. She insists on what poor mortals call the joy of life. You from your superior height may call it a sin But my partner does not see it in that light. Nor is she afraid of bearing more children to me. She has not the sense of responsibility that I flatter myself with the belief I have. My parents side more with my wife than with me, and there are daily quarrels. The denial of satisfaction to my wife has made her so peevish and so irritable that she flares up on the slightest pretext. My problem now is how to solve the difficulty. The children I have are too many for me. I am too poor to support them. The wife seems utterly irreconcilable If she does not have the satisfaction she demands, she may even go astray, or go mad, or commit suicide. I tell you, sometimes I feel that, if the law of the land permitted it, I would shoot down all unwanted children as you would stray

*Reprinted from *Young India*, April 26, 1928.

dogs. For the last three months I have gone without the second meal, without tiffin. I have business obligations which prevent me from fasting for days. I get no compassion from the wife because she considers I am a humbug. I know the literature on birth control. It is temptingly written. And I have read your book on self-restraint. I find myself between the devil and the deep sea."

The foregoing is a faithful paraphrase of a heart-rending letter from a young man who has given me his full name and address and whom I have known for some years. Being afraid to give his name, he tells me he wrote twice before anonymously, hoping that I would deal with his communications in the pages of *Young India*. I receive so many anonymous letters of this type that I hesitate to deal with them, even as I have considerable hesitation in dealing with this letter, although I know it to be perfectly genuine and know it to be a letter from a striving soul. The subject matter is so delicate. But I see that I may not shirk an obvious duty, claiming as I do claim a fair amount of experience of such cases and more especially because my method has given relief in several similar cases.

The condition in India, so far as English-educated Indians are concerned, is doubly difficult. The gulf between husband and wife from the point of view of social attainments is almost too wide to be bridgeable. Some young men seem to think that they have solved it satisfactorily by simply throwing their wives overboard, although they know that in their caste there is no divorce possible and therefore no remarriage on the part of their wives possible. Yet others — and this is the far more numerous class — use their wives merely as vehicles of enjoyment without sharing their intellectual life with them. A very small number — but daily growing — has a quickened conscience and is faced with the moral difficulty such as my correspondent is faced with.

In my opinion, sexual union to be legitimate is permissible only when both the parties desire it. I do not recognize the right of either partner to compel satisfaction. And if my position is correct in the case in point, there is no moral obligation on the part of the husband to yield to the wife's importunities. But this refusal at once throws a much greater and more exalted responsibility on the husband's shoulders. He will not look down upon his wife from his insolent height, but will humbly recognize that what to him is not a necessity is to her a fundamental necessity. He will therefore treat her with the utmost gentleness and love, and will have confidence in his own purity to transmute his partner's passion into energy of the highest type. He will therefore have to become her real friend, guide and physician. He will have to give her his fullest confidence, and with inexhaustible patience explain to her the moral basis of of his action, the true nature of the relationship that should subsist between husband and wife, and the true meaning of marriage. He will find in the process that many things that were not clear to him before will be clear, and he will draw his partner closer to him if his own restraint is truthful.

In the case in point I cannot help saying that the desire not to have more children is not enough reason for refusing satisfaction. It appears almost cowardly to reject one's wife's advances merely for fear of having to support children. A check upon an unlimited increase in the family is a good ground for both the parties jointly and individually putting a restraint upon sexual desire, but it is not sufficient warrant for one to refuse the privileges of a common bed to the other.

And why this impatience of children? Surely there is enough scope for honest, hard-working and intelligent men to earn enough for a reasonable number of children. I admit that for one like my correspondent, who is honestly trying to devote his whole time to the service of the country, it is difficult to support a large and growing family and at the same time to serve a country, millions of whose children are semi-starved. I have often expressed the opinion in these pages that it is wrong to bring forth progeny in India so long as she is in bondage. But that is a very good reason for young men and young women to abstain from marriage, not a conclusive reason for one partner refusing sexual co-operation to the other. That co-operation can be lawfully refused, it is a duty to refuse, when the call for *Brahmacharya* on the highest ground of pure religion is imperative. And when such a call has really come, it will have its healthy reaction upon the partner. Assuming, however, that it does not produce such reaction in time, it will still be a duty to adhere to restraint even at the risk of losing the life or the sanity of one's partner. The cause of *Brahmacharya* demands sacrifices no less heroic than, say, the cause of truth or of one's country. In view of what I have said above, it is hardly necessary to state that artificial control of birth is an immoral practice having no place in the conception of life that underlies my argument.

14

VOW OF BRAHMACHARYA*

After full discussion and mature deliberation I took the vow of *Brahmacharya* in 1906. I had not shared my thoughts with my wife until then, but only consulted her at the time of taking the vow. She had no objection. But I was hard put to it in making the final resolve. I had not the necessary strength. How was I to control my passions? The elimination of carnal relationship with one's wife seemed then a strange thing. But I launched forth with faith in the sustaining power of God.

As I looked back upon the twenty years of the vow, I am filled with pleasure and wonderment. The more or less successful practice of self-control had been going on since 1901. But the freedom and joy that came to me after taking the vow had never been experienced before 1906. Before the vow I had been open to being

*Reprint of Chapter VIII of the author's Autobiography, Part III.

overcome by temptation at any moment. Now the vow was a sure shield against temptation. The great potentiality of *Brahmacharya* daily became more and more patent to me. The vow was taken when I was in Phoenix. As soon as I was free from ambulance work, I went to Phoenix, whence I had to return to Johannesburg. In about a month of my returning there, the foundation of *Satyagraha* was laid. As though unknown to me, the *Brahmacharya* vow had been preparing me for it. *Satyagraha* had not been a preconceived plan. It came on spontaneously, without my having willed it. But I could see that all my previous steps had led up to that goal. I had cut down my household expenses at Johannesburg and gone to Phoenix, to take, as it were, the *Brahmacharya* vow.

The knowledge that a perfect observance of *Brahmacharya* means realization of *Brahman* I did not owe to the study of the *Shastras*. It slowly grew upon me with experience. The *Shastraic* texts on the subject I read only later in life. Every day of the vow has taken me nearer the knowledge that in *Brahmacharya* lies the protection of the body, the mind and the soul. For *Brahmacharya* was now no process of hard penance, it was a matter of consolation and joy. Every day revealed a fresh beauty in it.

But if it was a matter of ever increasing joy, let no one believe that it was an easy thing for me. Even while I am past fiftysix years, I realize how hard a thing it is. Every day I realize more and more that it is like walking on the sword's edge, and I see every moment the necessity for eternal vigilance.

Control of the palate is the first essential in the observance of the vow. I found that complete control of the palate made the observance very easy, and so I now pursued my dietetic experiments not merely from the vegetarian's but also the *Brahmachari's* point of view. As the result of these experiments I saw that the *Brahmachari's* food should be limited, simple, spiceless and, if possible, uncooked.

Six years of experiment have showed me that the *Brahmachari's* ideal food is fresh fruit and nuts. The immunity from passion that I enjoyed when I lived on this food was unknown to me after I changed that diet. *Brahmacharya* needed no effort on my part in South Africa when I lived on fruits and nuts alone. It has been a matter of very great effort ever since I began to take milk. How I had to go back to milk from a fruit diet will be considered in its proper place. It is enough to observe here that I have not the least doubt that milk diet makes the *Brahmacharya* vow difficult to observe. Let no one deduce from this that all *Brahmacharis* must give up milk. The effect on *Brahmacharya* of different kinds of food can be determined only after numerous experiments. I have yet to find a fruit substitute for milk which is an equally good muscle builder and easily digestible. The doctors, *vaidyas, hakims* have alike failed to enlighten me. Therefore, though I know milk to be partly a stimulant, I cannot for the time being advise anyone to give it up.

As an external aid to *Brahmacharya*, fasting is as necessary as selection and restriction in diet. So overpowering are the senses that they can be kept under control only when they are completely hedged in on all sides, from above and from beneath. It is common knowledge that they are powerless without food, and so fasting undertaken with a view to control the senses is, I have no doubt, very helpful. With some fasting is of no avail, because assuming that mechanical fasting alone will make them immune, they keep their bodies without food, but feast their minds upon all sorts of delicacies, thinking all the while as to what they will eat and what they will drink after the fast terminates. Such fasting helps them in controlling neither palate nor lust. Fasting is useful when mind cooperates with starving body, that is to say, when it cultivates a distaste for the objects that are denied to the body. Mind is at the root of all sensuality. Fasting, therefore, has a limited use, for a fasting man may continue to be swayed by passion. But it may be said that extinction of the sexual passion is as a rule impossible without fasting, which may be said to be indispensable for the observance of *Brahmacharya*. Many aspirants after *Brahmacharya* fail, because in the use of their other senses they want to carry on as those who are not *Brahmacharis*. Their effort is therefore identical with the effort to experience the bracing cold of winter in the scorching summer months. There should be a clear line between the life of a *Brahmachari* and of one who is not. The resemblance that there is between the two is only apparent. The distinction ought to be clear as daylight. Both use their eyesight, but whereas the *Brahmachari* uses it to see the glories of God, the other uses it to see the frivolity around him. Both use their ears, but whereas the one hears nothing but praises of God, the other feasts his ears upon ribaldry. Both often keep late hours, but whereas the one devotes them to prayer, the other fritters them away in wild and wasteful mirth. Both feed the inner man, but the one does so only to keep the temple of God in good repair, while the other gorges himself and makes the sacred vessel a stinking gutter. Thus both live as the poles apart, and the distance between them will grow and not diminish with the passage of time.

Brahmacharya means control of the senses in thought, word and deed. Every day I have been realizing more and more the necessity for restraints of the kind I have detailed above. There is no limit to the possibilities of renunciation, even as there is none to those of *Brahmacharya*. Such *Brahmacharya* is impossible of attainment by limited effort. For many, it must remain only as an ideal. An aspirant after *Brahmacharya* will always be conscious of his shortcomings, will seek out the passions lingering in the innermost recesses of his heart, and will incessantly strive to get rid of them. So long as thought is not under complete control of the will, *Brahmacharya* in its fulness is absent. Involuntary thought is an affection of the mind; and curbing of thought therefore means curbing of the mind which is even more difficult to curb than the wind. Nevertheless the existence of God within makes even control of the mind possible. Let no one think that it is impossible because it is difficult. It is the highest goal, and it is no wonder that the highest effort should be necessary to attain it.

But it was after coming to India that I realized that such *Brahmacharya* was impossible to attain merely by human effort. Until then I had been labouring under the delusion that fruit diet alone would enable me to eradicate all passions, and I had flattered myself with the belief that I had nothing more to do.

But I must not anticipate the chapter of my struggles. Meanwhile let me make it clear that those who desire to observe *Brahmacharya* with a view to realizing God need not despair, provided their faith in God is equal to their confidence in their own effort.

विपया विनिवर्तन्ते निराहारस्य देहिनः ।
रसवर्जं रसोऽप्यस्य परं दृष्ट्वा निवर्तते ॥

'The sense-objects turn away from an abstemious soul, leaving the relish behind. The relish also disappears with the realization of the Highest.' Therefore His name and His grace are the last resources of the aspirant after *moksha*. This truth came to me only after my return to India.

15

'STARTLING CONCLUSIONS'*

William R. Thurston, according to the publisher's preface, was a Major in the United States army, which he served for nearly ten years. And, during these years, he had varied experiences in several parts of the world, including China. During his travels he studied the effects of marriage laws and customs, as a result of which he felt the call to write a book on marriage. This book, which is called *Thurston's Philosophy of Marriage* and was published last year by the Tiffany Press, New York, contains only 32 pages of bold type, and can be read inside of an hour. The author has not entered into an elaborate argument, but has simply set forth his conclusions with just a dash of argument to support his conclusions which the publisher truly describes as 'startling'. In his foreword, the author claims to have based his conclusions on "personal observation, data obtained from physicians, statistics of social hygiene and medical statistics", compiled during the war. His conclusions are:

> 1 "That Nature never intended a woman to be bound to a man for life, and to be compelled to occupy the same bed or habitation with him, night after night, in pregnancy and out, in order to earn her board and lodging, and to exercise her natural right to bear children
>
> 2. "That the daily and nightly juxtaposition of the male and female, which is a result of present marriage laws and customs, leads to unrestrained sexual intercourse, which perverts the natural instincts of both male and female, and makes partial prostitutes of 90% of all married women. This condition arises from the fact that married women have been led to believe that such prostitution of themselves is right and natural because it is legal, and that it is necessary in order to retain the affections of their husbands"

The author then goes on to describe the effects of 'continual unrestrained sexual intercourse', which I epitomize as follows :

*Reprinted from *Young India*, 27-9-1928.

(*a*) "It causes the woman to become highly nervous, prematurely aged, diseased, irritable, restless, discontented, and incapable of properly caring for her children

(*b*) "Among the poorer classes, it leads to the propagation of many children who are not wanted . .

(*c*) "Among the higher classes, unrestrained sexual intercourse leads to the practice of contraception and abortion " *"If contraceptive methods, under the name of 'birth control' or any other name, are taught to the majority of the women of the masses, the race will become generally diseased, demoralized, depraved, and will eventually perish "* (The italics are the author's.)

(*d*) "Excessive sexual intercourse drains the male of the vitality necessary for earning a good living." *"At present there are approximately 2,000,000 more widows in the United States than there are widowers Comparatively few of these are war widows "* (The italics are the author's)

(*e*) "The excessive sexual intercourse incident to the present married state develops in the minds of both male and female a sense of futility." *"The poverty of the world today and the slums of the larger cities are not due to lack of profitable labour to be performed, but to excessive, unrestrained sexual intercourse, resulting from present marriage laws "* (The italics are the author's.)

(*f*) "Most serious of all from the standpoint of the future of the human race is sexual intercourse during pregnancy."

Then follows an indictment of China and India into which I need not go. This brings us to half of this booklet. The next half is devoted to the remedy.

The central fact of the remedy is that husband and wife must always live in separate rooms, therefore necessarily sleep in separate beds, and meet only when both desire progeny, but especially the wife. I do not intend to give the changes suggested in the marriage laws. The one thing common to all marriages throughout the world is a common room and a common bed, and this the author condemns in unmeasured terms, I venture to think, rightly. There is no doubt that much of the sensuality of our nature, whether male or female, is due to the superstition bearing a religious sanction that married people are bound to share the same bed and the same room. It has produced a mentality, the disastrous effect of which it is difficult for us, living in the atmosphere generated by that superstition, properly to estimate.

The author is equally opposed, as we have already seen, to contraceptive methods.

S. Ganesan, the enterprising publisher of Madras, has obtained the permission of the author to reprint the booklet for circulation in India. If he does so, the reader can possess a copy at a trifling price. He has secured also the rights of translation.

Many of the other remedies suggested by the author are, in my opinion, not of practical use to us, and in any case require legislative sanction. But every husband and wife can make a fixed resolution from today never to share the same room or the same bed at night, and to avoid sexual contact, except for the one supreme purpose for which it is intended for both man and beast. The beast observes the law invariably. Man having got the choice has grievously erred in making the wrong choice. Every woman can decline to have anything to do with contraception. Both man and woman should know that abstention from satisfaction of the sexual appetite results not in disease but in health and vigour, provided that mind cooperates with the body. The author believes that the present condition of marriage laws 'is responsible for the greater part of all the ills of the world today.' One need not share this sweeping belief with the author to come to the two final decisions I have suggested. But there can be no doubt that a large part of the miseries of today can be avoided, if we look at the relations between the sexes in a healthy and pure light, and regard ourselves as trustees for the moral welfare of the future generations.

BRAHMACHARYA or CHASTITY

The third among our observances is *Brahmacharya*. As a matter of fact all observances are deducible from Truth, and are meant to subserve it. The man, who is wedded to Truth and worships Truth alone, proves unfaithful to her, if he applies his talents to anything else. How then can he minister to the senses? A man, whose activities are wholly consecrated to the realization of Truth, which requires utter selflessness, can have no time for the selfish purpose of begetting children and running a household. Realization of Truth through self-gratification should, after what has been said before, appear a contradiction of terms.

If we look at it from the standpoint of *ahimsa* (nonviolence), we find that the fulfilment of *ahimsa* is impossible without utter selflessness. *Ahimsa* means Universal Love. If a man gives his love to one woman, or a woman to one man, what is there left for all the world besides? It simply means, "We two first, and the devil take all the rest of them." As a faithful wife must be prepared to sacrifice her all for the sake of her husband, and a faithful husband for the sake of his wife, it is clear that such persons cannot rise to the height of Universal Love, or look upon all mankind as kith and kin. For they have created a boundary wall round their love. The larger their family, the farther are they from Universal Love. Hence one who would obey the law of *ahimsa* cannot marry, not to speak of gratification outside the marital bond.

Then what about people who are already married? Will they never be able to realize Truth? Can they never offer up their all at the altar of humanity? There is a way out for them. They can behave as if they were not married. Those who have enjoyed this happy condition will be able to bear me out. Many have to my knowledge successfully tried the experiment.

If the married couple can think of each other as brother and sister, they are freed for universal service. The very thought that all the women in the world are one's sisters, mothers or daughters will at once ennoble a man and snap his chains. The husband and wife do not lose anything here, but only add to their resources and even to their family. Their love becomes free from the impurity of lust and so grows stronger. With the disappearance of this impurity, they can serve each other better, and the occasions for quarrel become fewer. There are more occasions for quarrel, where the love is selfish and bounded.

If the foregoing argument is appreciated, a consideration of the physical benefits of chastity becomes a matter of secondary importance. How foolish it is intentionally to dissipate vital energy in sensual enjoyment! It is a grave misuse to fritter away for physical gratification that which is given to man and woman for the full development of their bodily and mental powers. Such misuse is the root cause of many a disease.

Brahmacharya, like all other observances, must be observed in thought, word and deed. We are told in the *Gita*, and experience will corroborate the statement, that the foolish man, who appears to control his body but is nursing evil thoughts in his mind, makes a vain effort. It may be harmful to suppress the body, if the mind is at the same time allowed to go astray. Where the mind wanders, the body must follow sooner or later.

It is necessary here to appreciate a distinction. It is one thing to allow the mind to harbour impure thoughts; it is a different thing altogether if it strays among them in spite of ourselves. Victory will be ours in the end, if we non-cooperate with the mind in its evil wanderings.

We experience every moment of our lives that often while the body is subject to our control, the mind is not. This physical control should never be relaxed, and in addition we must put forth a constant endeavour to bring the mind under control. We can do nothing more, nothing less. If we give way to the mind, the body and the mind will pull different ways, and we shall be false to ourselves. Body and mind may be said to go together, so long as we continue to resist the approach of every evil thought.

The observance of *Brahmacharya* has been believed to be very difficult, almost impossible. In trying to find a reason for this belief, we see that the term *Brahmacharya* has been taken in a narrow sense. Mere control of animal passion has been thought to be tantamount to observing *Brahmacharya*. I feel that this conception is incomplete and wrong. *Brahmacharya* means control of all the organs of sense. He, who attempts to control only one organ and allows all the others free play, is bound to find his effort futile. To hear suggestive stories with the ears, to see suggestive sights with the eyes, to taste stimulating food with the tongue, to touch exciting things with the hands, and then at the same time expect to control the only remaining organ, is like putting one's hands in a fire, and then expecting to escape being burnt. He, therefore, who is resolved to control the one must be likewise determined to control the rest. I have always felt that much harm has been done by the narrow definition of *Brahmacharya*. If we practise simultaneous self-control in all directions, the attempt will be scientific and possible of success. Perhaps the palate is the chief sinner. That is why in the Ashram we have assigned to control of the palate a separate place among our observances.

Let us remember the root meaning of *Brahmacharya*. *Charya* means course of conduct; *Brahma-charya* conduct adapted to the search of *Brahma*, i. e., Truth. From this etymological meaning, arises the special meaning, viz., control of all the senses. We must entirely forget the incomplete definition which restricts itself to the sexual aspect only.

From Yeravda Mandir, Ch. III

17

BIRTH CONTROL (I)

A co-worker who is a careful reader of my writings was disturbed to read that I was likely to approve of the 'safe period' method of birth control. I endeavoured to make it clear to the friend that the safe period method did not repel me as did the use of contraceptives and that it was open largely only to married couples. But the discussion of the topic led us into much deeper waters than either of us had expected. The fact that my friend was repelled by the safe period method as much as by that of contraceptives showed to me that he believed in the possibility of ordinary persons practising the restraint imposed by the *Smritis*, i. e. that the union between husband and wife was permitted only when the parties really desired to have children. Whilst I knew the rule, I had never regarded it in the light that I began to do at the discussion. All these long years I had regarded it as a counsel of perfection not to be carried out literally, and had believed that so long as married couples carried on intercourse by mutual consent but without special regard to the desire for progeny, they were carrying out the purpose of marriage without breaking any positive injunction of the *Smritis*. But the new light in which I viewed the *Smriti* text was a revelation to me. I understood now as I never had done before the statement that married people, who strictly observed the injunction of the *Smritis*, were as much *Brahmacharis* as those who were never married and lived chaste lives.

The sole object of sexual intercourse according to the new light was the desire for progeny, never gratification of the sexual instinct. Simple gratification of the instinct would be counted according to this view of marriage as lust. This may appear to be a harsh expression to use for our enjoyment which has hitherto been regarded as innocent and legitimate. But I am not dealing with custom. I am dealing with the science of marriage as propounded by Hindu sages. Their presentation may be faulty, it may be altogether wrong. But for one like me who believes in several *Smriti* texts as inspired and based on experience, there is no escape from a full acceptance of their meaning. I know no other way of finding the truth of things and testing certain old texts in accordance with their full meaning, no matter how hard the test may appear and how harsh its deductions may sound.

In the light of what I have said above, birth control by contraceptives and the like is a profound error. I write thus with a full sense of my responsibility. I have great regard for Mrs. Margaret Sanger and her followers. She impressed me much by her great zeal for her cause. I know that she has great sympathy for the women who suffer because they have to bear the burden of carrying and rearing unwanted children. I know also that this method of birth control has the support of many Protestant divines, scientists, learned men and doctors, many of whom I have the honour of knowing personally and for whom I entertain high regard. But I should be false to my God who is Truth and nothing but Truth, if I concealed my belief from the reader or these great advocates of the method. Indeed, if I hid my belief, I should never discover my error — if my present belief is one. Moreover its declaration is due to those many men and women who accept my guidance and advice in many moral problems including this one concerning birth control.

That birth requires to be regulated and controlled is common cause between me and the advocates of contraceptives and the like. The difficulty of control through self-restraint is not to be denied. Yet there is no other way of attaining the end if mankind is to fulfil its destiny. It is my innermost conviction that if the method under discussion gains universal acceptance, mankind will suffer moral deterioration. This I say in spite of the evidence to the contrary that is often produced by the advocates of the method.

I believe I have no superstition in me. Truth is not truth merely because it is ancient. Nor is it necessarily to be regarded with suspicion because it is ancient. There are some fundamentals of life which may not be lightly given up because they are difficult of enforcement in one's life.

Birth control through self-control is no doubt difficult. But no one has yet been known seriously to dispute its efficacy and even superiority over the use of contraceptives.

Then, I feel that the full acceptance of the implication of the injunction of the *shastras* as to the strictly confined use of the sexual act, makes the observance of self-control much easier than if one regards the act itself as a source of supreme enjoyment. The function of the organs of generation is merely to generate progeny obviously of the highest type possible for a married couple. This can and should only take place when both parties desire, not sexual union but progeny, which is the result of such union. Desire for such union, therefore, without the desire for progeny, must be considered unlawful and should be restrained.

The possibility of such control for the ordinary man will be examined in the next issue.

Harijan, 14-3-1936

BIRTH CONTROL (II)

There is nothing in our society today which would conduce to self-control. Our very upbringing is against it. The primary concern of parents is to marry their children anyhow so that they may breed like rabbits. If they are girls, they are married at as early an age as they conveniently can be, irrespective of their moral welfare. The marriage ceremony is one long-drawn-out agony of feasting and frivolity. The householder's life is in keeping with the past life. It is a prolongation of self-indulgence. Holidays and social enjoyments are so arranged as to allow one the greatest latitude for sensuous living. The literature that is almost thrust on one generally panders to the animal passion. The most modern literature almost teaches that indulgence in it is a duty and total abstinence a sin.

Is it any wonder if control of the sexual appetite has become difficult if not almost impossible ? If then birth control through self-restraint is the most desirable and sensible and totally harmless method, we must change the social ideal and environment. The only way to bring about the desired end is for individuals who believe in the method of self-control to make the beginning themselves and with unquenchable faith to affect their surroundings. For them the conception of marriage I discussed last week has, it seems to me, the greatest significance. A proper grasp of it means a complete mental revolution. It is not meant merely for a few select individuals. It is presented as the law of the human species. Its breach reduces the status of human beings and brings swift punishment in the shape of multiplicity of unwanted children, a train of ever-increasing diseases, and disruption of man as a moral being responsible to his Maker. Birth control by contraceptives no doubt regulates to a certain extent the number of new-comers and enables persons of moderate means to keep the wolf from the door. But the moral harm it does to the individual and society is incalculable. For one thing, the outlook upon life for those who satisfy the sexual appetite for the sake of it is wholly changed. Marriage ceases to be a sacrament for them It means a revaluation of the social ideals hitherto prized as a precious treasure. No doubt this argument will make little appeal to those who regard the old ideals about marriage as a superstition. My argument is only addressed to those who regard marriage as a sacrament and woman not as an instrument of animal pleasure but as mother of man and trustee of the virtue of her progeny.

My experience of self-control by fellow-workers and myself confirms me in the view presented here. It assumes overwhelming force from the discovery in a vivid light of the ancient conception of marriage. For me *Brahmacharya* in married life now assumes its natural and inevitable position and becomes as simple as the fact of marriage itself. Any other method of birth control seems useless and unthinkable. Once the idea that the only and grand function of the sexual organ is generation, possesses man and woman, union for any other purpose they will hold as criminal waste of the vital fluid and cosequent excitement caused to man and woman as an equally criminal waste of precious energy. It is now easy to understand why the scientists of old have put such great value upon the vital fluid and why they have insisted upon its strong transmutation into the highest form of energy for the benefit of society. They boldly declare that one who has acquired a perfect control over his or her sexual energy strengthens the whole being, physical, mental and spiritual, and attains powers unattainable by any other means.

Let not the reader be disturbed by the absence of many or even any living specimens of such giant *Brahmacharis*. The *Brahmacharis* we see about us today are very incomplete specimens. At best they are aspirants who have acquired control over their bodies but not their minds. They have not become proof against temptation. This is not because *Brahmacharya* is so difficult of attainment. Social environment is against them, and the majority of those who are making an honest effort unknowingly isolate the control of the animal passion from all other passions, whereas the effort to be successful must include control over all the passions to which man is prey. Whilst *Brahmacharya* is not impossible of attainment by the average man and woman, it must not be supposed that it requires less effort, than that required by an average student who has set his heart upon becoming a master of any one of the sciences. Attainment of *Brahmacharya* in the sense here meant, means mastery of the Science of Life.

Harijan, 21-3-1936

19

MARRIED BRAHMACHARYA

A friend writes:

"I have long since held with you that self-control is the only sovereign method for attaining birth-control. That the sexual act is meant for procreation only, and apart from it, in any shape or form, would amount to unnatural gratification of lust, needs no proof. But sometimes this brings one up against a grave dilemma. Supposing that the sexual act, once or twice, fails to lead to conception, what is one to do then? Where is one to draw the limit? It is hard finally to give up all hope of begetting offspring. On the other hand, unlimited indulgence in the sexual act must result in the man being drained of all vitality. Again, should such a person be told to regard his failure to beget progeny on the first or the second chance, as a mark of adverse fate, and on that score to abstain from having any further intercourse thereafter? But that would require an exceptional degree of self-possession and spiritual strength on the part of the person concerned. Instances of people begetting progeny in their declining years after repeated failure during the years of manhood and youth, are by no means either unknown or rare. That makes the observance of complete abstinence still more difficult, and the position becomes further complicated when the parties happen to be otherwise healthy and free from any physical defect."

I admit the difficulty, but the difficulty is inherent in the problem itself. The road to any progress is strewn with such difficulty, and the story of man's ascent in the scale of evolution is co-extensive with the history of the successful overcoming of these difficulties. Take the story of the attempts to conquer the Himalayas. The higher you go the steeper becomes the climb, the more difficult the ascent, so much so that its highest peak still remains unvanquished. The enterprise has already exacted a heavy toll of sacrifice. Yet every year sees fresh attempts made only to end in failure like their predecessors. All that has, however, failed to damp the spirit of the explorers. If that is the case with the conquest of the Himalayas, what about the conquest of self, which is a harder job by far, even as the reward is richer? The scaling of the Himalayas can, at best, give a temporary feeling of elation and triumph. But the reward of the conquest of self is a spiritual bliss that knows no waning and grows ever more and more. It is a well-known maxim of the science of *Brahmacharya* that insemination in the case of a man who has properly kept the rules of *Brahmacharya* cannot, ought not to, fail to lead to conception. And this is just as it should be. When a man has completely conquered his animality, involuntary incontinence becomes impossible, and the desire for sexual gratification for its own sake ceases altogether. Sexual union then takes place only when there is a desire for offspring. This is the meaning of what has been described as 'Married *Brahmacharya*'. In other words, a person who obeys this rule, though leading a married life, attains the same state as and is equal in merit to one who completely abstains from the sexual act, which is only a means for procreation, never for self-indulgence. In practice, it is true, this ideal is seen to be rarely realized in its completeness. But in shaping our ideals we cannot think in terms of our weaknesses or the possible lapses. The present tendency, however, is to take a complete swing round, and the protagonists of contraceptives have almost set up self-indulgence as their ideal. Self-indulgence obviously can never be an ideal. There can be no limit to the practice of an ideal. But unlimited self-indulgence, as everybody would admit, can only result in certain destruction of the individual or the race concerned. Hence self-control alone can be our ideal, and it has been so regarded from the earliest times. Therefore we have to explore the means of its attainment, not to circumvent it.

It has become my settled conviction that most of the difficulties that are experienced in connection with the practice of *Brahmacharya* are due to our ignorance about its laws and would of themselves disappear if we discovered them. Let us, for instance, examine the poser propounded by our correspondent in the ideal light. In the ideal state, in the first place, such a contingency will never arise, because in a normally healthy couple, who have from their childhood upward observed the rules of *Brahmacharya*, sexual union can never prove infertile. In practice, however, anomalies do arise. The only rule that can be laid down in such instances is that the coitus may be permitted once at the end of the monthly period till coception is established.* If its object is achieved it must be abjured forthwith, for mere sensual gratification should never be its object. It is my faith based on my experience that bodily and mental health increases in the same ratio as bodily and mental chastity. Nor is it to be wondered at. A substance that is capable of producing such a wonderful being as man cannot but, when properly conserved, be transmuted into matchless energy

* The most illustrious example of this in European history is perhaps afforded by Ezenobia, the queen of Palmyra, equally renowned for her beauty and valour, about whom Gibbon has observed: "She never admitted her husband's embraces but for the sake of posterity. If her hopes were baffled, in the ensuing month she reiterated the experiment." — Pyarelal

and strength. Anyone can test for himself the truth of this observation of the *shastras* for himself by personal experience. And the rule holds good in respect of woman no less than man. The real difficulty, however, is that we vainly expect to be free from outward manifestations of lust, while harbouring it in our minds, with the result that physically and mentally we become utter wrecks, and our lives, in the words of the *Gita*, become a living lie or hypocrisy personified.

Harijan 20-3 1937.

20

THE CAUSE OF IT

A Bangalore correspondent asks:

> "You say that a married couple may have sexual union only when there is a mutual desire for a child and on no other account. Please let me know why one should wish for a child at all. Many people wish for children without fully realizing the responsibilities of parenthood, and many more wish for children fully knowing that they are incapable of discharging the responsibilies of a parent. Many persons who are physically and mentally unfit for parenthood wish for children. Don't you think that it is wrong for these persons to procreate?
>
> I should like to know the motive behind the desire for children. Many people wish for children to bequeath their possessions and to break the monotony of their life. A few people wish for a male child lest the gates of Heaven would not be opened for them. Are not these people wrong in wishing for a child?"

It is good to seek causes for things. But it is not always possible to discover them. The desire for children is universal. But I do not know any convincing cause, if to see oneself perpetuated through one's descendants is not a sufficient and convincing cause. My proposition, however, is not vitiated if the cause I give for the desire is not found sufficiently convincing. The desire is there. It seems to be natural. I am not sorry for having been born. It cannot be unlawful for me to see the best in me reproduced. Any way, till I see evil in procreation itself and till I see that the sexual act for mere pleasure is justifiable, I must hold that the sexual act is justified only where there is desire for children. I understand that this was so clear to the makers of the *Smritis* that Manu described only the first-born as children born of *dharma* and the rest of *kama*—lust. The more thought I give to the subject as dispassionately as is possible, the more convinced I feel about the correctness of the position I have taken and am enforcing. It is becoming clearer to me that the difficulty lies in our ignorance of the subject with which needless secrecy is being associated. Our thought is clouded. We dread to face consequences. We resort to half-measures as if they were perfect or final and thus render them most difficult of execution. If our thoughts were clear, if we became sure of our ground, our speech and action would be firm.

Thus, if I am sure that every morsel of food I take is for building and sustaining the body, I shall never desire to take food for the pleasure of the palate. I shall further realize that if I have any desire to eat things because they are tasty, and apart from hunger or the thought of sustaining the body, it is a token of disease and I should seek to cure myself of it and not satisfy it as if it was lawful or healthy. Even so if I am quite clear that the sexual act, apart from the unquestioned desire from progeny, is unlawful and detrimental to the body, mind and soul, surely resistance to the desire will become easy—far easier than when I am not clear whether the gratification of mere desire is or is not lawful and beneficial. If I am quite clear about the unlawfulness of the desire, I shall treat it as if it were a disease and repel its attacks with all my vigour. I shall feel the stronger for the resistance. They are wrong, even untruthful, who claim that they do not like the act but are helpless and therefore resistance leaves them weak and defeated. If all such people were to examine themselves, they would discover that their thoughts deceive them. Their thoughts cherish the desire, and their speech is a false interpreter of their thoughts. If on the other hand the speech is a true interpreter of the thoughts, there can be no such thing as weakness. Defeat there may be. Weakness never.

The correspondent's objection to procreation by unhealthy parents is perfectly valid. They can have or should have no desire for progeny. They are deceiving themselves and the world if they say that they perform the sexual act for progeny. In an examination of any subject truthfulness is always assumed. Desire for progeny must not be feigned in order to cover the pleasure of sexual union.

Harijan, 24-4-1937

21

FOR CONTRACEPTIVES

A correspondent writes:

"I would like to say a few words on the report of the interview between Mrs. Sanger and Mahatma Gandhi that appeared recently in the *Harijan*.

"The cardinal fact that I see missed in the interview is that it has not been taken into consideration that man is above all an artist and a creator. He is not satisfied with bare necessity, but must have beauty, colour and charm as well 'If ye have one pice only, buy bread of it, if two, one worth of bread and worth of flower,'—said Prophet Muhammad. In it is embodied a great psychological truth—the truth that man is by nature an artist. That is why we find him engaged in making his raiment something more than the mere necessity of sustaining his body. He has made every necessity into an art and has spent tons of blood on them. His creative instinct impels him to add to his difficulties and problems and solve them over again. He *cannot* be 'simple' as Rousseau, Ruskin, Tolstoy, Thoreau and Gandhiji would like him to be. War he must have as its necessary corollary which also he has transformed into a great art.

To appeal to him the example of nature would be in vain, for it is totally incompatible with his very being. 'Nature' *cannot* be his teacher. Those who appeal to it overlook that it does not only consist of hills and dales and flower-beds, but flood, cyclone and earthquake as well. 'From an artistic standpoint', says Nietzsche the iconoclast, "Nature is no model. It exaggerates, distorts and leaves gaps. Nature is the *accident*. To study 'from nature' seems to me a bad sign; thus lying in the dust before trivial facts is unworthy of a thorough artist. To see what is the function of another order of intellects, the *anti-artistic*, the matter-of-fact, one must know *who* one is!' We know that the wild beasts eat raw flesh out of the need of sustaining their bodies and not out of taste. We also know of the rutting season of nature outside which none meets sexually there. But it is, to quote our philosopher again, 'unworthy of a thorough artist' that man by nature is. To end sexual life when the need of propagation is no longer there, or to enjoin sex-communion expressly with the desire of begetting offspring, is too calculating, too natural, too 'matter-of-fact' as our philosopher just now said, to appeal to his strong artistic taste. Hence he has got quite another aspect of sexual love which is independent of the desire to multiply as has been revealed by such authorities as Havelock Ellis and Marie Stopes, but which, though originating in the soul, is nevertheless incomplete without the bodily union, so long as we do not get the soul all by itself, but through the instrument of the body. To cope with the *effect* of such a union is altogether a different problem, and herein is the task of the birth control movement. But if the task be shifted to a rearrangement of the soul itself — for 'self-control' is nothing different from this — by external discipline, we are not sanguine that it would prove all the purposes that are expected of it. Nor would the movement of control over birth without a firm psychological basis.

I would close with a further remark that by this I do not mean to underrate the value of the discipline of self-control or what is technically known as *brahmacharya*. I would always admire it as the art of the control of the sex instinct carried to perfection. But just as the perfection of other arts does not interfere with the *science* of life, with the *whole* life (in the Nietzschean sense of the term), with the proper scheme of all the values of life, — so also I will not allow the value of the ideal of *brahmacharya dominate* other values, far less use it as an *instrument* of solving problems, such as overpopulation. We have made such a hobgoblin of it! We have heard of the 'war-babies'. Should we refuse giving credit to those soldiers who brought victory for their countrymen by their blood because they happened to give birth to those war-babies? Nobody would. I believe it was with an eye to such a scheme of values that the scriptures (प्रश्नोपनिषत्) said, 'ब्रह्मचर्यमेव तद् यद् रात्रौ रत्या संयुज्यते', or 'there is *brahmacharya* where sexual union occurs only at night (i. e. as opposed to abnormal cohabitation during the day-time). Here normal sex life itself is spoken of as *brahmacharya*, the rigid conception of which began after we had already topsy-turvied the proper scheme of all the values of life "

I gladly publish this letter as I should any such letter that is not full of declamation, abuse or insinuations. The reader should have both the sides of the question to enable him to come to a decision. I am myself eager to know why a thing which is claimed to be scientific and beneficial and which has many distinguished supporters repels me notwithstanding my effort to see the bright side of it.

Thus it is not proved to my satisfaction that sexual union in marriage is in itself good and beneficial to the unionists. To the contrary effect I can bear ample testimony from my own experience and that of many friends. I am not aware of any of us having derived any benefit, mental, spiritual or physical. Momentary excitement and satisfaction there certainly was. But it was invariably followed by exhaustion. And the desire for union returned immediately the effect of exhaustion had worn out. Although I have always been a conscientious worker, I can clearly recall the fact that this indulgence interfered with my work. It was the consciousness of this limitation that put me on the track of self-restraint; and I have no manner of doubt that the self-restraint is responsible for the comparative freedom from illnesses that I have enjoyed for long periods and for my output of energy and work both physical and mental which eye-witnesses have described as phenomenal.

I fear that the correspondent has misapplied his reading. Man is undoubtedly an artist and creator. Undoubtedly he must have beauty and therefore colour. His artistic and creative nature at its best taught him to see art in self-restraint and ugliness in un-creative union. His instinct for the artistic taught him to discriminate and to know that any conglomeration of colours was no mark of beauty, nor every sense enjoyment good in itself. His eye for art taught man to seek enjoyment in usefulness. Thus he learnt at an early stage of his evolution that he was to eat not for its own sake as some of us still do, but that he should eat to enable him to live. At a later stage he learnt further that there was neither beauty nor joy in living for its own sake, but that he must live to serve his fellow-creatures and through them his Maker. Similarly, when he pondered over the phenomenon of the pleasurableness of sexual union, he discovered that, like every other organ of sense, this one of generation had its use and abuse. And he saw that its true function, its right use was to restrict it to generation. Any other use he saw, was ugly, and he saw further that it was fraught with very serious consequences as well to the individual as to the race. It is hardly necessary for me to prolong the argument.

The correspondent says well that man makes art out of his necessities. Necessity is not only the mother of invention, it is the mother also of art. We should therefore beware of that art which has not necessity as its basis.

Nor may we dignify every want by the name of necessity. Man's estate is one of probation. During that period he is played upon by evil forces as well as good. He is ever prey to temptations. He has to prove his manliness by resisting and fighting temptations. He is no warrior who fights outside foes of his imagination and is powerless to lift his little finger against the innumerable foes within or, what is worse, mistakes them for friends. "War he must have". But the correspondent is wrong when he says that 'as its necessary corollary he has transformed it into a great art." He has hardly yet learnt the art of war. He has mistaken false war for true, even as our forefathers, under a mistaken view of sacrifice, instead of sacrificing their base passions, sacrificed innocent non-human fellow creatures as many do even at the present day. We have yet to learn the art of true war. Surely there is neither beauty nor art in what is going on today on the

Abyssinian frontier. The correspondent has chosen unhappy (for him) names for his illustrations. Rousseau, Ruskin, Thoreau and Tolstoy were first-class artists of their time. They will live even after many of us are dead, cremated and forgotten.

The correspondent seems to have misapplied the word nature. When an appeal to man is made to copy or study nature, he is not invited to follow what the reptiles do or even what the king of the forest does. He has to study man's nature at its best, i.e. I presume his regenerate nature, whatever it may be. Perhaps it requires considerable effort to know what regenerate nature is. It is dangerous nowadays to refer to old teachers. I suggest to the correspondent that it is unnecessary to bring in Nietzsche or even *Prashnopanishad*. The question for me is past the stage of quotations. What has cold reason to say on the point under discussion? Is it or is it not correct to say that the only right use of the generative organ is to confine it solely to generation and that any other use is its abuse? If it is, no difficulty in achieving the right use and avoiding the wrong should baffle the scientific seeker.

FOR WOMEN REFORMERS

From a serious discussion I had with a sister I fear that my position on the use of contraceptives has not yet been sufficiently understood. My opposition is not due to their having come to us from the West. I thankfully use some western things when I know that they benefit us as they benefit those in the West. My opposition to contraceptives is based on merits.

I take it that the wisest among the protagonists of contraceptives restrict their use to married women who desire to satisfy their and their husbands' sexual appetite without wanting children. I hold this desire as unnatural in the human species and its satisfaction detrimental to the spiritual progress of the human family. As against this is often cited the following testimony among others of Lord Dawson of Penn:

> "Sex love is one of the clamant, dominating forces of the world. Here we have an instinct, so fundamental, so imperious that its influence is a fact which has to be accepted. suppress it you cannot. You may guide it into healthy channels, but an outlet it will have, and if that outlet is inadequate or unduly obstructed, irregular channels will be forced. Self-control has a breaking point, and if in any community marriage is difficult or late of attainment, an increase of irregular unions will inevitably result All are agreed that union of body should be in association with union of mind and soul, all are agreed that the rearing of children is a pre-eminent purpose. Has not sexual union over and over again been the physical expression of our love without thought or intention of procreation? Have we all been wrong? Or is it that the Church lacks that vital contact with the realities of life which accounts for the gulf between her and the people? Authority, and I include under authority the churches, will never gain the allegiance of the young unless their attitude is more frank, more courageous, and more in accordance with realities
>
> Sex love has, apart from parenthood, a purport of its own It is an essential part of health and happiness in marriage. If sexual union is a gift from God, it is worth learning how to use it. Within its own sphere it should be cultivated so as to bring physical satisfaction to both, not merely to one The attainment of mutual and reciprocal joy in their relations constitutes a firm

bond between two people and make for durability of their marriage tie. More marriages fail from inadequate and clumsy sex love than from too much sex love. Passion is a worthy possession; most men who are any good are capable of passion. Sex love without passion is a poor lifeless thing. Sensuality on the other hand is on a level with gluttony, a physical excess. Now that the revision of the Prayer Book is receiving consideration. I should like to suggest, with great respect, that an addition be made to the objects of marriage in the Marriage Service in these terms: 'The complete realization of the love of this man and this woman, the one for the other.'

I will pass on to consider the all-important question of birth control Birth control is here to stay. It is an established fact, and for good or evil has to be accepted. No denunciations will abolish it. The reasons which lead parents to limit their offspring are sometimes selfish, but more often honourable and cogent. The desire to marry and to rear children well-equipped for life's struggle, limited incomes, the cost of living, burdensome taxation, are forcible motives, and, further, amongst the educated classes there is the desire of women to take part in life and their husbands' careers, which is incompatible with oft-recurring pregnancies. Absence of birth control means late marriages, and these carry with them irregular unions and all the baneful consequences. It is idle to decry illicit intercourse and interpose obstacles to marriage at one and the same time. But say many, 'Birth control may be necessary, but the only control which is justifiable is voluntary abstention.' Such abstention would be either ineffective or, if effective, impracticable and harmful to health and happiness. To limit the size of a family to, say, four children, would be to impose on a married couple an amount of abstention which for long periods would almost be equivalent to celibacy, and when one remembers that owing to economic reasons the abstention would have to be most strict during the earlier years of marriage life when desires are strongest, I maintain a demand is being made which, for the mass of people, it is impossible to meet, that the endeavours to meet it would impose a strain hostile to health and happiness and carry with them grave dangers to morals The thing is preposterous. You might as well put water by the side of a man suffering from thirst and tell him not to drink it. No, birth control by abstention is either ineffective, or, if effective, is pernicious.

It is said to be unnatural and intrinsically immoral Civilization involves the chaining of natural forces and their conversion to man's will and uses. When anaesthetics were first used at child birth there was an outcry that their use was unnatural and wicked, because God meant woman to suffer. It is no more unnatural to control child-birth by artificial means. The use of birth control is good, its abuse bad. May I end by an appeal that the Church approach this question, in common with certain others, in the light of modern knowledge and the needs of a new world, and unhampered by traditions which have outworn their usefulness?"

Lord Dawson's eminence is not to be denied. But with all due respect to his greatness as a physician, I am tempted to question the value of his evidence, specially when it is pitted against the experience of men and women who have lived a life of continence without suffering any moral or physical harm. Physicians generally come across those who have so defied laws of health that they have contracted some illness. They, therefore, often successfully prescribe what sufferers should do to become well, but they cannot always know what healthy men and women can do in any particular direction. Lord Dawson's evidence, therefore, about the effect of continence on married people has to be taken with the greatest caution. No doubt the tendency among married people is to regard sexual satisfaction for itself as legitimate. But in the modern age in which nothing is taken for granted and everything is rightly scrutinized, it is surely wrong to take it for granted that, because we have hitherto indulged in the sexual appetite in married life, the practice is either legitimate or healthy. Many old practices have been discontinued with good results. Why should this particular practice be exempt from examination, especially in the light of the experience of those who, even as married men and women, are living a life of restraint with mutual benefit both physical and moral?

But I object to contraceptives also on special grounds in India. Young men in India do not know what sexual restraint is. It is not their fault. They are married early. It is the custom. Nobody tells them to exercise restraint in married life. Parents are impatient to see grandchildren. The poor girl wives are expected by their surroundings to bear children as fast as they can.

In such surroundings, the use of contraceptives can only further aggravate the mischief. The poor girls who are expected to submit to their husbands' desires are now to be taught that it is a good thing to desire sexual satisfaction without the desire to have children. And in order to fulfil the double purpose they are to have recourse to contraceptives!!!)

I regard this to be the most pernicious education for married women. I do not believe that woman is prey to sexual desire to the same extent as man. It is easier for her than for man to exercise self-restraint. I hold that the right education in this country is to teach woman the art of saying *no* even to her husband, to teach her that it is no part of her duty to become a mere tool or a doll in her husband's hands. She has rights as well as duties. Those who see in Sita a willing slave under Rama do not realize the loftiness of either her independence or Rama's consideration for her in everything. Sita was no helpless weak woman incapable of protecting herself or her honour. To ask India's women to take to contraceptives is, to say the least, putting the cart before the horse. The first thing is to free her from mental slavery, to teach her sacredness of her body, and to teach her dignity of national service and the service of humanity. It is not fair to assume that India's women are beyond redemption, and that they have therefore to be simply taught the use of contraceptives for the sake of preventing births and preserving such health as they may be in possession of.

Let not the sisters who are rightly indignant over the miseries of women who are called upon to bear children, whether they will or no, be impatient. Not even the propaganda in favour of contraceptives is going to promote the desired end overnight. Every method is a matter of education. My plea is for the right type.

Harijan, 2-5-1936.

23

SELF-CONTROL AGAIN

"Your recent articles on self-control have created quite a stir. Persons who are in sympathy with your views find it difficult to exercise self-control for any length of time. They argue that you are applying your own experience and practice to the whole mankind. And even you have admitted that you do not fulfil the definition of a complete *Brahmachari*. For you yourself are not free from animal passion. And since you admit the necessity of limiting the number of children a married couple may have, the use of contraceptives is the only practical method open to the vast majority of mankind."

Thus writes a correspondent.

I have admitted my own limitations. In this matter of self-control *v.* contraceptives, they constitute my qualifications. For my limitations show quite clearly that I am like the majority of earth earthy and can have no pretensions to any extraordinary gifts. The motive for my self-control was also quite ordinary, viz. the desire to limit the progeny for the purpose of serving the country or humanity. Inability to support a large family should be a greater incentive than the very distant one of serving one's country or humanity. That in spite of thirtyfive years of successful (from the present standpoint) self-control, the animal in me still needs watching, shows in an eminent degree that I am very much an ordinary mortal. I therefore do suggest that what has been possible for me is possible for any human being who would make the required effort.

My quarrel with the advocates of contraceptives lies in their taking it for granted that ordinary mortals cannot exercise self-control. Some of them even go so far as to say that even if they can, they ought not to do so. To them, no matter how eminent they may be in their own spheres, I say, in all humility but with utmost confidence, that they are talking without experience of the possibilities of self-control. They have no right to limit the capacity of the human soul. In such instances the positive evidence of one person like me, if it is reliable, is not only of greater value but decisive. To dismiss my evidence as useless because I am popularly regarded as a 'Mahatma', is not proper in a serious inquiry.

Far more weighty is the argument of a sister who says in effect: "We, the advocates of contraceptives, have come on the scene only recently. You self-controllers had the field all to yourselves all these long generations, — maybe thousands of years. What have you to show to your credit? Has the world learnt the lesson of self-control? What have you done to stop the misery of overburdened families? Have you heard the cry of wounded motherhood? Come, the field is even now open to you. We do not mind your advocacy of self-control. We may even wish you success, if perchance you save wives from the unwanted approaches of their husbands. But why should you seek to decry the methods which we employ, and which take note of, and make every allowance for common human weaknesses or habits, and which when properly employed almost never fail to accomplish their purpose?"

The taunt is dictated by the anguish of a sister filled with compassion for the families that are always in want because of the ever-increasing number of children. The appeal of human misery has been known to melt hearts of stone. How can it fail to effect high-souled sisters? But such appeals may easily lead one astray, if one is lifted off one's feet and, like a drowning man, catches any floating straw.

We are living in times when values are undergoing quick changes. We are not satisfied with slow results. We are not satisfied with the welfare merely of our own caste-fellows, not even of our own country. We feel or want to feel for the whole of humanity. All this is a tremendous gain in humanity's march towards its goal.

But we won't find the remedy for human ills by losing patience and by rejecting everything that is old because it is old. Our ancestors also dreamt, perhaps vaguely, the same dreams that fire us with zeal. The remedies they applied for similar ills, it is possible, are applicable even to the horizon that appears to have widened beyond expectations.

And my plea based on positive experience is that even as truth and *ahimsa* are not merely for the chosen few but for the whole of humanity to be practised in daily life, so exactly is self-control not merely for a few 'Mahatmas' but for the whole of humanity. And even as, because many people will be untruthful and violent, humanity may not lower its standard, so also, though many, even the majority, may not respond to the message of self control, we may not lower our standard.

A wise judge will not give a wrong decision in the face of a hard case. He will allow himself to appear to have hardened his heart because he knows that truest mercy lies in not making bad law.

We may not attribute the weaknesses of the perishable body or the flesh to the imperishable soul that resides in it. We have to regulate the body in the light of the laws that govern the soul. In my humble opinion, these laws are few and unchangeable, capable of being understood and followed by the whole of the human family. There would be differences of degree but not of kind in their application. If we have faith, we won't lose it, because it may take a million years before humanity realizes or makes the nearest or visible approach to its goal. In Jawaharlal's language, let us have the correct ideology.

The sister's challenge, however, remains to be answered. The 'self-controllers' are not idle. They are carrying on their propaganda. If their method is different in kind from the method of contraceptives, so is and must be their propaganda. 'Self-controllers' do not need clinics. They cannot advertize their cure for the simple reason that it is not an article to be sold or given. But their criticism of contraceptives and warning to the people against their use is part of their propaganda. The constructive side has always been there, but naturally in an unfelt and unseen manner. Advocacy of self-control has never been suspended. The most effective is that of example. The larger the number of honest persons who practise successful self-control, the more effective becomes the propaganda.

Harijan, 30-5-1936

24

BIRTH CONTROL THROUGH SELF-CONTROL

The following letter has been lying on my file for a considerable time:

> "The craze for birth control is today sweeping all over the world, and India is no exception. I have been closely following your articles in support of self-conrol in which I believe. Recently a 'Birth Control League' has been started in Ahmedabad. It advocates the use of modern contraceptive appliances to enable men and women to practise unlimited self-indulgence with impunity.
>
> It seems to me strange that good people who have themselves attained the afternoon of their life should favour a movement which must result in the vitality of the whole race being drained. How one wishes that instead of a 'Birth Control League' these friends had set up a 'Self-Control League' for realizing their goal. I would ask you when you visit Gujarat, to take up this matter and show the light to the women of Gujarat.
>
> Our doctors and *vaidyas* today seem to fight shy of taking their stand on self-control for fear of losing their bread. They do not seem to realize that if the new-fangled craze is left to pursue its course unchecked it will inevitably lead society into the abyss of self-destruction Only a timely adoption of the sovereign remedy of self-control can save it from a certain doom. A wide-spread use of contraceptives will and can only result in plunging the country into an orgy of self-indulgence and abuse, with the inevitable consequences of endless disease and misery."

I did not get any chance, during my recent brief visit to Ahmedabad, to take up the suggestion of this friend. But it is well-known that I hold strongly to the views attributed to me. Wherever contraceptive practices have taken root they have let loose a host of evils which even he who runs can see. But birth control enthusiasts fail to recognize this fact because they hold indulgence to be in itself good and have persuaded themselves that the spread of the birth control methods is morally desirable.)

I am afraid my correspondent has been led into exaggeration when he says that the Ahmedabad League advocates the use of modern contraceptive appliances to enable men and women to practise unlimited self-indulgence with impunity. But whatever the good motives of the promoters of the said League might be, their activity can only result in an aggravation of the evil of self-indulgence. For, as sure as water runs downhill, the use of contraceptives must result in the downhill path of self-indulgence.

Similarly, my correspondent also seems to have done an injustice to the doctors and *vaidyas* when he ascribes their failure to inculcate self-control purely to a fear of losing their bread. The fact is that the medical profession have so far regarded the subject of self-control as being outside their purview. But there are gathering signs of a coming healthy change in their outlook. The goal that the medical science has set before itself is the discovery of the cause and cure of disease. An honest pursuit of that goal is bound at last to bring it up against self-indulgence and lack of self-discipline as the prime cause of many diseases. For, with the advance of knowledge and insight, society is bound to insist more and more on prevention of disease by the removal of the root causes, rather than its cure alone. Complete eradication of disease is an utter impossibility unless the people learn to observe the elementary rule of self-discipline. The fact is so obvious that its recognition cannot be long delayed, and with its recognition will come greater emphasis on the part of the medical profession on self-discipline and self-control as a factor in a healthful existence. The Birth Control League of Ahmedabad should understand that spread of contraceptive knowledge and practice can only aid the growth of self-indulgence and abuse and its inevitable concomitants, misery and disease. I would therefore earnestly suggest to the promoters of the said League that if they will only utilize their time and energy to study deeply the evils of self-indulgence and inculcate upon the women the necessity and naturalness of practising self-control as a means of attaining birth control, they will find that they have discovered the best and quickest method of realizing their goal.

Harijan, 12-12-1936

25

WHAT IT IS LIKE

The recent debate between Dr. Sokhey and Dr. Mangaldas Mehta on the evergreen topic of birth control emboldens me to disclose the opinion of the late Dr. Ansari of revered memory supporting Dr. Mangaldas's position. It was now nearly a year ago, I wrote to the deceased asking him whether as a medical man, he could endorse the position I had taken up on the vexed question. Much to my agreeable surprise he wrote heartily supporting it. When I was in Delhi last, I had a brief discussion with him on the subject, and he promised at my request to contribute a series of articles showing by facts and figures from his own experience and that of other medical men, how the practice had hurt both men and women who were party to it. He gave a graphic account of the condition to which the men were reduced after they had mated for some time with their wives or other women who, they knew, were using contraceptives. Freedom from the fear of the natural consequence of condition had made them reckless in self-indulgence leading to an inordinate craving for seeing women which ended in dementia. Alas ! he died just when he was about to write the promised series.

Bernard Shaw is reported to have said that coition accompanied by the case of contraceptives was nothing less than sexual masturbation. A moment's reflection would show how accurate the description is.

I receive almost daily piteous letters from students and sometimes even from teachers complaining how they had become slaves to the habit and were being gradually reduced to loss of manhood. Recall, too, the correspondence published in these columns from the Principal of the Sanatan Dharma College, Lahore,* bitterly complaining of teachers practising unnatural vice on their pupils and the consequences of the practices on their health and character. The deduction I draw from these examples is that even the union between husband and wife bereft of the possibility of its natural consequence must cause the same ruination that invariably attends masturbation or unnatural vice.

It is the philanthropic motive that no doubt impels many birth control reformers to a whirlwind campaign in favour of the use of contraceptives. I invite them to contemplate the ruinous consequences of their misplaced philanthropy. Those whom they want to reach will never use them in any appreciable numbers. Those who ought not to use them will, without doubt, use them to the undoing of themselves and their partners. This would not matter in the least, if the use of contraceptives was incontestably proved to be right physically and morally. Dr. Ansari's opinion, if my testimony about it is accepted, is a grave warning to the reformers and would-be reformers.

Harijan, 12-9-1936

* See Chapters XXX and XXXI of this book.

*

26

A WITNESS FROM AMERICA

Miss Mabel E. Simpson of Montana (U. S. A.) writes to the Editor :

> "I wish to express my appreciation of your publication. What it lacks in size it more than makes up in quality I greatly enjoyed Mr. Gandhi's article on birth control displaying his usual clear sight into the heart of things. If he had visited America twenty years ago when birth control was disapproved and now when it is in full swing, he would know that it brings moral deterioration. But he would not be able to convince anybody of it, for it also brings a blindness to both moral and spiritual perception that makes it impossible for its followers to discern with sensitivity along high moral and spiritual lines. If India follows the West in this, she will surely lose two of her most priceless and beautiful jewels : affection for little children and reverence for parenthood. America has lost both — and does not know it. Could you print a statement of the meaning of *brahmacharya* ? I have been asked about it, and while I have an idea I am not sure enough to attempt to explain it to others Thank you "

The reader may place what value he or she chooses on this piece of evidence. I suggest, however, that such evidence against the use of contraceptives is worth far more than that of those who claim to derive benefit from their use. The reason is obvious. The benefit in the sense that advent of children is often checked is not denied. What is contended is that the moral harm the use does is incalculable. Miss Simpson has given us a measure of such harm.

Now for the definition — the meaning — of *brahmacharya*. Its root meaning may be given thus : that conduct which puts one in touch with God.

The conduct consists in the fullest control over all the senses. This is the true and relevant meaning of the word.

Popularly it has come to mean mere physical control over the organ of generation. This narrow meaning has debased *brahmacharya* and made its practice all but impossible. Control over the organ of generation is impossible without proper control over all the senses. They are all interdependent. Mind on the lower plane is included in the senses. Without control over the mind mere physical control, even if it can be attained for a time, is of little or no use.

Harijan, 13-6-1936

27

'A VOICE IN THE WILDERNESS'

"Just lately I read a review of your conference with Mrs. Sanger, the birth control advocate. I was so deeply moved that I am writing you to express my appreciation for your stand. God bless you for your courage.

For the past thirty years I have been teaching boys. I have always advocated the control of the body, and urged boys to live unselfishly.

When Mrs. Sanger was in my neighbourhood, the high school boys and girls took advantage of the information to carry on their illicit intercourse with no fear of results. Should Mrs. Sanger have her way, the time would come when the whole world would seek the sensual and love would die. I realize it will take centuries to educate the public to higher ideals, but there is no time like the present to begin. I fear she mistakes passion for love, for love is of the spirit and never born of lust.

Dr. Alexis Carrel agrees with you, in that sex control is not harmful except to those who feed their passions and are already unbalanced. Mrs. Sanger is wrong in saying that most doctors believe abstinence is harmful. I find many leading doctors and scientists belonging to the American Social Hygiene Association hold that control is beneficial.

You are doing a noble work. I have followed with interest all the vicissitudes of your long life struggle. You are one of the few who have this higher spiritual viewpoint on the sex question. I want you to know I reach out to you across the great waters in fellowship.

Let us keep up the good work so that youth may know the truth, for the hope of the future is in their hands.

I add a quotation from one of my talks to boys :

'Create — always create. To create is noble, uplifting, inspiring. But the moment you seek to gratify the senses by merely enjoying the creative powers, you begin to cheat creation and to destroy all those higher spiritual forces within you. It can end only in disappointment.

'Creation, physical, mental and spiritual, is joy and life. If you are merely seeking the sensations of the flesh with no thought of creating, or even trying to avoid the aim of creation, you are perverting nature and killing your spiritual powers.

'The result will be passion, uncontrolled,—exhaustion, disappointment and defeat. It can never bring out those finer qualities on which we can build a new race of spiritual men and women.'

I know this is like a prophet crying in the wilderness, but I am convinced of the truth of it, and I can but point the way."

This is one of the letters which I occasionally get from America in condemnation of the use of contraceptives. Current literature that India imports weekly from the Far West would have us believe that in America none but idiots and imbeciles oppose the use of this modern method of deliverance from the bondage of the superstition which imprisons the body and crushes it by denying it its supreme enjoyment. That literature produces as much momentary intoxication as the act which it teaches and incites us to perform without incurring the risk of its ordinary result. I do not put before the readers of *Harijan* merely letters of individual condemnation received from the West. They have their use for me as a seeker but very little for the general reader. This letter, however, from a teacher of boys with thirty years' experience behind him has a definite value. It should serve as a guide for Indian teachers and the public—men and women—who are carried away by the overwhelming tide. The use of contraceptives is infinitely more tempting than the whisky bottle. But it is no more lawful than the sparkling liquid for its fatal temptation. Nor can opposition to the use of either be given up in despair because their use seems to be growing. If the opponents have faith in their mission, it has to be pursued. A voice in the wilderness has a potency which voices uttered in the midst of 'the madding crowd' lack. For the voice in the wilderness has meditation, deliberation and unquenchable faith behind it, whilst the babel of voices has generally nothing but the backing of the experience of personal enjoyment or the false and sentimental pity for the unwanted children and their suffering mothers. Argument of personal experience has as much weight as an act of a drunkard. The argument of pity is a trap into which it is dangerous to fall. Sufferings of unwanted children and of equally unwanted motherhood are punishments or warnings devised by beneficent nature. Disregard of the law of discipline and restraint is suicide. Ours is a state of probation. If we refuse to bear the yoke of discipline, we court failure like cowards, we avoid battle and give up the only joy of living.

Harijan, 27-3-1937

28

WONDERFUL IF TRUE

During our morning and evening walks, Khansaheb Abdul Gaffar Khan and I often talk on matters of common interest. Having travelled in the frontier territories as far as Kabul and beyond and knowing the frontier tribes well, he often describes to me the habits and customs of these simple folk. He tells me that these tribesmen who are untouched by the so-called civilization live principally on maize and barley bread and lentils supplemented at times by buttermilk. They get meat but rarely. The only way I could account for their well-known hardiness was their open-air life and invigorating climate. Khansaheb promptly added, "That is not enough. The secret of their strength lies in their chaste lives. They marry, both men and women, after full maturity. Unfaithfulness, adultery or unmarried love are practically unknown. Union out of wedlock is punishable by death. The injured party has the right to take the life of the wrong-doer."

If this chastity is so universal as Khansaheb describes it, it furnishes us in India a lesson that we should take to heart. I suggested to Khansaheb that if the fine physique of the tribesmen was largely due to their continence, there must be perfect co-operation between the mind and the body. For if the mind hankered after satisfaction of the flesh and the body resisted, there must be tremendous waste of vital energy leaving the body thoroughly exhausted. Khansaheb agreed that that was a fair deduction and that, so far as he was able to judge, he felt that the tribesmen were so habituated to continence outside marriage that young men and women never seemed to desire sexual satisfaction outside marriage. Khansaheb also told me that the women in the tribal areas never observed the purdah, there was no false prudery there, the women were fearless, roamed about anywhere freely, were well able to take care of themselves and defend their honour without seeking or needing male protection.

Khansaheb, however, admits that this continence not being based on reason or enlightened faith breaks down when these men and women of the hills come in contact with civilized or soft life where departure from the custom carries no punishment and public opinion looks upon unfaithfulness and adultery with more or less indifference. This opens up reflections which I must not discuss just now. My purpose in writing this just now is to seek corroboration and further light from those who know these tribesmen as Khansaheb does, and to suggest to young men and women of the plains that observance of continence, if it is really natural to the tribesmen, as Khansaheb thinks it is, should be equally natural to us, if only we would inhabit our thought world with the right kind of thoughts and deal summarily with the intruders. Indeed if the right kind settle down in sufficiently large numbers, the intruders will be crowded out no doubt. The process requires courage. But self-restraint never accrues to the faint-hearted. It is the beautiful fruit of watchfulness and ceaseless effort in the form of prayer and fasting. The prayer is not vain repetition nor fasting mere starvation of the body. Prayer has to come from the heart which knows God by faith, and fasting is abstinence from evil or injurious thought, activity or food. Starvation of the body when the mind thinks of a multiplicity of dishes is worse than useless.

Harijan, 10-4-1937.

29

SEXUAL PERVERSION

Some years ago the Bihar Government in its Education Department had an inquiry into the question of unnatural vice in its schools, and the Committee of Inquiry had found the existence of the vice even among teachers who were abusing their position among their boys in order to satisfy their unnatural lust. The Director of Education had issued a circular prescribing departmental action on such vice being found to exist in connection with any teacher. It would be interesting to know the results, if any, issuing from the circular.

I have had literature too sent to me from other provinces inviting my attention to such vice and showing that it was on the increase practically all over India in public as well as private schools. Personal letters received from boys have confirmed the information.

Unnatural though the vice is, it has come down to us from times immemorial. The remedy for all secret vice is most difficult to find. And it becomes still more difficult when it affects guardians of boys which the teachers are. 'If the salt loses its savour, wherewith shall it be salted?' In my opinion departmental action, necessary as it is in all proved cases, can hardly meet the case. The levelling of public opinion alone can cope with the evil. But in most matters there is no such thing as effective public opinion in this country. The feeling of helplessness that pervades political life has affected all other departments. We therefore pass by many a wrong that is being perpetrated in front of us.

A system of education that puts an exclusive emphasis on literary equipment, not only is ill-adapted to deal with the evil but actually results in promoting it. Boys who were clean before they went to public schools have been found to have become unclean, effeminate and imbecile at the end of their school course. The Bihar Committee has recommended the 'instilling into the minds of boys a reverence for religion'. But who is to bell the cat? The teachers alone can teach reverence for religion. But they themselves have none. It is therefore a question of a proper selection of teachers. But a proper selection of teachers means either a much higher pay than is now given, or reversion to teaching not as a career but as a life-long dedication to a sacred duty. This is in vogue even today among Roman Catholics. The first is obviously impossible in a poor country like ours. The second seems to me to be the only course left open. But that course is not open to us under a system of government in which everything has a price and which is the costliest in the world.

The difficulty of coping with the evil is aggravated because the parents generally take no interest in the morals of their children. Their duty is done when they send them to school. The outlook before us is thus gloomy. But there is hope in the fact that there is only one remedy for all evil, viz., general purification. Instead of being overwhelmed by the magnitude of the evil, each one of us must do the best one can by the scrupulous attention to one's own immediate surroundings, taking self as the first and the immediate point of attack. We need not hug the comfort to ourselves that we are not like other men. Unnatural vice is not an isolated phenomenon. It is but a violent symptom of the same disease. If we have impurity within us, if we are sexually depraved, we must right ourselves before expecting to reform our neighbours. There is too much sitting in judgment upon others and too much indulgence towards self. The result is a vicious circle. Those who realize the truth of it must get out of it, and they will find that progress though never easy becomes sensibly possible.

Young India, 27-6-1929

30

A GROWING VICE?

The Principal of the Sanatan Dharma College, Lahore, writes:

> "Allow me to request you to peruse the accompanying newspaper cutting, notices, etc., which speak for themselves. The Youths' Welfare Association is doing very useful work here in the Punjab. It has attracted notice in academic and administrative quarters, while it has secured the active interest of enlightened guardians of boys. Pandit Sitaram Das of Bihar is the leading spirit of this movement which counts very many distinguished people here among its patrons.
>
> The evil of juvenile seduction is admittedly more rampant in the Punjab and N. W. F. Province than elsewhere in India.
>
> May I pray that you will draw the attention of the country to this canker through a note or letter in the *Harijan* or in any other newspaper?"

The Secretary of the Youth League wrote to me long ago on this very delicate subject. On receiving his letter I entered into correspondence with Dr. Gopichand who confirmed the statements made in the League Secretary's letter. But I could not see my way clear to discussing the problem in these columns or elsewhere. I had known of the evil but was not sure that a newspaper discussion could deal with it to any purpose. Nor am I sure now. But I may not resist the appeal of the Principal of the College.

The vice is not new. It is wide-spread. As it is necessarily kept secret, it is not possible to detect it easily. It goes hand in hand with easy life. In the case referred to by the Principal, the teachers are alleged to be the corruptors of their own wards. 'When the salt loses its savour wherewith shall it be salted?'

This is a matter which no Commission, no Government can deal with successfully. It is the function of the moral reformer. The parents have to be awakened to a sense of their responsibility. The students should be brought in close touch with clean life. The idea that ethics and clean living are the foundation of true education, should be seriously propagated. Trustees of educational institutions have to exercise the greatest care in the selection of teachers, and having selected them, they have to see to it that they remain up to the mark. These are some of the ways in which the awful vice can be brought under control even if it cannot be eradicated.

Harijan, 27-4-1935

31

DUTY OF REFORMERS

I gladly publish the following letter from the Principal, Sanatan Dharma College, Lahore:

"In all earnestness I beg to draw your attention to the horror of the atrocities connected with cases of unnatural offence committed on children.

As you are well aware, very few of these cases are reported to the police or taken to law courts. Of late there seems to have been an orgy of such cases in the Punjab. The enclosed newspaper cuttings, which report only the most flagrant of the very rare cases that come to law courts, will fully reveal to you the magnitude of this menace to our young boys and girls. Some months back daring attempts were made in Lahore by *gundas* to abduct little school-boys from the very gates of some schools in broad daylight. Even now special vigilence arrangements are necessary for them while going to and returning from school. The circumstances of the assaults narrated in the reports of the cases tried, are of rare and diabolical cruelty and daring.

The feeling of the public in general is either one of apathy or of helplessness and lack of self-confidence in the matter of organized effort to crush these crimes.

The enclosed copy of a circular issued by the Government of the Punjab will show you how the Government feel helpness in the face of the apathy of the public as well as of their departmental officers.

You rightly remarked in your editorial notes in *Young India* of the 9th September 1926, and of the 27th June 1929, that the time was ripe for a public discussion of the subject of sexual offences of this class, and that only a levelling up of public opinion all over the country could cope with the evil. The only effective way to such levelling up of public opinion is publicity through newspapers.

I submit most respectfully that this is the least that the horrible situation demands; and I appeal to you to give a lead to our press by raising your powerful voice for mobilizing an intensive press campaign against this horror."

There can be no doubt that there must be a relentless war waged against this vice. I have gone through the gruesome reports enclosed with this letter. These are of a different type from those dealt with by me in the articles to which the Principal refers. They had reference to cases exclusively of seduction by teachers. The reports now sent mostly deal with cases of unnatural assaults committed by *gundas* on boys of tender age and then murdered. Though the cases of unnatural assaults followed by murder appear more hedious, I believe that they are more capable of being dealt with than the cases in which boys become willing victims of their teachers. Both require incessant vigilance by the reformer and the rousing of public conscience against the commission of this disgusting crime. It is the duty of leaders in the Punjab in which this crime seems to flourish most, to get together irrespective of race or creed, and devise methods of protecting the youth of the land of five rivers from criminals whether as seducers or ravishers and murderers. It is no use passing resolutions condemning the criminals. All crimes are different kinds of diseases and they should be treated as such by the reformers. That does not mean that the police will suspend their function of regarding such cases as public crimes, but their measures are never intended to deal with causes of these social disturbances. To do so is the special prerogative of the reformer. And unless the moral tone of society is raised, in spite of whatever may be written in the newspapers, such crimes will flourish, if only for the simple reason that the moral sense of these perverts has become blunt and they rarely read newspapers, especially those portions which contain fervent exhortation against such vices. The only effective way I can conceive of, therefore, is for some enthusiastic reformers like the Principal of the Sanatan Dharma College, if he is one, to gather together other reformers and take concerted measure to deal with the evil.

Harijan, 19-10-1935

32

FOR THE YOUNG

It is the fashion in some quarters nowadays for the young to discredit whatever may be said by old people. I am not prepared to say that there is absolutely no justification for this belief. But I warn the youth of the contry against always discounting whatever old men or women may say, for the mere fact that it is said by such persons. Even as wisdom often comes from the mouths of babes, so does it often come from the mouths of old people. The golden rule is to test everything in the light of reason and experience, no matter from whom it comes. I want to revert to the subject of birth control by contraceptives. It is dinned into one's ears that gratification of the sex urge is a solemn obligation like the obligation of discharging debts lawfully incurred, and that, not to do so would involve the penalty of intellectual decay. This sex urge has been isolated from the desire for progeny, and it is said by the protagonists of the use of contraceptives that conception is an accident to be prevented except when the parties desire to have children. I venture to suggest that this is a most dangerous doctrine to preach anywhere; much more so in a country like India where the middle class male population has become imbecile through abuse of the creative function. If satisfaction of the sex urge is a duty, the unnatural vice of which I wrote some time ago and several other ways of gratification would be commendable. The reader should know that even persons of note have been known to approve of what is commonly known as sexual perversion. He may be shocked at the statement. But if it somehow or other gains the stamp of respectability, it will be the rage among boys and girls to satisfy their urge among members of their own sex. For me the use of contraceptives is not far removed from the means to which persons have hitherto resorted for the gratification of their sexual desire with the results that very few know. I know what havoc secret vice has played among school boys and school girls. The introduction of contraceptives under the name of science and the *imprimatur* of known leaders of society have intensified the complication and made the task of reformers who work for purity of social life, well-nigh impossible for the moment. I betrary no confidence when I inform the reader that there are unmarried girls of impressionable age studying in schools and colleges who study birth control literature and magazines with avidity and even possess contraceptives. It is impossible to confine their use to married women. Marriage loses its sanctity when its purpose and highest use is conceived to be the satisfaction of the animal passion without contemplating the natural result of such satisfaction.

I have no doubt that those learned men and women who are carrying on propaganda with missionary zeal in favour of the use of contraceptives, are doing irreparable harm to the youth of the country under the false belief that they will be saving thereby, the poor women who may be obliged to bear children against their will. Those who need to limit their children will not be easily reached by them. Our poor women have not the knowledge or the training that the women of the West have. Surely the propaganda is not being carried on on behalf of the middle class women, for they do not need the knowledge, at any rate so much as the poor classes do.

The greatest harm, however, done by that propaganda lies in its rejection of the old ideal and substitution in its place of one which, if carried out, must spell the moral and physical extinction of the race. The horror with which ancient literature has regarded the fruitless use of the vital fluid was not a superstition born of ignorance. What shall we say of a husbandman who will sow the finest seed in his possession on stony ground or of the owner of a field who will receive, in his field rich with fine soil, good seed under conditions that will make it impossible for it to grow? God has blessed man with seed that has the highest potency and woman with a field richer than the richest earth to be found anywhere on this globe. Surely it is criminal folly for man to allow his most precious possession to run to waste. He must guard it with a care greater than he will bestow upon the richest pearls in his possession. And so is a woman guilty of criminal folly who will receive the seed in her life-producing field with the deliberate intention of letting it run to waste. Both he and she will be judged guilty of misuse of the talents given to them and they will be dispossessed of what they have been given. Sex urge is a fine and noble thing. There is nothing to be ashamed of in it. But it is meant only for the act of creation. Any other use of it is a sin against God and humanity. Contraceptives of a kind there were before and there will be hereafter; but the use of them was formerly regarded as sinful. It was reserved for our generation to glorify vice by calling it virtue. The greatest disservice protagonists of contraceptives are rendering to the youth of India is to fill their minds with what appears to me to be wrong ideology. Let the young men and women of India who hold her destiny in their hands beware of this false god and guard the treasure with which God has blessed them and use it, if they wish, for the only purpose for which it is intended.

Harijan, 28-3-1936

33

HEADING FOR PROMISCUITY

Thus writes a young man:

"You want everyone to become moral in order to change the world. I do not exactly know what you mean by morality—whether you confine it to matters sexual, or whether it covers the whole field of human conduct. I suspect the former, because I do not see you pointing out to your capitalist and landlord friends, the great injustice and harm they are doing by making huge profits at the expense of labourers and tenants, while you are never tired of castigating young men and women for their moral lapses in sexual matters and upholding before them the virtues of celibacy. You claim to know the mind of Indian youth. I do not claim to represent anybody, but as a solitary young man I beg to challenge your claim. You do not seem to know through what environment, the modern middle-class youth is passing, what with long spells of unemployment, crushing social customs and traditions, and temptations of co-education! It is all a conflict between the old and the new ideas, resulting usually in the defeat and misery of youth. I humbly request you to be kind and compassionate to the youth and not to judge them by your puritanic standards of morality. After all, I think, every act, when it is performed with mutual consent and mutual love, is moral whether it is performed within marriage or without. Since the invention of contraceptives the sexual basis of the institution of marriage has been knocked down. It has now become an institution mainly for the protection and welfare of children. You will, perhaps, be shocked at these ideas I would here venture to ask you not to forget your own youth when judging the present-day youth. You were an over-sexed individual given to excessive indulgence, which seems to have created in you a sort of disgust towards the sexual act, and hence your asceticism and the idea of sin. Compared to you, I think many young men of today are better in this respect."

This is from a typical letter. To my knowledge the writer has gone through several changes even during the past three months that I have known him. He is still passing through a crisis. The extract quoted is from a long letter which, together with many of his other writings, he would gladly have me publish. But what I have quoted just represents the attitude of many a youth.

Of course my sympathies are with young men and young women. I have a vivid recollection of the days of my own youth. And it is because of my faith in the youth of the country that I am never tired of dealing with problems that face them.

For the morals, ethics and religion are convertible terms. A moral life without reference to religion is like a house built upon sand. And religion divorced from morality is like 'sounding brass' good only for making a noise and breaking heads. Morality includes truth, *ahimsa* and continence. Every virtue that mankind has ever practised is referable to and derived from these three fundamental virtues. Non-violence and continence are again derivable from Truth, which for me is God.

Without continence a man or woman is undone. To have no control over the senses is like sailing in a rudderless ship, bound to break to pieces on coming in contact with the very first rock. Hence my constant insistence on continence. My correspondent is right in saying in effect that the coming in of contraceptives has changed the ideas about sexual relations. If mutual consent makes a sexual act moral whether within marriage or without, and by parity of reasoning, even between members of the same sex, the whole basis of sexual morality is gone and nothing but 'misery and defeat' awaits the youth of the country. Many young men and women are to be found in India who would be glad to be free from the craving for mutual intercourse in whose grip they find themselves. This craving is stronger than the strongest intoxicant which has ever enslaved man. It is futile to hope that the use of contraceptives will be restricted to the mere regulation of progeny. There is hope for a decent life only so long as the sexual act is definitely related to the conception of precious life. This rules out of court perverted sexuality and to a lesser degree promiscuity. Divorce of the sexual act from its natural consequence must lead to hideous promiscuity and condonation, if not endorsement, of unnatural vice.

Since my own experiences are relevant to the consideration of the sex problem, let me just warn the reader who has not read my autobiographical chapters against drawing the conclusion that my correspondent has drawn about my sins of indulgence. Whatever over-indulgence there was with me, it was strictly restricted to my wife. And I was living in a big joint family where there was hardly any privacy except for a few hours at night. I awoke to the folly of indulgence for the sake of it even when I was twentythree years old, and decided upon total *brahmacharya* in 1899, i. e., when I was thirty years old. It is wrong to call me an ascetic. The ideals that regulate my life are presented for acceptance by mankind in general. I have arrived at them by gradual evolution. Every step was thought out, well considered, and taken with the greatest deliberation. Both my continence and non-violence were derived from personal experience and became necessary in response to the calls of public duty. The isolated life I had to lead in South Africa whether as a householder, legal practitioner, social reformer or politician, required, for the due fulfilment of these duties, the strictest regulation of sexual life and a rigid practice of non-violence and truth in human relations, whether with my own countrymen or with the Europeans. I claim to be no more than an average man with less than average ability. Nor can I claim any special merit for such non-violence or continence as I have been able to reach with laborious research. I have not the shadow of a doubt that any man or woman can achieve what I have, if he or she would make the same effort and cultivate the same hope and faith. Work without faith is like an attempt to reach the bottom of a bottomless pit.

Harijan, 3-10-1936

34

A YOUTH'S DIFFICULTY

A correspondent who prefers to remain anonymous seeks an answer to a question arising out of my article in *Harijan* addressed to the young. Although it is a sound rule to ignore anonymous correspondence, I do sometimes make an exception when the question put is substantial as in the present case.

The letter is in Hindi and is longer than it need have been. Its purport is:

> "From your writing I doubt if you understand the young mind. What has been possible for you is not possible for all young men. I happen to be married. I can restrain myself. My wife cannot. She does not want children, but she does want to enjoy herself. What am I to do? Is it not my duty to satisfy her? I am not generous enough to look upon her satisfying her desire through other channels. I read from the papers that you are not averse to promoting marriages and blessing them. Surely you know or ought to know that they are not contracted with the high purpose that you have mentioned."

The correspondent is right. The fact that I bless so many marriages when they satisfy the tests that I have set as to age, economy, etc., perhaps shows somewhat that I know the youth of the country to an extent that would justify my guiding them when they seek my guidance.

My correspondent's case is typical. He deserves sympathy. That the sole purpose of sexual connection is procreation is in the nature of a new discovery for me. Though I had known the rule, I had never before given it the weight it deserved. I must have till recently regarded it as a mere pious wish. I now regard it as a fundamental law of married state, which is easy of observance if its paramount importance is duly recognized. My object will be fulfilled when the law is given its due place in society. To me it is a living law. We break it always and pay heavily for its breach. If my correspondent realizes its inestimable value and if he has love for his wife and has faith in himself, he will convert her to his view. Is he sincere when he says he can restrain himself? Has the animal passion become transmuted in his case into a higher passion, say, for service of fellow beings? Does he naturally refrain from doing anything to excite the passion in his wife? Let him know that Hindu science denotes eight kinds of unions which include sexual suggestions made even by signs. Is the correspondent free from these? If he is not, and if he is sincerely desirous that his wife should be weaned from the sexual desire, let him surround her with the purest love, let him explain the law to her, let him explain the physical effects of union without the desire for procreation, let him tell her what the vital fluid means. Let him further engage his wife in healthy pursuits and strive to regulate her diet, exercise, etc., so as to still the passion in her. Above all, if he is a man of religion, he will try to transmit to his companion his own living faith. For, I must confess that the observance of the law of continence is impossible without a living faith in God which is living Truth. It is the fashion nowadays to dismiss God from life altogether and insist on the possibility of reaching the highest kind of life without the necessity of a living faith in a living God. I must confess my inability to drive the truth of the law home to those who have no faith in and no need for a Power infinitely higher than themselves. My own experience has led me to the knowledge that fullest life is impossible without an immovable belief in a living Law in obedience to which the whole universe moves. A man without that faith is like a drop thrown out of the ocean bound to perish. Every drop in the ocean shares its majesty and has the honour of giving us the ozone of life.

Harijan, 25-4-1936.

35

FOR STUDENTS

"With reference to your note entitled 'A Student's Difficulty appearing in the *Harijan* dated January 9, 1937, I submit the following in all humility for your kind consideration. I feel you have not done justice to the student in question. The problem defies easy solution. Your reply to his question is vague and general. You ask students to shake off false notions of dignity and rank themselves among the common labourers. All this general talk does not carry one far and is certainly not worthy of a supremely practical man like you. Please consider the problem at greater length and offer a detailed, practical and comprehensive solution with special reference to the following case

I am a student of M A. (Ancient Indian History) in the University of Lucknow. I am about 21 years of age. I have a love for learning and want to do as much of it as possible in my life-time. I am also inspired by your ideology of life. In about a month's time when the final M. A. Exminations come off I will have done with my education, and will have to enter life, as they say. Besides a wife, I have 4 brothers (all younger, one of them married), 2 sisters (both below twelve years of age) and my parents to support. There is no capital to fall back upon. The landed property is very small. What should I do for the education of the sisters and brothers? Then the sisters will have to be married sooner rather than later. Above all, where are the food and clothing to come from? I am not a lover of the so-called standard of living. I want just a healthy condition of life, besides provision for emergencies for myself and for those who depend on me. It is more or less only a question of two healthy meals and tidy clothes I want to lead an economically honest life. I don't want to earn a living by usury or by selling flesh. I have an ambition for patriotic service also. I am willing to fulfil your conditions laid down in the note referred to above to the best of my ability. But I do not know what to do! Where and how to begin? My education has been ruinously academic, and theoretical. I sometimes think of spinning, your pet panacea, but then I do not know how to learn it and what to do with the spun yarn, etc.

Yes, under the circumstances in which I am placed, will you suggest my adopting contraceptive methods? I may assure you I believe in self-control and *brahmacharya*. But then it will be some time before I become a *brahmachari*. I am afraid unless I adopt artificial contraceptive methods during the period before the desired consummation of full self-control, I may get children and invite economic ruination thereby. And, moreover, I feel that just now it is not quite proper in the interests of a normally healthy emotional life of my wife to impose on her a life of rigorous self-control. After all, sex has its place in the lives of normal men and women. I am not an exception to it, much less my wife who has not the equipment to read and understand your great writings on *brahmacharya* or dangers of indulgence, etc.

I regret the letter has been a little too lengthy. But then I wanted to avoid brevity at the cost of clarity. You are at liberty to make what use you like of this letter."

Though this letter was received about the end of February last, I am able to deal with it only now. It raises issues of great importance, each demanding large enough space for two columns of *Harijan*. But I must be brief.

The very difficulties the student raises, though serious in their setting, are of his own making. The very mention of them must show the falsity of his position and of the educational system in our country. It turns education into a purely commercial product to be converted into money. For me education has a much nobler purpose. Let the student count himself as one among the millions, and he will discover that millions of young men and women of his age cannot fulfil the conditions which he will have his degree to do. Why should he make himself responsible for the maintenance of all the relatives he mentions? Why should the grown-up ones, if of sound body, not labour for their maintenance? It is wrong to have many drones to one busy bee—though a male.

The remedy lies in his unlearning many things. He must revise his ideas of education. His sisters ought not to repeat the expensive education that he had. They can develop their intelligence through lerning some handicraft in a scientific manner. The moment they do so, they have development of the mind side by side with that of the body. And if they will learn to regard themselves as servants of humanity rather than its exploiters, they will have development of the heart i. e. the soul as well. And they will become equal earners of bread with their brother.

I might as well discuss here his sister's marriage to which reference has been made in the letter. I do not know what is meant by marriage taking place 'sooner rather than later'. In no case need it take place before they are 20 years old. It is no use thinking so many years in advance. And if he will revise the whole scheme of life, he will have the sisters to choose their partners, and the ceremony need never cost more than five rupees each, if that. I have been present at several such ceremonies. And the husbands or their elders have been graduates in fair circumstances.

It is pathetic to find the student so helpless as not to know how and where to have spinning lessons. Let him make a diligent search in Lucknow and he will find that there are young men enough to teach him. But he need not confine himself to spinning; though it too is fast becoming a full-time occupation able to give a village-minded man or woman his or her livelihood. I hope I have said here sufficient to enable him to dot the i's and cross the t's.

And now for contraceptives. Even here, the difficulty is imaginary. He is wrong in underrating his wife's intelligence. I have no doubt whatsoever that if she is the ordinary type of womanhood, she will readily respond to his self-restraint. Let him be true to himself and ask himself whether he has enough of it himself. All the evidence in my possession goes to show that it is man who lacks the power of self-restraint more than woman. But there is no need for belittling his own inability to exercise restraint. He must manfully face the prospect of a large family and discover the best means of supporting them. He must know that against the millions who are strangers to the use of contraceptives, there are possibly a few thousand who use them. The millions are in no dread of having to breed their children though the latter may not all be wanted. I suggest that it is cowardly to refuse to face the consequences of one's acts. Persons who use contraceptives will never learn the virtue of self-restraint. They will not need it.

Self-indulgence with contraceptives may prevent the coming of children but will sap the vitality of both men and women—perhaps more of men than of women. It is unmanly to refuse battle with the devil. Let my correspondent resolve upon self-restraint as the only sure and honourable method of avoiding unwanted children. What though he and his fail in the effort a hundred times? Joy is in the battle. The result comes by the grace of God.

Harijan, 17-4-1937

36

A MORAL DILEMMA

A friend writes:

"About two and a half years ago this city was convulsed by a social tragedy. A *Vaishya* gentleman had a sixteen years old daughter. She had a maternal uncle aged twentyone years studying in college in the same city. The two fell secretly into love with each other. The girl is said to have become pregnant. When the true state of affairs at last became known, the lovers committed suicide by taking poison. The girl died immediately but the boy died a couple of days afterwards in the hospital. The incident raised a storm of controversy and set all tongues wagging, so much so that it became difficult for the bereaved parents of the hapless girl to dwell in the city. In the course of time the storm blew over. But the memory of the event still lingers in the people's minds and is raked up every now and then, whenever a similar topic arises. At the time when the storm was at its height and nobody had a kind word to say about the deceased unfortunate lovers, I shocked everybody by expressing my opinion that under the afore-mentioned circumstances the young lovers ought to have been allowed to have their way. But mine remained a voice in the wilderness. What is your opinion in the matter?"

I have deliberately kept back the name of the correspondent and the place at the request of the writer, as he did not want old sores to be reopened by a revival of an old controversy. All the same I feel that a public discussion of this delicate topic is necessary. In my opinion such marriages as are interdicted in a particular society, cannot be recognized all at once or at the will of an individual. Nor has society or relatives of parties concerned any right to impose their will upon, and forcibly curtail the liberty of action of the young people who may want to contract such marriages. In the instance cited by the correspondent, both the parties had fully attained maturity. They could well think for themselves. No one had a right forcibly to prevent them from marrying each other if they wanted to. Society could at the most refuse to recognize the marriage, but it was the height of tyranny to drive them to suicide.

Marriage taboos are not universal and are largely based on social usage. The usage varies from province to province and as between different divisions. This does not mean that the youth may ride roughshod over all established social customs and inhibitions. Before they decide to do so, they must convert public opinion to their side. In the meantime, the individuals concerned ought patiently to bide their time or, if they cannot do that calmly and quietly, to face the consequences of social ostracism.

At the same time it is equally the duty of society not to take up a heartless, step-motherly attitude towards those who might disregard or break the established conventions. In the instance described by my correspondent, the guilt of driving the young couple to suicide certainly rests on the shoulders of society if the version that is before me is correct.

Harijan, 29-5-1937

37

THE MARRIAGE IDEAL

A friend writes:

"In the current issue of the *Harijan Sevak* in your article entitled 'A Moral Dilemma' you have observed, 'Many marriage taboos appear to have grown out of social customs. They are nowhere seen to rest on any vital, moral or religious principle. My own instinct based upon my experience tells me that probably these taboos were promulgated out of eugenic considerations. It is a well-known principle of the science of eugenics that the issue resulting from the crossing of exogamous elements is eugenically fitter than the product of endogamous unions. That is the reason why in Hinduism *Sagotra* (सगोत्र) and *Sapinda* (सपिण्ड) marriages are interdicted. On the other hand, if we admit social custom with all its kaleidoscopic variety and change to be the sole reason for these taboos, we are left with no strong reason why marriages between paternal uncle and niece, or for the matter of that, between brother and sister, should absolutely be tabooed. If, as you say, the begetting of progeny be the only legitimate object of marriage, then the choice of partners would become purely a question of eugenic harmony. Are all other considerations to be ruled out of court as relatively unimportant? If not, what should be their order of precedence? I would set it down as follows:

(1) Mutual attraction or love;

(2) Eugenic fitness;

(3) Approval and consent of the respective families concerned; and consideration for the interest of the social order to which one belongs;

(4) Spiritual development.

What do you say to it?

The Hindu *shastras* have emphatically set down procreation as the sole end of marriage, as the ancient benediction that is pronounced upon the prospective housewife by her elders at the time of marriage, viz., 'May you be blessed with eight children!' shows. This bears out your contention that cohabitation in marriage should only be for the purpose of begetting offspring, never for sensual gratification. But then, would you expect a married couple to be satisfied with only one offspring irrespective of whether it is male or female? Besides the longing to perpetuate one's line which you have very properly recognised, there also has existed amongst us, a strong feeling that this can be properly done only through a male issue. And the birth of a girl, therefore, is less welcome than that of a boy. In view of this very widespread craving for a male issue, don't you think that your ideal of having only one offspring should be modified so as to include the begetting of a male issue in addition to the possible female ones?

I entirely agree with you that a married person who confines the sex act strictly to the purpose of procreation, should be regarded as a *brahmachari*. I also hold with you that in the case of a married couple who have practised the rule of purity and self-control before and after marriage, a single act of union must lead to conception. In support of your first point there is in our *shastras* the celebrated story of Vishwamitra and Arundhati, the wife of Vasishtha who, in spite of her one hundred sons, was greeted by Vishwamitra as a perfect *brahmacharini*, whose command even the elements were bound to obey because her connubial relations with her husband were purely directed to the attainment and discharge of the function of motherhood. But I doubt whether even the Hindu *shastras* would support your ideal of having only one offspring, irrespective of whether it is male or female. It seems to me, therefore, that if you liberalize your ideal of married life so as to include the begetting of one male offspring in addition to the possible female ones, it would go a long way towards satisfying many married couples. Otherwise, I am afraid, most people would find it to be harder to limit sexual relationship to the procreation of the first child and then, irrespective of its sex, practise complete abstention for the rest of life than never to marry at all. I am being slowly forced to the view that sexuality is man's primitive nature, self-control is a cultivated virtue representing a step in his upward evolution towards religion and spirituality which is the natural law of his development. That is why self-control has been held in such high regard. I honour the person who lives up to the ideal of regarding sexual union only as a means for procreation. I also agree that coming together under any other circumstance would be sensual indulgence. But I am not prepared to condemn it as a heinous sin or to regard a husband and wife who cannot help their nature as fallen creatures to be treated with cheap pity or high-brow contempt."

I do not know what the scientific basis for the various taboos in respect of marriage relationships is. But it seems to me clear that a social custom or usage that helps the practice of virtue and self-control, should have the sanctity of a moral law. If it is eugenic considerations that are at the root of interdiction of marriages between brother and sister, then they ought to apply equally to cousin-marriages. A safe rule of conduct, therefore, would be as a rule to respect such taboos where they exist in a particular society. I accept generally the conditions for an ideal marriage enumerated by my correspondent. But I would change their order of importance and put 'love' last in the list. By giving it the first place, the other conditions are liable to be overshadowed by it altogether and rendered more or less nugatory. Therefore, spiritual development ought to be given the first place in the choice for marriage. Service should come next, family considerations and the interest of the social order should have the third place, and mutual attraction or 'love', the fourth and the last place. This means that 'love' alone, where the other three conditions are not fulfilled, should not be held as a valid reason for marriage. At the same time, marriage, where there is no love, should equally be ruled out even though all the other conditions are fully complied with. I should score out the condition of eugenic fitness, because the begetting of offspring being the central purpose of marriage, eugenic fitness cannot be treated merely as a 'condition'; it is the *sine qua non* of marriage.

Hindu *shastras* certainly show a marked bias in favour of the male offspring. But this originated at a time when physical warfare was the order of the day and adequate man-power was a *sine qua non* of success in the struggle for existence. The number of sons that a man had was, therefore, then looked upon as a mark of virility and strength, and to facilitate the begetting of numerous offspring, even polygamy was sanctioned and encouraged. But if we regard marriage as a sacrament, there is room in it only for one offspring, and that is why in our *shastras* the first offspring is described as धर्मज, i. e. 'duty-born', all subsequent issues being referred to as कामज, i. e. 'lust-born'. I make no distinction between son and daughter. Such distinction is, in my opinion, invidious and wrong. The birth of a son or a daughter should be welcome alike.

The story of Vishwamitra and Vasishtha is good as an illustration of the principle that the sexual act, performed solely for the purpose of begetting offspring is not inconsistent with the highest ideal of *brahmacharya*. But the whole of that story need not be taken literally. Sexual intercourse for the purpose of carnal satisfaction is reversion to animality, and it should therefore be man's endeavour to rise above it. But failure to do so as between husband and wife, cannot be regarded as a sin or a matter of obloquy. Millions in this world eat for the satisfaction of their palate; similarly, millions of the husbands and wives indulge in the sex act for their carnal satisfaction and will continue to do so and also pay the inexorable penalty in the shape of numberless ills with which nature visits all violations of its order. The ideal of absolute *brahmacharya* or of married *brahmacharya* is for those who aspire to a spiritual or higher life; it is the *sine qua non* of such life.

Harijan, 5-6-1937

38

SEX EDUCATION

Shri Maganbhai Desai, who received the other day the degree equivalent to Master of Arts from the Gujarat Vidyapith, wrote to me a Gujarati letter dated 7th October from which I cull the following:

> "May I invite you to discuss in the columns of the *Harijanbandhu* a question which you have so far left more or less untouched, I mean the question of imparting sex instruction to young people? As you know, Shri — is regarded as a great advocate in its favour in Gujarat. Personally I have had always my doubts. But apart from them, I am not sure whether this particular gentleman is at all fitted for the task. The results at any rate are not at all encouraging. According to this gentleman it would seem as if the lack of sex education was at the root of all our educational problems and social ills. He and people of his way of thinking simply pounce upon the teaching of modern psychology that dormant libido is the motive spring of all human activity, and without further ado, set to exalt and almost deify it. —, that imp of our Ashram, remarked to me the other day, 'What do you know of the demon of sex which is in every breast?' His remark seemed to me to betray a dulling rather than awakening of his

moral sensibility. No end of mischief is today being insidiously done in the name of sex education Books are written on the subject, their successive editions follow close upon one another, each edition running into several thousands. Some weeklies owe their very existence to a successful exploitation of this theme. They sell like hot cakes. The resulting havoc can be easily imagined. One may, of course, say that society only gets what it wants and deserves. That, however, can hardly be a consolation to the reformer whose task is rendered extremely difficult by the spate of libidinous literature that masquerades under the name of sexual science

I would therefore request you to publicly discuss this question. Should sex education be included in the educational curricula of our children? Who should impart it? What would be the necessary qualification for the task? Should this subject be taught in a matter-of-fact manner to all and sundry just like geography or arithmetic? Or is there any limit? And if so, who is to draw the line and where? Again, should the aim of sex education be to combat the onset of libido or simply to recognize it as an inevitable fact of nature which has to be accepted and submitted to?"

Sex complex is today steadily gaining ground in Gujarat as in the rest of India. And what is more, those who fall under its sway feel as if there is something meritorious about it. When a slave begins to take pride in his fetters and hugs them like precious ornaments, the triumph of the slave-owner is complete. But this success of Cupid, spectacular though it may be, will, I am convinced, prove to be short-lived and ignoble, and at long last end in inanition, even like a scorpion whose venom is spent. But that does not mean that we can in the meantime, afford to sit with folded hands. The certainty of its defeat need not, must not, lull us into a false sense of security. The conquest of lust is the highest endeavour of a man or woman's existence. Without overcoming lust man cannot hope to rule over self. And without rule over self there can be no Swaraj or *Ramaraj*. Rule of all without rule of oneself would prove to be as deceptive and disappointing as a painted toy-mango, charming to look at outwardly but hollow and empty within. No worker who has not overcome lust can hope to render any genuine service to the cause of Harijans, communal unity, khadi, cow-preservation or village reconstruction. Great causes like these cannot be served by intellectual equipment alone; they call for spiritual effort or soul-force. Soul-force comes only through God's grace, and God's grace never descends upon a man who is a slave to lust.

What place has then instruction in sexual science in our educational system, or has it any place there at all? Sexual science is of two kinds — that which is used for controlling or overcoming the sexual passion, and that which is used to stimulate and feed it. Instruction in the former is as necessary a part of a child's education as the latter is harmful and dangerous and fit therefore only to be shunned. All great religions have rightly regarded '*kama*' as the arch-enemy of man, anger or hatred coming only in the second place. According to the *Gita*, the latter is an offspring of the former. The *Gita*, of course, uses the word '*kama*' in its wider sense of desire. But the same holds good of the narrow sense in which it is used here.

This, however, still leaves unanswered the question, i. e. whether it is desirable to impart to young pupils a knowledge about the use and function of generative organs. It seems to me that it is necessary to impart such knowledge to a certain extent. At present they are often left to pick up such knowledge anyhow with the result that they are misled into abusive practices. We cannot properly control or conquer the sexual passion by turning a blind eye to it. I am therefore strongly in favour of teaching young boys and girls, the significance and right use of their generative organs. And in my own way I have tried to impart this knowledge to young children of both sexes for whose training I was responsible.

But the sex education that I stand for, must have for its object the conquest and sublimation of the sex passion. Such education should automatically serve to bring home to children, the essential distinction between man and brute, to make them realize that it is man's special privilege and pride to be gifted with the faculties of head and heart both; that he is a thinking no less than a feeling animal, as the very derivation of the word मनुष्य shows, and to renounce the sovereignty of reason over the blind instincts is therefore to renounce a man's estate. In man, reason quickens and guides the feeling. In brute, the soul lies ever dormant. To awaken the heart is to awaken the dormant soul, to awaken reason, and to inculcate discrimination between good and evil.

Who should teach this true science of sex? Clearly, he who has attained mastery over his passions. To teach astronomy and kindred sciences we have teachers who have gone through course of training in them and are masters of their art. Even so must we have as teachers of sexual science, i. e. the science of sex-control, those who have studied it and have acquired mastery over self. Even a lofty utterance, that has not the backing of sincerity and experience, will be inert and lifeless, and will utterly fail to penetrate and quicken the hearts of men, while the speech that springs from self-realization and genuine experience is always fruitful.

Today our entire environment — our reading, our thinking, our social behaviour — is generally calculated to subserve and cater for the sex-urge. To break through its coils is no easy task. But it is a task worthy of our highest endeavour. Even if there are a handful of teachers endowed with practical experience, who accept the ideal of attaining self-control as the highest duty of man, and are fired by a genuine and undying faith in their mission, and are sleeplessly vigilant and active, their labour will light the path of the children of Gujarat, save the unwary from falling into the mire of sexuality, and rescue those who might be already engulfed in it.

Harijan, 21-11-1936

39

AN UNNATURAL FATHER

A young man has sent me a letter which can be given here only in substance. It is as under:

> "I am a married man. I had gone out to a foreign country. had a friend whom both I and my parents implicitly trusted. During my absence he seduced my wife who has now conceived of him. My father now insists that the girl should resort to abortion; otherwise, he says, the family would be disgraced. To me it seems that it would be wrong to do so. The poor woman is consumed with remorse She cares neither to eat nor drink, but is always weeping. Will you kindly tell me as to what my duty is in the case?"

I have published this letter with great hesitation. As everybody knows, such cases are by no means unfrequent in society. A restrained public discussion of the question, therefore, does not seem to me to be out of place.

It seems to me clear as daylight that abortion would be a crime. Countless husbands are guilty of the same lapse as this poor woman, but nobody ever questions them. Society not only excuses them but does not even censure them. Then, again, the woman cannot conceal her shame while man can successfully hide his sin.

The woman in question deserves to be pitied. It would be the sacred duty of the husband to bring up the baby with all the love and tenderness that he is capable of and to refuse to yield to the counsels of his father. Whether he should continue to live with his wife is a ticklish question. Circumstances may warrant separation from her. In that case he would be bound to provide for her maintenance and education and to help her to live a pure life. Nor should I see anything wrong in his accepting her repentance if it is sincere and genuine. Nay, further, I can imagine a situation when it would be the sacred duty of the husband, to take back an erring wife who has completely expiated for and redeemed her error.

Young India, 3-1-1929.

40

A RENUNCIATION

In 1891 after my return from England I virtually took charge of the children of the family and introduced the habit of walking with them — boys and girls — putting my hands on their shoulders. These were my brothers' children. The practice continued even after they grew old. With the extension of the family, it gradually grew to proportions sufficient to attract attention.

I was unconscious of doing any wrong, so far as I can recollect, till some years ago at Sabarmati an inmate of the Ashram told me that my practice, when extended to grown-up girls and women, offended the accepted notions of decency. But after discussion with the inmates it was continued. Recently two co-workers who came to Wardha suggested that the practice was likely to set a bad example to others and that I should discontinue it on that account. Their argument did not appeal to me. Nevertheless I did not want to ignore the friends' warning. I, therefore, referred it for examination and advice to five inmates of the Ashram. Whilst it was taking shape, a decisive event took place. It was brought to my notice that a bright university student was taking all sorts of liberties in private with a girl who was under his influence, on the plea that he loved her like his own sister and could not restrain himself from some physical demonstration of it. He resented the slightest suggestion of impurity. Could I mention what the youth had been doing, the reader would unhesitatingly pronounce the liberties taken by him as impure. When I read the correspondence, I and those who saw it, came to the conclusion that either the young man was a consummate hypocrite or was self-deluded.

Anyway the discovery set me athinking. I recalled the warning of the two co-workers and asked myself, how I would feel if I found that the young man was using my practice in his defence. I may mention that the girl who is the victim of the youth's attentions, although she regards him as absolutely pure and brotherly, does not like them, even protests against them, but is too weak to resist his action. The self-introspection induced by the the event resulted, within two or three days of the reading of the correspondence, in the renunciation of the practice, and I announced it to the inmates of the Wardha Ashram on the 12th instant. It was not without a pang that I came to the decision. Never has an impure thought entered my being during or owing to the practice. My act has always been open. I believe that my act was that of a parent and has enabled the numerous girls under my guidance and wardship to give their confidences which perhaps no one else has enjoyed in the same measure. Whilst I do not believe in a *brahmacharya* which ever requires a wall of protection against the touch of the opposite sex and will fail it exposed to the least temptation, I am not unaware of the dangers attendant upon the freedom I have taken.

The discovery quoted by me has, therefore, prompted me to renounce the practice, however pure it may have been in itself. Every act of mine is scrutinized by thousands of men and women, as I am conducting an experiment requiring ceaseless vigilance. I must avoid doing things which may require a reasoned defence. My example was never meant to be followed by all and sundry. The young man's case has come upon me as a warning. I have taken it in the hope that my renunciation will set right those who may have erred, whether under the influence of my example or without it. Innocent youth is a priceless possession, not to be squandered away for the sake of a momentary excitement, miscalled pleasure. And let the weak girls like the one in this picture be strong enough to resist the approaches, though they may be declared to be innocent, of young men who are either knaves or who do not know what they are doing.

Harijan, 21-9-1935.

41

NOTHING WITHOUT GRACE

By the grace of medical friends and self-constituted gaolers, Sardar Vallabhbhai and Jamnalalji, I am now able by way of trial to resume to a limited extent my talks with the readers of *Harijan*. The restrictions that they have put on my liberty and to which I have agreed, are that for the time being at any rate, I shall not write for *Harijan* more than I may consider to be absolutely necessary and that too, not involving more than a few hours' writing per week. I shall not carry on private correspondence with reference to correspondents' personal problems or domestic difficulties, except those with which I have already concerned myself, and I shall not accept public engagements or attend or speak at public gatherings. There are positive directions about sleep, recreation, exercise and food, with which the reader is not concerned and with which, therefore, I need not deal. I hope that the readers of *Harijan* and correspondents will cooperate with me and Mahadev Desai, who has in the first instance to attend to all correspondence, in the observance of these restrictions.

It will interest the reader to know something about the origin of the breakdown and the measures taken to cope with it. So far as I have understood the medical friends, after a very careful and painstaking examination of my system, they have found no functional derangement. Their opinion is that the breakdown was most probably due to deficiency of proteins and carbohydrates in the form of sugar and starches, coupled with overstrain for a prolonged period, involving long hours and concentration on numerous taxing private problems in additon to the performance of daily public duty. So far as I can recollect, I had been complaining for the past twelve months or more that if I did not curtail the volume of ever-growing work, I was sure to break down. Therefore, when it came, it was nothing new to me. And it is highly likely that the world would have heard little of it but for the overanxiety of one of the friends who, on seeing me indisposed, sent a sensational note to Jamnalalji who gathered together all the medical talent that was available in Wardha, and sent messages to Nagpur and Bombay for further help.

The day I collapsed, I had a warning on rising in the morning that there was some unusual pain about the neck, but I made light of it and never mentioned it to anybody. I continued to go through the daily programme. The final stroke was a most exhausting and serious conversation I had with a friend whilst I was having the daily evening stroll. The nerves had already been sufficiently taxed during the preceding fortnight, with the consideration and solution of problems which for me were quite as big and as important as, say, the paramount question of Swaraj.

Even if no fuss had been made over the collapse, I would have taken nature's peremptory warning to heart, given myself moderate rest and tided over the difficulty. But looking back upon the past, I feel that it was well that the fuss was made. The extraordinary precaution advised by the medical friends and equally extraordinary care taken by the two gaolers, enforced on me the exacting rest which I would not have taken and which allowed ample time for introspection. Not only have I profited by it, but the introspection has revealed vital defects in my following out of the interpretation of the *Gita* as I have understood it. I have discovered that I have not approached with adequate detachment, the innumerable problems that have presented themselves for solution. It is clear that I have taken many of them to heart and allowed them to rouse my emotional being and thus affect my nerves. In other words, they have not, as they should have, in a votary of the *Gita*, left my body or mind untouched. I verily believe that one who literally follows the prescription of the eternal mother, need never grow old in mind. Such a one's body will wither in due course like leaves of a healthy tree, leaving the mind as young and as fresh as ever. That seems to me to be the meaning of Bhishma delivering his marvellous discourse to Yudhishthira, though he was on his death-bed. Medical friends were never tired of warning me against being excited over or affected by events happening around me. Extra precautions were taken to keep from me news of a tragic character. Though I think I was not quite so bad a devotee of the *Gita* as their precautions lead me to suppose, there was undoubtedly substance behind them. For I discovered, with what a wrench I accepted Jamnalalji's conditions and demand that I should remove from Maganwadi to Mahila Ashram. Anyway I had lost credit with him, for detached action. The fact of the collapse was for him eloquent enough testimony for discrediting my vaunted detachment. I must plead guilty to the condemnation.

The worst, however, was to follow. I have been trying to follow *brahmacharya* consciously and deliberately since 1899. My definition of it is purity, not merely of body but of both speech and thought also. With the exception of what must be regarded as one lapse, I can recall no instance, during more than thirtysix years' constant and conscious effort, of mental disturbance such as I experienced during this illness. I was disgusted with myself. The moment the feeling came I acquainted my attendants and the medical friends with my condition. They could give me no help. I expected none. I broke loose after the experience from the rigid rest that was imposed upon me. The confession of the wretched experience brought much relief to me. I felt as if a great load had been raised from over me. It enabled me to pull myself together before any harm could be done. But what of the *Gita*? Its teaching is clear and precise. A mind that is once hooked to the Star of Stars becomes incorruptible. How far I must be from Him, He alone knows. Thank God my much vaunted Mahatmaship has never fooled me. But this enforced rest has humbled me as never before. It has brought to the surface my limitations and imperfections. But I am not so much ashamed of them, as I should be of hiding them from the public. My faith in the message of the *Gita* is as bright as ever. Unwearied, ceaseless effort is the price that must be paid for turning that faith into rich infallible experience. But the same *Gita* says without any equivocation that the experience is not to be had without divine grace. We should develop swelled heads if Divinity had not made that ample reservation.

Harijan, 29-2-1936

42

HOW NON-VIOLENCE WORKS

A Congress leader said to me the other day, in the course of our conversations, "How is it that in quality, the Congress is not what it used to be in 1920-25? It has deteriorated. Ninety per cent of the members are not carrying out the Congress discipline. Can you not do something to mend this state of things?"

The question is apposite and timely. I can't shirk responsibility by saying, 'I am no longer in the Congress. I have gone out of it for the purpose of serving it better.' I know that I still influence the Congress policy. As the author of the Congress constitution of 1920, I must hold myself responsible for such deterioration as is avoidable.

The Congress started with an initial handicap in 1920. Very few believed in truth and non-violence as a creed. Most members accepted them as a policy. It was inevitable. I had hoped that many would accept them as their creed after they had watched the working of the Congress under the new policy. Only some did, not many. In the beginning stages, the change that came over the foremost leaders was profound. Readers will recall the letters from the late Pandit Motilal Nehru and Deshbandhu Das reproduced in the *Young India*. They had experienced a new joy and a new hope in a life of self-denial, simplicity and self-sacrifice. The Ali Brothers had almost become faqirs. As we toured from place to place, I watched with delight the change that was coming over the brothers. What was true of these four leaders was true of many others whom I can name. The enthusiasm of the leaders had infected the rank and file.

But this phenomenal change was due to the spell of 'Swaraj in one year'. The conditions I had attached to the fulfilment of the formula were forgotten. Khwaja Saheb Abdul Majid even went so far as to suggest that, as the general of the Satyagraha army which the Congress had then become, and still is (if only Congressmen realize the meaning of Satyagraha), I should have made sure that the conditions were such that they would be fulfilled. Perhaps he was right. Only I had no such prevision in me. The use of non-violence on a mass scale and for political purposes was, even for myself, an experiment. I could not therefore dogmatize. My conditions were meant to be a measure of popular response. They might or might not be fulfilled. Mistakes, miscalculations were always possible. Be that as it may, when the fight for Swaraj became prolonged and Khilafat ceased to be a live issue, enthusiasm began to wane, confidence in non-violence even as a policy began to be shaken, and untruth crept in. People who had no faith in the twin virtues or the Khadi clause stole in, and many even openly defied the Congress constitution.

The evil has continued to grow. The Working Committee has been making some attempt to purge the Congress of the evil but has not been able to put its foot down and risk the loss of numbers on the Congress register. I myself believe in quality rather than quantity.

But there is no such thing as compulsion in the scheme of non-violence. Reliance has to be placed upon ability to reach the intellect and the heart—the latter rather than the former.

It follows that there must be power in the word of a Satyagraha general—not the power that the possession of limitless arms gives, but the power that purity of life, strict vigilance and ceaseless application produce. This is impossible without the observance of *brahmacharya.* It must be as full as it is humanly possible. *Brahmacharya* here does not mean mere physical self-control. It means much more. It means complete control over all the senses. Thus an impure thought is a breach of *brahmacharya*; so is anger. All power comes from the preservation and sublimation of the vitality that is responsible for creation of life. If the vitality is husbanded instead of being dissipated, it is transmuted into creative energy of the highest order. This vitality is continuously and even unconsciously dissipated by evil, or even rambling, disorderly, unwanted thoughts. And since thought is the root of all speech and action, the quality of the latter corresponds to that of the former. Hence perfectly controlled thought is itself power of the highest potency and can become self-acting. That seems to me to be the meaning of the silent prayer of the heart. If man is after the image of God, he has but to will a thing in the limited sphere allotted to him and it becomes. Such power is impossible in one who dissipates his energy in any way whatsoever, even as steam kept in a leaky pipe yields no power. The sexual act divorced from the deliberate purpose of generation is a typical and gross form of dissipation and has therefore been specially and rightly chosen for condemnation. But in one who has to organize vast masses of mankind for non-violent action, the full control described by me has to be attempted and virtually achieved.

This control is unattainable save by the grace of God. There is a verse in the second chapter of the *Gita* which freely rendered means: "Sense-effects remain in abeyance whilst one is fasting or whilst the particular sense is starved; but the hankering does not cease except when one sees God face to face." This control is not mechanical or temporary. Once attained it is never lost. In that state vital energy is stored up without any chance of escaping by the innumerable outlets.

It has been said that such *brahmacharya*, if it is at all attainable, can be so only by cave-dwellers. A *brahmachari*, it is said, should never see, much less touch, a woman. Doubtless a *brahmachari* may not think of, speak of, see or touch a woman *lustfully*. But the prohibition, one finds in books on *brahmacharya*, is mentioned without the important adverb. The reason for the omission seems to be that man is no impartial judge in such matters, and therefore, cannot say when he is or is not affected by such contacts. Cupid's visitations are often unperceivable. Difficult though, therefore, *brahmacharya* is of observance when one freely mixes with the world, it is not of much value, if it is attainable only by retirement from the world.

Anyway, I have practised *brahmacharya* for over thirty years with considerable success though living in the midst of activities. After the decision to lead the life of a *brahmachari*, there was little change in my outward practice, except with my wife. In the course of my work among the Indians in South Africa, I mixed freely with women. There was hardly an Indian woman in the Transvaal and Natal whom I did not know. They were so many sisters and daughters to me. My *brahmacharya* was not derived from books. I evolved my own rules for my guidance and that of those who, at my invitation, had joined me in the experiment. If I have not followed the prescribed restrictions, much less have I accepted the description found even in religious literature of woman as the source of all evil and temptation. Owing as I do all the good there may be in me to my mother, I have looked upon woman, never as an object for satisfaction of sexual desire, but always with the veneration due to my own mother. Man is the tempter and aggressor. It is not woman whose touch defiles man, but he is often himself too impure to touch her. But recently a doubt has seized me as to the nature of the limitations that a *brahmachari* or *brahmacharini* should put upon himself or herself, regarding contacts with the opposite sex. I have set limitations which do not satisfy me. What they should be, I do not know. I am experimenting. I have never claimed to have been a perfect *brahmachari* of my definition. I have not acquired that control over my thoughts that I need for my researches in non-violence. If my non-violence is to be contagious and infectious, I must acquire greater control over my thoughts. There is perhaps a flaw somewhere which accounts for the apparent failure of leadership adverted to in the opening sentence of this writing.

My faith in non-violence remains as strong as ever. I am quite sure that not only should it answer all our requirements in our country, but that it should, if properly applied, prevent the bloodshed that is going on outside India and is threatening to overwhelm the Western world.

My aspiration is limited. God has not given me the power to guide the world on the path of non-violence. But I have imagined that He has chosen me as His instrument for presenting non-violence to India for dealing with her many ills. The progress already made is great. But much more remains to be done. And yet I seem to have lost the power to evoke the needed response from Congressmen in general. It is a bad carpenter who quarrels with his tools. It is a bad general who blames his men for faulty workmanship. I know I am not a bad general. I have wisdom enough to know my limitations. God will give me strength enough to declare my bankruptcy if such is to be my lot. He will perhaps take me away when I am no longer wanted for the work which I have been permitted to do for nearly half a century. But I do entertain the hope that there is yet work for me to do, that the darkness that seems to have enveloped me will disappear, and that, whether, with another battle more brilliant than the Dandi March or without, India will come to her own demonstrably through non-violent means. I am praying for the light that will dispel the darkness. Let those who have a living faith in non-violence join me in the prayer.

Harijan, 23-7-1938

43

STUDENTS' SHAME

There is a most pathetic letter from a college girl in the Punjab lying on my file for nearly two months. Want of time was but an excuse for shirking the answer to the girl's question. Somehow or other I was avoiding the task, though I knew the answer. Meanwhile I received another letter from a sister of great experience, and I felt that I could no longer evade the duty of dealing with the college girl's very real difficulty. Her letter is written in chaste Hindustani. I must try to do as much justice as I can to the letter, which gives me a perfect picture of her deep feeling. Here is my rendering of a portion of the letter:

"To girls and grown-up women there come times, in spite of their wish to the contrary, when they have to venture out alone, whether they are going from one place to another in the same city, or from one town to another. And when they are thus found alone, evil-minded people pester them. They use improper or even indecent language whilst they are passing by. And if fear does not check them, they do not hesitate to take further liberty. I should like to know what part non-violence can play on such occasions. The use of violence is of course there. If the girl or the woman has sufficient courage, she will use what resources she has and teach miscreants a lesson. They can at least kick up a row that would draw the attention of the people around, resulting in the miscreants being horse-whipped. But I know that the result of such treatment would be merely to postpone the agony, not a permanent cure Where you know the people who misbehave, I feel sure that they will listen to reason, the gesture of love and humility. But what about a fellow cycling by, using foul language on seeing a girl or a woman unaccompanied by a male companion? You have no opportunity of reasoning with him. There is no likelihood of your meeting him again. You may not even recognize him. You do not know his address. What is a poor girl or a woman to do in such cases? By way of example I want to give you my own experience of last night (26th October). I was going with a girl companion of mine on a very special errand at about 7-30 P. M. It was impossible to secure a male companion at the time and the errand could not be put off. On the way a Sikh young man passed by on his cycle and continued to murmur something till we were within hearing distance. We knew that it was aimed at us. We felt hurt and uneasy. There was no crowd on the road. Before we had gone a few paces the cyclist returned. We recognized him at once whilst he was still at a respectful distance He wheeled towards us; heaven knows whether he had intended to get down or merely pass by us. We felt that we were in danger. We had no faith in our physical prowess. I myself am weaker than the average girl. But in my hands I had a big book. Somehow or other courage came to me all of a sudden. I hurled the heavy book at the cycle and roared out, 'Dare you repeat your pranks?' He could with difficulty keep his balance, put on speed and fled from us. Now if I had not flung the book at his cycle, he might have harassed us by his filthy language to the end of our journey. This was an ordinary, perhaps insignificant, occurrence; but I wish you could come to Lahore and listen to the difficulties of us unfortunate girls. You would surely discover proper solution. First of all, tell me how, in the circumstances mentioned above, can girls apply the principle of *ahimsa* and save themselves. Secondly, what is the remedy for curing youth of the abominable habit of insulting womenfolk? You would not suggest that we should wait and suffer till a new generation, taught from childhood to be polite to their womenfolk, comes into being. The Government is either unwilling or unable to deal with this social evil. The big leaders have no time for such questions. Some, when they hear of a girl bravely castigating ill-behaved youth, say, 'Well done. That is the way all girls should behave.' Sometimes a leader is found eloquently lecturing against such misbehaviour of students. But no one applies himself continuously to the solution of this serious problem. You will be painfully surprised to know that during Diwali and such other holidays, newspapers come out with notices warning women from venturing outdoors even to see the illuminations. This one fact should enable you to know to what straits we are reduced in this part of the world! Neither the writers nor the readers of such warnings have any sense of shame that they should have to be issued."

Another Punjabi girl to whom I gave the letter to read, supports the narrative from her own experiences of her college days and tells me that what my correspondent has related is the common experience of most girls.

The other letter from an experienced woman relates the experiences of her girl friends in Lucknow. They are molested in cinema theatres by boys sitting in the row behind them, using all kinds of language which I can only call indecent. They are stated to resort even to practical jokes which have been described by my correspondent but which I must not reproduce here.

If the immediate personal relief was all that was needed, no doubt, the remedy that the girl who describes herself to be physically weak adopted, i.e. of flinging her book at the cyclist, was quite correct. It is an age-long remedy. And I have said in these columns that when a person wants to become violent, physical weakness does not come in the way of its effective use even against a physically powerful opponent. And we know that in the present age, there have been invented so many methods of using physical force that even a little girl with sufficient intelligence can deal death and destruction. The fashion nowadays is growing of training girls to defend themselves in situations, such as the one described by my correspondent. But she is wise enough to know that even though she was able to make effective use for the moment, of the book she had in her hand as a weapon of defence, it was no remedy for the growing evil. In the cases of rude remarks, there need be no perturbation but there should be no indifference. All such cases should be published in the papers. Names of the offenders should be published when they are traced. There should be no false modesty about exposing the evil. There is nothing like public opinion for castigating public misconduct. There is no doubt that, as the correspondent says, there is great public apathy about such matters. But it is not the public alone that are to blame. They must have before them examples of rudeness. Even as stealing cannot be dealt with, unless cases of thieving are published and followed up, so also is it impossible to deal with cases of rude behaviour if they are suppressed. Crime and vice generally require darkness for prowling. They disappear when light plays upon them.

But I have a fear that the modern girl loves to be Juliet to half a dozen Romeos. She loves adventure. My correspondent seems to represent the unusual type. The modern girl dresses not to protect herself from wind, rain and sun but to attract attention. She improves upon nature by painting herself and looking extraordinary. The non-violent way is not for such girls. I have often remarked in these columns that definite rules govern the development of the non-violent spirit in us. It is a strenuous effort. It marks a revolution in the way of thinking and living. If my correspondent and the girls of her way of thinking will revolutionize their life in the prescribed manner, they will soon find that young men, who at all come in contact with them, will learn to respect them and to put on their best behaviour in their presence. But if perchance they find, as they may, that their very chastity is in danger of being violated, they must develop courage enough to die rather than yield to the brute in man. It has been suggested that a girl who is gagged or bound so as to make her powerless even for struggling, cannot die as easily as I seem to think. I venture to assert that a girl who has the will to resist can burst all the bonds that may have been used to render her powerless. The resolute will gives her the strength to die.

But this heroism is possible only for those who have trained themselves for it. Those who have not a living faith in non-violence will learn the art of ordinary self-defence and protect themselves from indecent behaviour of unchivalrous youth.

The great question, however, is why should young men be devoid of elementary good manners so as to make decent girls be in perpetual fear of molestation from them ? I should be sorry to discover that the majority of young men have lost all sense of chivalry. But they should, as a class, be jealous of their reputation and deal with every case of impropriety occuring among their mates. They must learn to hold the honour of every woman as dear as that of their own sisters and mothers. All the education they receive will be in vain if they do not learn good manners.

And is it not as much the concern of professors and schoolmasters to ensure gentlemanliness among their pupils as to prepare them for the subjects prescribed for the class-room ?

Harijan, 31-12-1938

44

THE MODERN GIRL

I have received a letter written on behalf of eleven girls whose names and addresses have been sent to me. I give it below with changes that make it more readable without in any way altering the meaning:

"Your comments on the letter of a lady student captioned 'Students' Shame' and published in the *Harijan* of the 31st December, 1938, deserve special attention. The modern girl, it seems, has provoked you to the extent that you have disposed of her finally as one playing Juliet to half a dozen Romeos. This remark which betrays your idea about women in general is not very inspiring.

"In these days when women are coming out of closed doors to help men and take an equal share of the burden of life, it is indeed strange that they are still blamed even when they are maltreated by men. It cannot be denied that instances can be cited where the fault is equally divided. There may be a few girls playing Juliets to half a dozen Romeos. But such cases presuppose the existence of half a dozen Romeos, moving about the streets in quest of a Juliet. And it cannot or should never be taken that modern girls are categorically all Juliets or modern youths all Romeos. You yourself have come in contact with quite a number of modern girls and may have been struck by their resolution, sacrifice and other sterling womanly virtues.

"As for forming public opinion against such misdemeanours as pointed out by your correspondent, it is not for girls to do it, not so much out of false shame as from its ineffectiveness.

"But a statement like this from one revered all over the world, seems to hold a brief once more for that worn out and unbecoming saying 'woman is the gate of Hell'

"From the foregoing remarks, however, please do not conclude that modern girls have no respect for you. They hold you in as much respect as every young man does. To be hated or pitied is what they resent much. They are ready to mend their ways if they are really guilty. Their guilt, if any, must be conclusively proved before they are anathematized. In this respect they would neither desire to take shelter under the covering of 'ladies, please,' nor would they silently stand and allow the judge to condemn them in his own way. Truth must be faced; the modern girl or 'Juliet', as you have called her, has courage enough to face it."

My correspondents do not perhaps know that I began service of India's women in South Africa more than forty years ago when perhaps none of them was born. I hold myself to be incapable of writing anything derogatory to womanhood. My regard for the fair sex is too great to permit me to think ill of them. She is, what she has been described to be in English, the better half of mankind. And my article was written to expose students' shame, not to advertise the frailties of girls. But in giving the diagnosis of the disease, I was bound if I was to prescribe the right remedy, to mention all the factors which induced the disease.

The modern girl has a special meaning. Therefore there was no question of my restricting the scope of my remark to some. But all the girls who receive English education are not modern girls. I know many who are not at all touched by the 'modern girl' spirit. But there are some who have become modern girls. My remark was meant to warn India's girl students against copying the modern girl and complicating a problem that has become a serious menace. For, at the time I received the letter referred to, I received also a letter from an Andhra girl student bitterly complaining of the behaviour of Andhra students which, from the description given, is worse than what was described by the Lahore girl. This daughter of Andhra tells me that the simple dress of her girl friends gives them no protection, but they lack the courage to expose the barbarism of the boys who are a disgrace to the institution they belong to. I commend this complaint to the authorities of the Andhra University.

The eleven girls I invite to initiate a crusade against the rude behaviour of students. God helps only those who help themselves. The girls must learn the art of protecting themselves against the ruffianly behaviour of man.

Harijan, 4-2-1939

45

OBSCENE ADVERTISEMENTS

A sister, sending me a cutting from a well-known magazine containing the advertisement of a most objectionable book, writes:

> "The enclosed came under my eye when glancing over the pages of —. I do not know if you get this magazine. I do not suppose you ever have time to glance at it even if it is sent to you. Once before I spoke to you about 'obscene advertisements'. I do wish you would write about them some time. That books of the type advertised, are flooding the market today is only too true, but should responsible journals like — encourage their sale? My woman's modesty is so utterly repelled by these things that I cannot write to anyone but you. To think that what God has given to woman with intent for an express purpose, should be advertised for abuse is too degrading for words. . . .I wish you would write about the responsibility of leading Indian newspapers and journals in this respect. This is not the first by any means that I could have sent to you for criticism."

From the advertisement I do not propose to reproduce any portion except to tell the reader that it describes as obscenely as it can the suggestive contents of the book advertised. Its title is 'Sexual Beauty of the Female Form', and the advertising firm tells the reader that it will give away free to the buyer two more books called 'New Knowledge for the Bride' and 'The Sexual Embrace or How to Please Your Partner'.

I fear that in relying on me in any way to affect the course of the advertisers of such books or to move the editors or publishers from their purpose of making their productions yield profits, she relies on a broken reed. No amount of appealing by me to the publishers of the objectionable books or advertisements of them will be of any use. But what I would like to tell the writer of the letter and other learned sisters like her, is to come out in the open and to do the work that is peculiarly and specially theirs. Very often a bad name is given to a person and he or she in course of time begins to believe in the badness. To call a woman a member of 'the weaker sex' is a libel. In what way is woman the weaker sex I do not know. If the implication is that she lacks the brute instinct of man or does not possess it in the same measure as man, the charge may be admitted. But then woman becomes, as she is, the nobler sex. If she is weak in striking, she is strong in suffering. I have described woman as the embodiment of sacrifice and *ahimsa*. She has to learn not to rely on man to protect her virtue or her honour. I do not know a single instance of a man having ever protected the virtue of a woman. He cannot even if he would. Rama certainly did not protect the virtue of Sita, nor the five Pandavas of Draupadi. Both these noble women protected their own virtue by the sheer force of their purity. No person loses honour or self-respect but by his consent. A woman no more loses her honour or virtue because a brute renders her senseless and ravishes her than a man loses his because a wicked woman administers to him a stupefying drug and makes him do what she likes.

It is remarkable that there are no books wrttten in praise of male beauty. But why should there always be literature to excite the animal passions of man? May it be that woman like to live up to the titles that man has chosen to bestow upon her? Does she like to have the beauty of her form exploited by man? Does she like to look beautiful of form before man, and why? These are questions I would like educated sisters to ask themselves. If these advertisements and literature offend them, they must wage a relentless war against them and they will stop them in a moment. Would that woman will realize the power she has latent in her for good, if she has also for mischief. It is in her power to make the world more livable both for her and her partner, whether as father, son or husband, if she would cease to think of herself as weak and fit only to serve as a doll for man to play with. If society is not to be destroyed by insane wars of nations against nations and still more insane wars on its moral foundations, the woman will have to play her part not manfully, as some are trying to do, but womanfully. She won't better humanity by vying with man in his ability to destroy life mostly without purpose. Let it be her privilege to wean the erring man from his error which will envelope in his ruin that of woman also. This wretched advertisement is merely a straw showing which way the wind is blowing. It is a shameless exploitation of woman. It would not leave alone even "the beauty of female form of savage races of the world."

Harijan, 14-11-1936

46

HOW TO STOP OBSCENE ADVERTISEMENTS?

A correpondent who saw my article on obscene advertisements writes:

> "You can do much in preventing obscene advertisements by exposing the names of the papers and magazines which advertise such shameless things as you have mentioned."

I can't undertake the censorship my correspondent advises, but I can suggest a better way. If public conscience is alive, subscribers can write to their respective papers, if they contain objectionable advertisements, drawing their attention to them and stopping their subscriptions if the offence is not cured. The reader will be glad to know that the sister who complained to me about the obscene advertisement wrote also to the editor of the offending magazine who expressed his regret for the inadvertent admission of the obnoxious advertisement and promised to remove it forthwith.

I am glad also to be able to say that my caution has found support from some other papers. Thus the editor of the *Nispruha* of Nagpur writes:

> "I have not only read with great care your article in the *Harijan* regarding obscene advertisements but have given a detailed translation of it in the *Nispruha*. I have also added a short editorial comment thereon.
>
> I am enclossing a typical advertisement which, though not obscene, is yet immoral in a sense. The advertisement is obviously bogus and it is generally the villager who falls a prey to it. I have always refused such advertisements and I am also writing

to this party similarly. If an editor must supervise the reading matter that he will allow, it is as much his duty to supervise the advertisments, and no editor can permit his paper to be used by people desirous of duping the simple villagers"

Harijan, 2-1-1937.

47

FAMINES AND BIRTH RATE

Major Gen. Sir John McGaw, President, India Office Medical Board, is reported by a correspondent to have said:

> "Famines in India will recur, in fact India is today facing perpetual famine. Unless something is done to decrease the birth rate in India, the country will be leading straight for a calamity."

The correspondent asks what I have to say on this grave issue.

For me, this and some other ways of explaining away famines in India, is to divert the attention from the only cause of recurring famines in this benighted land. I have stated and repeat here that famines of India are not a calamity descended upon us from nature but is a calamity created by the rulers—whether through ignorant indifference or whether consciously or otherwise does not matter. Prevention against draught is not beyond human effort and ingenuity. Such effort has not proved ineffective in other countries. In India a sustained intelligent effort has never been made.

The bogey of increasing birth rate is not a new thing. It has been often trotted out. Increase in population is not and ought not to be regarded as a calamity to be avoided. Its regulation or restriction by artificial methods is a calamity of the first grade whether we know it or not. It is bound to degrade the race, if it becomes universal, which, thank God, it is never likely to be. Pestilence, wars and famines are cursed antidotes against cursed lust which is responsible for unwanted children. If we would avoid this three-fold curse we would avoid too the curse of unwanted children by the sovereign remedy of self-control. The evil consequences of artificial methods are being seen by discerning men even now. Without however encroaching upon the moral domain, let me say that propagation of the race rabbit-wise must undoubtedly be stopped; but not so as to bring greater evils in its train. It should be stopped by methods which in themselves ennoble the race. In other words, it is all a matter of proper education which would embrace every department of life; and dealing with one curse will take in its orbit all the others. A way is not to be avoided becuse it is upward and therefore uphill. Man's upward progress necessarily means ever increasing difficulty, which is to be welcomed.

Harijan 31-3-1946.

48

SELF-RESTRAINT IN MARRIAGE

The same correspondent from the Patidar Ashram, Surat, who put a question to Shri Narahari Parikh, has also asked the following:

"To marry and not have sexual commerce until Swaraj is attained is surely an inconsistency. He who wants to refrain has no need to marry and *vice versa*. Man is a civilized being. By introducing the institution of marriage, he has attempted to establish an ordered and just society. If there were no such institution as marriage, people would be quarrelling about matters of sex. Of course, marriage does not mean sexual license. There is room for self-restraint which adorns married life. The main purpose of married life is that man and woman should live together and thereby help each other's growth. It cannot be gainsaid that in this growth the sexual side must be satisfied but with due control. When, however, you ask a married couple to pledge themselves to complete sexual restraint until Swaraj is attained, it is really putting a premium on hypocrisy. There is even danger of moral perversion for the couple concerned. Exceptional men and women will refuse to be bound in marriage. Those who desire marriage are of the ordinary run of human beings. It is good that the particular bridegroom made it clear later on that he could not deny to his wife the right of motherhood. This sentence really saved Gandhiji's face. One cannot expect anything other than hypocrisy in the guise of celibacy in marriage.

"Gandhiji ought to explain clearly the implications of the vow of celibacy until the attainment of Swaraj. To me it appears quite ridiculous."

It is deplorable that the correspondent seems to take it for granted that the main thing in marriage is the satisfaction of the sexual urge. Rightly speaking, the true purpose of marriage should be and is intimate friendship and companionship between man and woman. There is in it no room for sexual satisfaction. That marriage is no marriage which takes place for the satisfaction of the sex desire. That satisfaction is a denial of true friendship. I know of English marriages undertaken for the sake of companionship and mutual service. If a reference to my own married life is not considered irrelevant, I may say that my wife and I tested the real bliss of married life when we renounced sexual contact, and that, in the heyday of youth. It was then that our companionship blossomed and both of us were enabled to render real service to India and humanity in general. I have written about this in my "Experiments with Truth". Indeed this self-denial was born out of our great desire for service.

Of course, innumerable marriages take place in the natural course of event and such will continue. The physical side of married life is given pre-eminence in these. Innumerable persons eat in order to satisfy the palate; but such indulgence does not therefore become one's duty. Very few eat to live but they are the ones who really know the law of eating. Similarly, those only really marry who marry in order to experience the purity and sanctity of the marriage tie and thereby realize the divinity within.

The correspondent does not seem to be conversant with the full details of the Tendulkar-Indumati marriage. The vow of sexual restraint was an outcome of mature deliberation. The text was written in Hindustani. The papers put in their own English translations of it. The original provided for sexual intercourse if the wife desired progeny. This much is certain that both desired to observe restraint even after marriage. The union was for promotion of joint service. They had known each other for many years. Shri Indumati's parents gave their consent to this marriage after much testing. Then jail life prolonged the agony. Both parties as well as their elders were keen that the ceremony should take place in Sevagram Ashram, where Shri Indumati had lived for some time and derived solace. I am unaware of their whereabouts today. I have no reason to suspect hypocrisy in the transaction. But even if it is discovered, it would not prove that the vow of *brahmacharya* in married life is at fault. The fault lies in hypocrisy. An English poet has well said, "Hypocrisy is an ode to virtue". Wherever there are true coins, counterfeit ones will also be found. Where there is virtue, there will be hypocrisy, i.e. vice masquerading as virtue. How tragic and surprising that a virtuous action should be sought to be stopped because of the fear of hypocrisy!

Harijan, 7-7-1946

49

HOW DID I BEGIN IT ?

Readers must have noticed that last week I started writing for the *Harijan.* How long I shall be able to continue it, I do not know. God's will be done in this as in other things.

When I think of it, the circumstances under which I stopped writing for the *Harijan* have not altered. Pyarelalji is far away from me and in my opinion is doing very important work in Noakhali. He is taking part in what I have called *Mahayagna.* Parsuramji, the English typist who had become used to the work has gone to Ahmedabad of his own choice to help Jivanji. Kanu Gandhi was of much help, but he is also taking part in the *Mahayagna* of Noakhali. Most of the other helpers are also unable to help under the stress of circumstances or other causes. To resume writing for the *Harijan* under these adverse conditions would be ordinarily considered madness. But what appears unpractical from the ordinary standpoint is feasible under divine guidance. I believe I dance to the divine tune. If this is delusion, I treasure it.

Who is this Divinity ? I would love to discuss the question; only not today.

The question that is foremost with us all, I discuss every evening after the prayer. This writing will come before the readers after seven days. This interval would be considered too long in connection with the pressing problem. Therefore, in these columns for the moment, I must confine myself to things of eternal value. One such is *brahmacharya.* The world seems to be running after things of transitory value. It has no time for the other. And yet when one thinks a little deeper, it becomes clear that it is the things eternal that count in the end.

What is *brahmacharya* ? It is the way of life which leads us to Brahma (God). It includes full control over the process of reproduction. The control must be in thought, word and deed. If the thought is not under control, the other two have no value. There is a saying in Hindustani: "He whose heart is pure has all the purifying waters of the Ganges in his house." For one whose thought is under control, the other is mere child's play. The *brahmachari* of my conception will be healthy and will easily live long. He will not even suffer from so much as a headache. Mental and physical work will not cause fatigue. He is ever bright, never slothful. Outward neatness will be an exact reflection of the inner. He will exhibit all the attributes of the steadfast one described in the *Gita*. It need cause no worry if not one person is met with answering the description.

Is it strange that one who is able completely to conserve and sublimate the vital fluid which has the potentiality of creating human beings, should exhibit all the attributes described above? Who can measure the creative strength of such sublimation, one drop of which has the potentiality of bringing into being a human life? Patanjali has described five disciplines. It is not possible to isolate any one of these and practise it. It may be posited in the case of Truth, because it really includes the other four. And for this age the five have been expanded into eleven. Acharya Vinoba has put them in the form of a Marathi verse: They are non-violence, truth, non-stealing, *brahmacharya*, non-possession, bread labour, control of the palate, fearlessness, equal regard for all religions, *swadeshi* and removal of untouchability.

All these can be derived from Truth. But life is complex. It is not possible to enunciate one grand principle and leave the rest to follow of itself. Even when we know a proposition, its corollaries have to be worked out.

It is well to bear in mind that all the disciplines are of equal importance. If one is broken, all are. There seems to be a popular belief amongst us that breach of truth or non-violence is pardonable. Non-stealing and non-possession are rarely mentioned. We hardly recognize the necessity of observing them. But a fancied breach of *brahmacharya* excites wrath and worse. There must be something seriously wrong with a society in which values are exaggerated and underestimated. Moreover, to use the word *brahmacharya* in a narrow sense is to detract from its value. Such detraction increases the difficulty of proper observance. When it is isolated, even the elementary observance becomes difficult, if not impossible. Therefore, it is essential that all the disciplines should be taken as one. This enables one to realize the full meaning and significance of *brahmacharya*.

Harijan 8-6-1947

50

WALLS OF PROTECTION

Let us ask ourselves what walls should be erected to protect *brahmacharya* of which I wrote last week. The answer seems clear. It is not *brahmacharya* that needs walls of protection. To say this is easy enough and sounds sweet. But it is difficult to understand the import of the statement and more so to act accordingly.

It is true that he who has attained perfect *brahmacharya* does not stand in need of protecting walls. But the aspirant undoubtedly needs them, even as a young mango plant has need of a strong fence round it. A child goes from its mother's lap to the cradle and from the cradle to the push-cart, till he becomes a man who has learnt to walk without aid. To cling to the aid when it is needless is surely harmful.

I made it clear last week that *brahmacharya* is one of the eleven observances. It follows, therefore, that the real aid to *brahmacharya* are the remaining ten observances. The difference between them and the walls of protection is that the latter are temporary, the former permanent. They are an integral part of *brahmacharya*.

Brahmacharya is a mental condition. The outward behaviour of a man is at once the sign and proof of the inner state. He who has killed the sexual urge in him will never be guilty of it in any shape or form. However attractive a woman may be, her attraction will produce no effect on the man without the urge. The same rule applies to woman. But he or she who has not conquered lust should not turn the eyes even towards a sister or a brother or a daughter or a son. This advice I have given to friends who have profited by it.

As for myself I have to admit with great shame that while the sight of women had ceased to rouse any sexual urge in me in South Africa, in the early days of my return to India, past recollections roused the urge against which I had to battle fairly hard. The same is true of the vague fear which is so unbecoming in man.

I was cowardly by nature. I was frightened to sleep in the dark. To sleep alone in a room was an act of bravery for me. I hope I have lost that cowardliness. Yet I do not know what would be my state if I lost my way and had to wander alone in a thick forest on a dark night and if I were to forget that God was ever with me. If this childhood's fear has not completely gone from me, it would be certainly more difficult for me to be fearless in a lonely jungle than to control the sex urge.

There are certain rules laid down in India for the would-be *brahmachari*. Thus he may not live among women, animals and eunuchs, he may not teach a woman only or even a group, he may not sit on the same mat as a woman, he may not look at any part of a woman's body, he may not take milk, curds, *ghee* or any fatty substance nor indulge in baths and oily massage. I read about these when I was in South Africa. There I came in touch with some men and women who, while they observed *brahmacharya*, never knew that any of the above-named restraints were necessary. Nor did I observe them and I was none the worse for the non-observance. I did give up milk, *ghee* and other animal substances but for different reasons. I failed in this attempt after two or three years after my return to India. But if today I could find any effective vegetable substitute for milk and *ghee*, I would gladly renounce all animal products. But this is another story.

A perfect *brahmachari* never loses his vital fluid. On the contrary, he is able to increase it day by day and, what is more, he conserves it; he will, therefore, never become old in the accepted sense and his intellect will never be dimmed.

It appears to me that even the true aspirant does not need the above-mentioned restraints. *Brahmacharya* is not a virtue that can be cultivated by outward restraints. He who runs away from a necessary contact with a woman, does not understand the full meaning of *brahmacharya*.

Let not the reader imagine for one moment that what I have written is to serve as the slightest encouragement to life without the law of real restraint. Nor is there room in any honest attempt for hypocrisy.

Self-indulgence and hypocrisy are sins to be avoided.

The true *brahmachari* will shun false restraints. He must create his own fences according to his limitations, breaking them down when he feels that they are unnecessary. The first thing is to know what true *brahmacharya* is, then to realize its value and lastly to try to cultivate this priceless virtue. I hold that true service of the country demands this observance.

Harijan, 15-6-1947.

51

A PERPLEXITY

"I have developed a curious mentality about the relations between men and women. I believe in certain checks upon these. Yet my condition is very like that of a man suspended in mid-air. I often feel that if these relations were more natural than they are, probably there would be less sinfulness. Yet something within me tells me that every touch, be it ever so superficial, is bound to lead to the eruption of animal passion. When one examines the court cases here even about brother and sister or even father and daughter, the beginning seems to have been quite innocent. In my opinion the glow of mere touch drags down inside of a month, even a week, one who is not endowed with extra purity. A good man may take even ten years but he is sure to go down the incline of vice. There is a constant conflict between the habit which we have inherited and the study of modernist books The question often arises — can society altogether abjure contact between the sexes? I have not been able to come to a decision. Such in short is my sorry plight."

This is the usual state of many youths and young women. There is only one way for such young people. They have to avoid all contact of the opposite sex. The checks and restraints described in our books were the result of experience gained during those times. They were, no doubt, necessary for the writers and their readers. Today every aspirant has to pick out from them the necessary items and add new ones which experience may make necessary. If we draw a circle round the goal to be reached, we shall find many ways leading to the goal, each one according to his needs.

An aspirant who may not know his own mind will certainly fail if he blindly copies another.

Having said so much by way of caution, I must add that to find the true way to *brahmacharya* through a study of court cases and erotic literature is as fruitless as the effort to find the proverbial flower in the heavens above. The true way is not to be found in English law courts or in the novels. They have their use in their limited field, but they are of no use to the aspirant after *brahmacharya*. English men and women who tread the difficult path are not afflicted by the imaginings of the correspondent quoted above. Those whom I have in mind have their God enthroned in their hearts. They are neither self-deceived nor would they deceive others. To them their sisters and mothers are ever thus and for them all women are in the place of sisters and mothers. It never occurs to them that every contact with them is sinful or that it is fraught with danger They see in all women the same God they see in themselves. It will betray lack of humility to say that such specimens do not exist because we have not come across them. Lack of belief in the possibility would also amount to lowering the standard of *brahmacharya*. There is as much error in saying that there is no God because we have not seen Him face to face or because we have not met men who have had that experience, as there is in rejecting the possibilities of *brahmacharya* because our own evidence is to the contrary.

Harijan, 6-7-1947

52
IN DEFENCE

The correspondent from whose letter I had quoted the other day writes :

> "I entirely agree with the opinion you have expressed on the views set forth in a letter I wrote eleven years ago. Nevertheless, I lacked the courage to act up to them I often say to myself, 'Why enter the black hole at all ?' In spite of your presenting society with the ideal man of your imagination for its own good, it seems to me that that good would be better served by keeping intact the restraints handed down by men of experience. It is true that sex-consciousness should be removed. It is also true that the feeling of ownership of women should likewise go. But in propagating these fundamental rules, persons have been known to have damaged our society to a great extent. It seems to me to be dangerous. X objects even to sitting on the same mat with women. He may be an example of faith in our old wisdom. Nevertheless, the idea is not to be lightly set aside. The sage advice of the *Gita* that whatever the great in a society do, common people will follow, is unforgettable. Therefore, it seems to me that it is wisdom for those who have reached a higher state to act in accordance with the capacity of those many who belong to a lower state and this they will do, in order to avoid the risk of the lower state people resorting to thoughtless imitation. I admit, however, one apt argument in defence of your position, viz., that if there was nobody to demonstrate the feasibility of the higher state, society would never develop faith in that state. Therefore, someone has got to demonstrate the feasibility of reaching the high state. I seem to reach the conclusion that every great person has got to model his behaviour after due appreciation of the *pros* and *cons*."

I like the above criticism. Everyone should learn how to measure his own weakness. He, who, knowing his own weakness, imitates the strong, is bound to fail. Hence have I contended that everyone should construct his own restraints.

I do not think that X goes so far as to object to squatting on the same mat as women. I should be surprised if your statement proved true. I could not appreciate such prohibition. I have never known him to defend it.

I can only detect ignorance in likening woman to the black hole. The very thought is insulting to both man and woman. May not her son sit side by side with his mother or the man share the same bench in a train with his sister ? He who suffers excitement through such juxtaposition is surely worthy of pity.

Although I believe that for the sake of social good one should abandon many things, I feel that there is room for wise discretion even in the observance of such restraints. In Europe there is a society of men which advocates stark nakedness. I was asked to join that society and I refused to do so. My objection was that the proposition was intolerable and that unless a measure of self-control had become an established fact, the exhibition of nakedness was not desirable. This I said although I believe that theoretically speaking, there is nothing harmful in both the sexes going about in utter nakedness. It is said that in their state of innocence Adam and Eve had not even a fig leaf to cover their nakedness. But immediately they became aware of their nakedness, they began to cover themselves and were hurled from Paradise. Are we not in that inherited fallen state ? If we were to forget that, we would surely harm ourselves. I consider this an instance of observing prohibition for the sake of social good.

Contrarywise, for the very sake of society it was just and proper to give up untouchability although it was fashionable among people of accepted merit. Marriage of nine-year-old girls used to be defended on the ground of social good. So was prohibition against crossing the seas. Such instances can be multiplied. Every custom has to be examined on its own merits.

Restraints must not be such as to perpetuate sex-consciousness. In most of our daily transactions such consciousness is absent. Such occasion, so far as I am aware, is only one. If the consciousness afflicted us the whole day long, we should be considered to have a corrupt mind and such a mind is not conducive to social welfare. If the villagers were continuously sex-conscious, they would be useless for advancement of self and society.

Harijan 27-7-1947.

53

ON CONTRACEPTIVES

During Gandhiji's Bengal tour, while answering questions in one of the workers' meetings, he said that a woman who really and truly prepared her children for the service of the motherland, need not do anything more. A friend interpreted this remark as a confirmation of the popular belief that woman's one duty was to look after the home and bring up the children properly. Gandhiji laughed and said: "People always interpret things in the way that suits them. Men and women given to animal enjoyment can never prepare their children for the service of the motherland. It is only those whose law of life is self-control that can do so and such will always find time for service outside the domestic sphere."

He holds strong views against birth control with the help of contraceptives. "Contraceptives," he says, "are an insult to womanhood. The difference between a prostitute and a woman using contraceptives is only this that the former sells her body to several men, the latter sells it to one man. Man has no right to touch his wife so long as she does not wish to have a child, and the woman should have the will power to resist even her own husband."

S. N.

Harijan, 5-5-1946

SELF-RESTRAINT *V.* SELF-INDULGENCE

PART II

EXTRACTS FROM MAHADEV DESAI'S
WEEKLY LETTERS

I

ON THE THRESHOLD OF MARRIED LIFE

The annual meeting of the Gandhi Seva Sangh at Hubli, disturbed by incessant rain, was important for various reasons. I propose to speak of it at length in the next issue. I am going to confine myself in this issue to the two marriages and sacred thread ceremonies we had under the blessings of the members of the Sangh. For me it is a matter of personal gratefulness that prompts me to write these lines. But there were about these apparently private ceremonies things in which the public are likely to be interested, and I therefore make no apology for occupying a part of these columns.

The Sangh itself is an ethical body—a body of public workers who approach the problems of work in a predominantly religious spirit, and their discussions are always full of self-introspection. It was in the fitness of things that Gandhiji decided to perform the marriage ceremonies of his grand-daughter and my sister and the thread ceremonies of my brother and son under the auspices of the Sangh. Nothing could contribute better to the understanding, on the part of the young parties concerned, of the seriousness of the life on which they were about to embark,—above all to a conviction that the ceremonies were no festivities but solemn consecration ceremonies. All outward show and ceremony was eschewed, no invitations to friends or relations were issued, and the parties came in the conviction that they would prize much more the blessings of a body of serious-minded, self-sacrificing public workers than the blessings of relations and friends which they should get as a matter of course. The ceremonies were performed by two *Shastris*. Shastri Rambhatji of Belgaum and Shastri Laxman Joshi of the famous Prajna Pathashala at Wai, who offered their services without the thought of a reward. They knew the meaning of every part of the ceremonies, and Shri

Laxman Shastri translated every *mantra* in very lucid Hindi and insisted on the parties understanding every word that they repeated.

Contrary to his wont, Gandhiji did not address his remarks to the married couples in the presence of the audience, but privately. But they will interest all married couples and I summarize them here as best I can.

"You must know," he said, "that I do not believe in ceremonies except to the extent that they awaken in us a sense of duty. I have had that attitude of mind ever since I began to think for myself. The *mantras* you have repeated and the vows you have taken, were all in Sanskrit, but they were all translated for you. We had the Sanskrit text because I know that the Sanskrit word has a power under the influence of which one would love to come.

"One of the wishes expressed by the husband during the ceremony is that the bride may be the mother of a good and healthy son. The wish did not shock me. It does not mean that procreation is obligatory, but it means that if progeny is wanted, marriage performed in a strictly religious spirit is essential. He who does not want a child need not marry at all. Marriage for the satisfaction of sexual appetite is no marriage. It is *vyabhichara* — concupiscence. Today's ceremony, therefore, means that the sexual act is permitted only when there is a clear desire by both for a child. The whole conception is sacred. The act has therefore to be performed prayerfully. It is not preceded by the usual courtship designed to provide sexual excitement and pleasure. Such union may only be once in a life-time, if no other child is desired. Those who are not morally and physically healthy, have no business to unite, and if they do, it is *vyabhichara* — concupiscence. You must unlearn the lesson, if you have learnt it before, that marriage is for the satisfaction of animal appetite. It is a superstition. The whole ceremony is performed in the presence of the sacred fire. Let the fire make ashes of all the lust in you.

"I would also ask you to disabuse yourselves of another superstition which is rampant nowadays. It is being said that restraint and abstinence are wrong and free satisfaction of the sexual appetite and free love is the most natural thing. There was never a more ruinous superstition. You may be incapable of attaining the ideal, your flesh may be weak; but do not therefore lower the ideal, do not make irreligion your religion. In your weak moments remember what I am telling you. The remembrance of this solemn occasion may well steady and restrain you. The very purpose of marriage is restraint and sublimation of the sexual passion. If there is any other purpose, marriage is no consecration, but marriage for other purposes besides having progeny.

"You are being united in marriage as friends and equals. If the husband is called *swamin*, the wife is *swamini*—each master of the other, each helpmate of the other, each co-operating with the other in the performance of life's tasks and duties. To you, boys, I would say that if you are gifted with better intellects and richer emotions, infect the girls with them. Be their true teachers and guides, help them and guide them, but never hinder them or misguide them. Let there be complete harmony of thought and word and deed between you, may you have no secrets from each other, may you be one in soul.

"Don't be hypocrites, don't break your health in the vain effort of performing what may be impossible for you. Restraint never ruins one's health. What ruins one's health is not restraint but outward suppression. A really self-restrained person grows every day from strength to strength and from peace to more peace. The very first step in self-restraint is the restraint of thoughts. Understand your limitations and do only as much as you can. I have placed the ideal before you—the right angle. Try as best you can to attain the right angle. But if you fail, there is no cause for grief or shame. I have simply explained to you that marriage is a consecration, a new birth, even as the sacred thread ceremony is a consecration and a new birth. Let not what I have told you alarm you or weaken you. Always aim at complete harmony of thought and word and deed. Always aim at purifying your thoughts and everything will be well. There is nothing more potent than thought. Deed follows word and word follows thought. The world is the result of a mighty thought, and where the thought is mighty and pure, the result is always mighty and pure. I want you to go hence armed with the armour of a noble ideal, and I assure you no temptation can harm you, no impurity can touch you.

"Remember the various ceremonies that have been explained to you. Look at the simple-looking ceremony of *madhuparka*. The whole world is full of *madhu*—sweet nectar or honey—if only you will partake of it after the rest of the world has taken its share of it. It means 'enjoyment by means of renunciation.'

"But if there is no desire for progeny, should there be no marriage?" asked one of the bridegrooms.

"Certainly not. I do not believe in Platonic marriages. In certain rare cases, men are known to have married women to protect the latter and not for any physical union at all. But those cases are very rare indeed. You must read all that I have written on pure married life. What I read in the *Mahabharata* is daily growing upon me. Vyasa is described therein as having performed *niyoga* He is not described as beautiful, but he was the reverse of it. His form is represented as terrible, he made no amorous gestures, but he smeared his whole body with ghee before he performed the union. He performed the act not for lust but for procreation. The desire for a child is perfectly natural, and once the desire is satisfied, there should be no union.

"Manu has described the first child as *dharmaja*—born out of a sense of duty, and children born after the first as *kamaja*—carnally born. That gives in a nutshell the law of sexual relations. And what is God but the Law? And to obey God is to perform the Law. Remember that you were thriced asked to repeat: 'I will not transgress the Law in any respects.' Even if we had a handful of men and women prepared to abide by the Law, we should have a race of men and women stalwart and true.

"Remember that I really came to enjoy my married life after I ceased to look at Ba sexually. I took the vow of abstinence when I was in the prime of youth and health, when I was young enough to enjoy married life in the accepted sense of the term. I saw in a flash that I was born, as we all are, for a sacred mission. I did not know this when I was married. But on coming to my sense I felt that I must see that the marriage subserved the mission for which I was born. Then indeed did I realize true *dharma*. True happiness came into our lives only after the vow was taken. Ba, though she looks frail, has a fine constitution and toils from morning until night. She would never have done so, had she continued to be the object of my lust.

"And yet I woke up late in the sense that I had lived the married life for some years. You are lucky enough to be aroused in good time. Circumstances, when I was married, were as unpropitious as they could be. For you they are as propitious as they could be. There was one thing, though, that I possessed and that carried me through. It was the armour of truth. That protected me and saved me. Truth has been the very foundation of my life. *Brahmacharya* and *ahimsa* were born later out of truth. Whatever, therefore, you do, be true to yourselves and to the world. Hide not your thoughts. If it is shameful to reveal them, it is more shameful to think them."

Harijan, 24-4-1937.

II

A BIRTH CONTROL ENTHUSIAST

Quite a striking contrast to the old peasant who had brought his all in the service of the poor was Mrs. How-Martyn, the birth control enthusiast from England, who had brought her gospel for the relief of the poor in India and who came to convert Gandhiji or be converted. Of course, she has come to India for the first time and has hardly seen anything of the poor. So she talked of her experience of the British slums and put in a strong plea for the 'poor woman' who had to submit to the strong man.

On her very first premise Gandhiji joined issue. "There is no *poor* woman. Poor woman is mightier than man, and I am quite prepared to demonstrate it to you if you come to the villages of India. Any woman there would tell you that, if she did not want it, there was no man born of woman who could compel her. I can say this from my own experience in relation to my wife, and mine is no solitary instance. If the will to die rather than to yield is there, no monster can make the woman yield. No, it is a mutual affair. Men and women both are a mixture of the brute and the divine, and if we can subdue the brute, it is well and good."

"But what is the woman to do, if the man for the sake of having not more children goes to another woman?"

"So now you are shifting your own ground. If you misconceive your premises, you are bound to come to wrong conclusions. Don't assume things and try to unman man and unwoman woman. Let me understand the basis of your gospel. When I said your birth control propaganda was sufficient introduction, there was some seriousness behind the joke, for, I know that there are some men and women who think that in birth control lies our salvation. Let me, therefore, understand the basis from you."

"I do not see in it the salvation of the world," said Mrs. How-Martyn, "but what I say is that without some form of birth control there is no salvation. You would do it in one way, I would do it in another. I advocate your method as well, but not in all cases. You seem to regard a beautiful function as something objectionable Two animals are nearest to the divine when they are going to create new life. There is something very beautiful in the act."

"Here again you are labouring under a confusion," said Gandhiji. "The creation of a new life is nearest the divine, I agree. All I want is that one should approach that act in a divine way. That is to say, man and woman must come together with no other desire than that of creating a new life. But if they come together merely to have a fond embrace, they are nearest the devil. Man unfortunately forgets that he is nearest the divine, hankers after the brute instinct in himself and becomes less than the brute."

"But why must you cast aspersion on the brute?"

"I do not. The brute fulfils the law of his own nature. The lion in his majesty is a noble creature and he has a perfect right to eat me up; but I have none to develop paws and pounce upon you. Then I lower myself and become worse than the brute."

"I am sorry," said Mrs. How-Martyn, "I have expressed myself very badly. I confess that in a majority of cases it is not going to be their salvation, but a factor which will conduce to higher life. You understand what I mean, though I am afraid I have not been able to make myself quite clear."

"Oh, no. I do not want to take any undue advantage of you. But I want you to understand my viewpoint. Do not run away with misconceptions. Man must choose either of the two courses, the upward or the downward; but as he has the brute in him, he will more easily choose the downward course than the upward, especially when the downward course is presented to him in a beautiful garb. Man easily capitulates when sin is presented in the garb of virtue, and that is what Marie Stopes and others are doing. If I were to popularize the religion of indulgence, I know that men would simply clutch at it. I know that, if people like you in selfless zeal cried themselves hoarse upholding your doctrine, you might even ride to apparent victory; but I also know that you will ride to certain death, of course totally unconscious of the mischief you are doing. The downward instinct requires no advocacy, no argument. It is there embodied in them, and unless you regulate and control it, there is danger of disease and pestilence."

Mrs. How-Martyn, who until now seemed to accept the distinction between the divine and the devilish, contended that there was really none and that they were much more allied than people imagined. That really is the thing at the back of all birth control philosophy, and the enthusiasts forget that that is their Achilles' heel.

"So you think the devil and the divine are the same? Do you believe in the sun? And if you do, don't you think you must believe in the shadow?" asked Gandhiji.

"Why should you call 'shadow' devil?"

"You may call it 'no-God', if you like."

"I do not think there is no-God in the shadow. There is life everywhere."

"There is a thing like absence of life. Do you know that Hindus will reduce the body of the dearest one to ashes as soon as life in it is extinct? There is an essential unity in all life, but there is diversity, too, and one has to penetrate it and find the unity behind — but not by intellect, as you are trying to do. Where there is truth, there must be untruth; where there is light, there must be shadow. You cannot realize the wider consciousness, unless you subordinate completely reason and intellect, and the body, too."

Mrs. How-Martyn looked puzzled, and time was fast running against her. But Gandhiji said: "No. I am prepared to give you more time. But for that you must come to Wardha and stay with me. I am as great an enthusiast as you, and you must not leave India until you have converted me or converted yourself."

As I listened to the rapturous discourse, which other engagements had to bring to an end, I was reminded of the great words of St. Francis of Assisi: "Light looked down and beheld darkness. 'Thither will I go,' said Light. Peace looked down and beheld War; 'Thither will I go,' said Peace. Love looked down and beheld Hatred; 'Thither will I go,' said Love—and the Word was made Flesh and dwelt among us."

Harijan, 1-2-1935.

III

PROBLEM OF BIRTH CONTROL

But how the villager and the villages haunt Gandhiji's days and dreams, will appear most vividly in a discourse that he had with Swami Yoganand, who has just returned home after a long stay in America. On his way to Ranchi he halted here for a couple of days and had long conversations with Gandhiji. His mission in America was purely spiritual and he said he had tried everywhere to show by preaching and example the spiritual message of India to the world. It is his conviction that 'Crucified India will mean the salvation of the world.'

Two problems he wanted to discuss with Gandhiji—the problem of Evil and the problem of Birth Control. He had seen a good deal of the seamy side of American life and knew Judge Lindsay intimately. . . .

'I shall now change the subject,' said the Swami. 'You would prefer self-control to birth control?'

'I think artificial birth control or birth control according to methods suggested today and recommended in the West is suicidal. When I say 'suicidal', I do not mean resulting in the extinction of the race; I mean suicidal in a higher sense of the term, that is to say, these methods make man lower than the brute; they are immoral.'

'But how long are we to tolerate indiscriminate procreation? I know a man who used to purchase a *seer* of milk, and went on diluting it with water in order to divide it between his children whose number increased every year. Don't you think this was a sin?'

'It is a sin to bring forth unwanted children, but I think it is a greater sin to avoid the consequences of one's own action. It simply unmans man.'

'What then is the most practical method of telling man this truth?'

'The most practical method is to live the life of self-control. Example is better than precept.'

'But the West asks us, "Why is it that you have greater child mortality and lower life average than we, though you regard yourselves as more spiritual than the West?" Do you believe in many children, Mahatmaji?'

'I believe in no children.'

'Then the whole race will be extinct.'

'It won't be extinct, it will be transformed into something better. But it can never happen, for we have inherited from eternity the sex instinct from our progenitors. It means a tremendous effort to check this habit of ages, and yet it is a simple effort. Absolute renunciation, absolute *brahmacharya* is the ideal state. If you dare not think of it, marry by all means, but even then live a life of self-control.'

'Have you any working method to teach this to the masses?'

'It is, as I said a moment ago, to attain complete self-control and go and live that life amongst the masses. A life of self-restraint and denial of all luxuries cannot but have its effect on the masses. There is an indissoluble connection between self-control and the control of the palate. The man who observes *brahmacharya* will be controlled in every one of his acts and will be humble.'

'I see what you mean,' said the Swami. 'The masses do not know the happiness of self-control and we have to teach them that. But what about the argument of the West I referred to before?'

'I do not think that we are more spiritually-minded than the West. If we were, we should not have fallen so low. But because the average life of a Westerner is much higher than ours, it does not prove the spirituality of the West. Whoever is spiritually-minded must show a better, not necessarily a longer, life.'

Harijan, 7-9-1935

IV

MRS. SANGER AND BIRTH CONTROL

IN SEVERAL ASPECTS

Since the time Mrs. Margaret Sanger, the famous leader of the Birth Control movement, paid a visit to Wardha, I have seen several different aspects of her. First as she appeared to me there during those remarkable interviews with Gandhiji - interviews in which she appealed to Gandhiji as a great moral teacher "to advise something practical, something that can be applied to solve the problem of too frequent child-bearing," "to give some message for those who are not yet sure but who are anxious to limit their families." She seemed, during those conversations into which Gandhiji poured his whole being, desperately anxious to find out some point of contact with Gandhiji, to find out the utmost extent to which he could go with her. And he did indicate the extent. Her second aspect is revealed in her article in the *Illustrated Weekly of India* in which she ridicules what she calls Gandhiji's "amazing boast" of having known the experiences and the aspirations of thousands of women in India." Mrs. Sanger approached Gandhiji in Wardha for solution of a tough problem, because, as she herself said, "there were thousands, millions, who regard your word as that of a saint," and yet she ridicules his claim to know these women's aspirations and experiences," thousands of whom marched to jail at his word. All she is concerned about in this article is to prove that Gandhiji does not know the women of India. She utters not a word about the points of agreement she sought at the interview, and the extent to which Gandhiji said he was prepared to go with her. The third aspect is revealed in an address on " Woman of the Future " that she delivered before the World Fellowship of Faiths. I shall come to this later in my article.

THE INTERVIEW

To come to the interview. As I have already said, Gandhiji poured his whole being into his conversation. He revealed himself inside out, giving Mrs. Sanger an intimate glimpse of his own private life. He also declared to her his own limitations, especially the stupendous limitation of his own philosophy of life – a philosophy that seeks self-realization through self-control, and said that from *him* there could be one solution and one alone. " I could not recommend the remedy of birth control to a woman who wanted my approval. I should simply say to her : "My remedy is of no use to you. You must go to others for advice." Mrs. sanger cited some hard cases. " I agree, " said Gandhiji, " there are hard cases. Else birth control enthusiasts would have no case. But I would say, do devise remedies by all means, but the remedies should be other than the ones you advise. If you and I as moral reformers put our foot down on this remedy and said, 'You must fall back on other remedies,' those would surely be found. " Both seemed to be agreed that woman should be emancipated, that woman should be the arbiter of her destiny. But Mrs. Sanger would have Gandhiji work for woman's emancipation through her pet device, just as believers in violence want Gandhiji to win India's freedom through violence, since they seem to be sure that non-violence can never succeed.

She forgets this fundamental difference in her impatience to prove that Gandhiji does not know the women of India. And she claims to prove this on the ground that he makes an impossible appeal to the women of

India — the appeal to resist their husbands. Well, this is what he said: "My wife I made the orbit of all women. In her I studied all women. I came in contact with many European women in South Africa, and I knew practically every Indian woman there. I worked with them. I tried to show them they were not slaves either of their husbands or parents, not only in the political field but in the domestic as well. But the trouble was that some could not resist their husbands. The remedy is in the hands of women themselves. The struggle is difficult for them, and I do not blame them. I blame the men. Men have legislated against them. Man has regarded woman as his tool. She has learned to be his tool and in the end found it easy and pleasurable to be such, because when one drags anothor in his fall the descent is easy . . . I have felt that during the years still left to me, if I can drive home to women's minds the truth that they are free, we will have no birth control problem in India. If they will only learn to say 'no' to their husbands when they approach them carnally, I do not suppose all husbands are brutes, and if women only know how to resist them, all will be well. I have been able to teach women who have come in contact with me how to resist their husbands. The real problem is that many do not want to resist them . . . No resistance bordering upon bitterness will be necessary in 99 out of 100 cases. If a wife says to her husband, 'No, I do not want it,' he will make no trouble. But she hasn't been taught. Her parents in most cases won't teach it to her. There are some cases, I know, in which parents have appealed to their daughters' husbands not to force motherhood on their daughters. And I have come across amenable husbands too. I want woman to learn the primary right of resistance. She thinks now that she has not got it."

What is there in this to show that Gandhiji did not know the women of India or did not know women, I do not understand. Jesus, who set the seal of his own blood upon his precept "Love thine enemy", and "Resist not evil", would be held to have uttered the precept in ignorance of mankind, simply because we are far away from realization of that principle!

Mrs. Sanger raises the phantasmagoria of "irritations, disputes, and thwarted longings that Mr. Gandhi's advice would bring into the home", of the absence of "loving glances" and of "tender good night kisses" and of "words of endearment", forgetting all the while that birth control and all its tender or vulgar accompaniments have contributed in America to countless irritations and disputes, divorces and worse. But the America we know through books of a realist reformer like Upton Sinclair would seem to be different from the America that Mrs. Sanger claims to know. She cited cases of great nervous and mental breakdowns as a result of the practice of self-control. Gandhiji spoke from a knowledge of the numerous letters he received every mail, when he said to her that "the evidence is all based on examination of imbeciles. The conclusions are not drawn from the practice of healthy-minded people. The people they take for examples, have not lived a life of even tolerable continence. These neurologists assume that people are expected to exercise self-restraint while they continue to lead the same ill regulated life. The consequence is that they do not exercise self-restraint but become lunatics. I carry on correspondence with many of these people and they describe their own ailments to me. I simply say that if I were to present them with this method of birth control they would lead far worse lives."

He told her that when she went to Calcutta she would be told by those who knew what havoc contraceptives had worked among unmarried young men and women. But evidently for the purpose of the conversation, at any rate, Mrs. Sanger confined herself to propagation of knowledge of birth control among married couples only.

Mrs. Sanger mocks at what she calls Mr. Gandhi's "appalling fear of licentiousness and over-indulgence" following upon a life of unrestrained birth control, and she pointedly asks: "Has he ever thought that the same frequency can occur during the nine months of a woman's pregnancy ?" I must say that in advancing this argument Mrs. Sanger is less than fair to her own sex. None but the most abnormally lewd or suppressed would submit to even legitimate sexual advances during pregnancy.

What was to be done with couples who wanted to resist the impulse of sex and yet could not do so ?

SEX-LOVE AND SEX-LUST

Mrs. Sanger was thus led on to her apotheosis of "sex-love", which she said "is a relationship which makes for oneness, for completeness between husband and wife and contributes to a finer understanding and a greater spiritual harmony." An obviously harmless proposition, but full of confusion when in the same breath one identifies love with lust and then tries to separate the one from the other. The distinction that Gandhiji drew between love and lust will be evident from the following extracts from the coversation :

G. : When both want to satisfy animal passion without having to suffer the consequences of their act it is not love, it is lust. But if love is pure, it will transcend animal passion and will regulate itself. We have not had enough education of the passions. When a husband says, "Let us not have children, but let us have relations," what is that but animal passion ? If they do not want to have more children, they should simply refuse to unite. Love becomes lust the moment you make it a means for the satisfaction of animal needs. It is just the same with food. If food is taken only for pleasure, it is lust. You do not take chocolates for the sake of satisfying your hunger. You take them for pleasure and then ask the doctor for an antidote. Perhaps you will tell the doctor that whisky befogs your brain and he gives you an antidote. Would it not be better not to take chocolates or whisky ?

Mrs. S. : No. I do not accept the analogy.

G. : Of course you will not accept the analogy because you think this sex expression without desire for children is a need of the soul, a contention I do not endorse.

Mrs. S. : Yes, sex expression is a spiritual need and I claim that the quality of this expression is more important than the result, for, the quality of the relationship is there regardless of results. We all know that the great majority of children are born as an accident, without the parents having any desire for conception. Seldom are two people drawn together in the sex act by their desire to have children. . . . Do you think it possible for two people who are in love, who are happy together, to regulate their sex act only once in two years, so that relationship would only take place when they wanted a child? Do you think it possible?

G. : I had the honour of doing that very thing and I am not the only one.

Mrs. Sanger thought it was illogical to contend that sex union for the purpose of having children would be love, and union for the satisfaction of the sexual appetite was lust, for the same act was involved in both. Gandhiji immediately capitulated and said he was ready to describe all sexual union as partaking of the nature of lust. He made the whole thing abundantly clear by citing facts from his own life. "I know," he said, "from my own experience that as long as I looked upon my wife carnally, we had no real understanding. Our love did not reach a high plane. There was affection between us always, but we came closer and closer the more we or rather I became restrained. There never was want of restraint on the part of my wife. Very often she would show restraint, but she rarely resisted me although she showed disinclination very often. All the time I wanted carnal pleasure I could not serve her. The moment I bade good-bye to a life of carnal pleasure our whole relationship became spiritual. Lust died and love reigned instead."

But Mrs. Sanger probably regards every free embrace an act of love and a married life without sexual relationship and its blandishments a dull lifeless affair. Gandhiji's own personal witness made no impression upon her. She dismissed it as that of an 'idealist', as appears from her veiled sneer at "that small group of idealists who have sublimated their sex energies into creative action, into the activities of his own National Congress." I do not think during all his conversation Gandhiji even once referred to the Congress or Congressmen. Mrs. Sanger forgets that all moral advancement has proceeded on the practice of a "small group of idealists" and that even the apparent progress of her own movement depends a lot on the clever way in which she idealizes her nostrum and describes it as the upward path "demanding of us who inhabit this globe all that we possess in intelligence, knowledge, courage, vision and responsibility," the road that "leads to the fulfilment of human destiny on this planet!"

A POSSIBLE WAY OUT

Mrs. Sanger is so impatient to prove that Gandhiji is a visionary that she forgets the practical ways and means that Gandhiji suggested to her.

"Must the sexual union take place only three or four times in an entire lifetime?" she asked.

"Why should people not be taught," replied Gandhiji, "that it is immoral to have more than three or four children and that after they have had that number they should sleep separately? If they are taught this, it would harden into custom. And if social reformers cannot impress this idea upon the people, why not a law? If husband and wife have four children, they would have had sufficient animal enjoyment. Their love may then be lifted to a higher plane. Their bodies have met. After they have had the children they wanted, their love transforms itself into a spiritual relationship. If these children die and they want more, then they may meet again. Why must people be slaves of this passion when they are not of others? When you give them education in birth control, you tell them it is a duty. You say to them that if they do not do this thing, they will interrupt their spiritual evolution. You do not even talk of regulation. After giving them education in birth control you do not say to them 'thus far and no further'. You ask people to drink temperately, as though it was possible to remain temperate. I know these temperate people."

And yet as Mrs. Sanger was so dreadfully in earnest Gandhiji did mention a remedy which could conceivably appeal to him. That method was the avoidance of sexual union during unsafe periods, confining it to the 'safe' period of about ten days during the month. That had at least an element of self-control which had to be exercised during the unsafe period. Whether this appealed to Mrs. Sanger or not I do not know. But therein spoke Gandhiji the truth-seeker. Mrs. Sanger has not referred to it anywhere in her interviews or her *Illustrated Weekly* article. Perhaps if birth controllers were to be satisfied with this simple method, the birth control clinics and propagandists would find their trade gone.

INCONSISTENT ?

But I come to a third aspect of Mrs. Sanger. Her address to the World Fellowship of Faiths is most revealing. She frankly speaks there on behalf of her country where "there are more criminal abortions performed than in any other country in the world. The national total of abortions has been estimated to top 2,000,000 per year. This total does not include the number brought about by drugs or by instruments used by the pregnant woman herself." Let it be remembered that it is not only the married woman who is thought of here. It is the unmarried woman too, and Mrs. Sanger would not really mind arming her with contraceptives. "The infinitely more complicated problem of abortion" can be only solved, she says, "by a proper, safe, dependable means of birth control." In the present state of society abortions are inevitable, and so birth control is also inevitable ! The vicious circle is complete. Mrs. Sanger makes a fervent appeal for preventing the " misuse and tragic waste of the greatest creative force within human nature itself." She forgets that contraceptives will provide the most infernal engine of that waste and misuse.

But I have come across in her address a startling argument which would take away from the seriousness of all her arguments. "Japan is breaking her own record for population increase ! The whole crisis in the Far East — so menacing to the peace of the world at large — grows out of this 'full speed ahead' cradle competition between Asiatic races. Is it not time for the League of Nations or the World Court to turn on this red traffic light? Japan's determination to find an outlet for this surplus population precipitates the so-called 'undeclared war' against the Chinese, the creation of the puppet State of Manchukuo, the breaking of solemn treaties, the sowing of the seeds of another World War." Another yellow peril? Is it a humanitarian that speaks here, or someone vastly different therefrom? I wonder.

Harijan, 25-1-1936

* * *

MRS. SANGER'S LETTER

Mrs. Sanger has sent me a letter which I must publish in fairness to her :

Dear Mr. Desai,

In your article giving out the interview between Mr. Gandhi and myself you say that in my article in the *Illustrated Weekly* I wrote only on one point of the conversation In this you are quite correct That was all I meant to give out or to discuss in that article

May I also say that before I sent the article I read it to a dear and loyal friend of yours and Mr. Gandhi's, Muriel Lester, who was the one who suggested what you called a "veiled sneer". Please be assured that I have only the highest regard and respect for all those brave men and women who are working for India's freedom. If you will look up my own record, you will find my name among that first group of men and women in America who in 1917 organized themselves to help over there for the freedom of India here.

The next point in your article in which I think you are also in error is that you seem to indicate that Mr. Gandhi accepted in our conversation the method of the Safe Period. I think you will look over the typed statement. You will find him saying "It does not repel me as the other does," but he did not commit himself beyond that, though I pressed for a more definite statement. I would not consider it fair to Mr. Gandhi to make the statements you have given out for publicity. Nor do I think Mr. Gandhi would agree to your last paragraph about the propagandist "trade". That sentence and intimation is not worthy of one like yourself who has worked selflessly in a cause for humanity.

The birth control workers have battled and are still working selflessly and without remuneration for a cause they consider to be a fundamental human right, and a cause for human liberty and progress, and it is unfair, unkind and untrue to play to the opposition by making a trite remark which has no foundation in fact.

Sincerely yours,
MARGARET SANGER

As regards the "veiled sneer", I gladly and gratefully stand corrected. I must say, however, that the generally querulous and flippant tone of her article justified me in reading a sneer where I now understand, none was meant.

As regards the other "error", I would request Mrs. Sanger to remember that whilst she concerned herself with "only one point of the conversation", I could not. I do not think that in saying that Gandhiji would tolerate the "Safe Period" method because it involved a certain measure of self-control, I committed him to a thing he would not have liked to. I simply wanted to show Gandhiji's readiness to agree with his adversary as much as he could. The very reason why he said that "the method does not repel me as the other does", is of the very essence in this matter. Whereas Mrs. Sanger's method leaves one free to indulge oneself all the days of the month, this particular one seemed to have the credit of imposing on one certain measure of self-control.

I see that Mrs. Sanger resents the suggestion about "trade". I did not mean to attribute any "trade" motives to Mrs. Sanger personally. I know that *she* has fought bravely and selflessly for her cause. But there is absolutely no untruth in the statement that there is altogether too much of unseemly propaganda about birth control and all kinds of contraceptives and attractive-looking but shoddy literature which is the stock-in-trade of the average birth control enthusiast. All this serves but to vitiate the cause which Mrs. Sanger is espousing selflessly.

Harijan, 22-2-1936

V

WRONG APOTHEOSIS OF WOMEN*

Gandhiji next dwelt on a topic on which he had spoken in the Subjects Committee, but could not have any resolution thereon as he did not find the proper atmosphere. The occasion was a letter addressed to him by the ladies in charge of a women's movement called *Jyoti Sangh*. The letter enclosed copy of a resolution they had passed condemning the present-day tendencies in literature ragarding the presentation of women. There was, Gandhiji felt, considerable force in the complaint, and he said : "The gravamen of their charge is that the present-day writers give an entirely false picture of women. They are exasperated at the sickly sentimentality with which you delineate them, at the vulgar way in which you dwell on their physical form. Does all their beauty and their strength lie in their physical form, in their capacity to please the lustful eye of men ? Why, the writers of the letter justly ask, should we be eternally represented as meek, submissive women for whom all the menial jobs of the household are reserved, and whose only deities are their husbands ? Why are they not delineated as they really are ? We are, they say, neither aetherial damsels, nor dolls nor bundles

* From an account of the proceedings of the Gujarat Literary Conference held at Ahmedabad in November, 1936.

of passions and nerves. We are as much human beings as men are, and we are filled with the same urge for freedom. I claim to know them and their minds sufficiently well. There was a time in South Africa when I was surrounded by numerous women, all their men-folk having gone to jails. There were some sixty inmates and I had become the brother and father of all the girls and women. Let me tell you that they grew in strength and spirit under me, so much so that they ultimately marched to jails themselves.

"I am told that our literature is full of even an exaggerated apotheosis of women. Let me say that it is an altogether wrong apotheosis. Let me place one simple test before you. In what light do you think of them when you proceed to write about them? I suggest that before you put your pens to paper, think of woman as your own mother, and I assure you the chastest literature will flow from your pens even like the beautiful rain from heaven which waters the thirsty earth below. Remember that a woman was your mother before a woman became your wife. Far from quenching their spiritual thirst some writers stimulate their passions, so much so that poor ignorant women waste their time wondering how they might answer to the description our fiction gives of them. Are detailed descriptions of their physical form an essential part of literature, I wonder? Do you find anything of the kind in the Upanishads, the Quran or the Bible? And yet do you know that the English language would be empty without the Bible? Three parts Bible and one part Shakespeare is the description of it. Arabic would be forgotten without the Quran. And think of Hindi without Tulsidas! Do you find in it anything like what you find in present-day literature about women?"

Harijan, 21-11-1936.

Appendix I

GENERATION AND REGENERATION *

(By William Loftus Hare)

I. GENERATION IN BIOLOGY

Microscopic observation of unicellular life has revealed the fact that in the lowest forms reproduction takes place by fission. Growth follows on nourishment until the maximum size for the species is reached, and then the organism divides its nucleus into two, and soon afterwards its body. Given the normal conditions — water and nourishment — this appears to exhaust its functions but in the case of denial of these conditions there is sometimes observed a reconjunction of two cells, from which rejuvenation but not reproduction may result.

In multicellular life there is nourishment and growth as in the life below it, but a new phenomenon is observed. The group of cells constituting the body are mostly differentiated to separate functions some for obtaining nourishment, some for its distributions, some for locomotion and some for protection, as for instance, the skin The primitive function of fission is abandoned by those to whom new duties are assigned, but is preserved by those cells which occupy a more interior position in the organism. These are guarded and served by the others which have undergone varied differentiation, while they themselves remain as they were. They divide as before, but *within* the multicellular body, and at length some are extruded from it. They have, however, gained a new power, instead of dividing in two as their ancestors did, they undergo segmentation or multiplication of nuclei without separation. This process continues until the organism has reached the normal size and structure of its multicellular species. But in the body we may observe a new feature, the original deposit of germ-cells are not only or chiefly extruded for external reproduction, they themselves supply a continuous stream of fresh units from

* Reprinted from *The Open Court* (Chikago), March, 1926.

their group for interior differentiation, wheresoever they are needed. These undifferentiated germ-cells are thus performing two functions simultaneously, namely: internal reproduction for the building up of the body and external reproduction for the continuation of the species. Here we may clearly distinguish two processes, which we shall call *regeneration* and *generation*. One point more is important here: the regenerative process—internal reproduction—is fundamental for the individual, and therefore necessary and primary the generative process is due to a superfluity of cells, and is therefore secondary. Probably both are closely dependent on nourishment · for if this be low, there will be a deficiency of internal reproduction and no necessity for, or possibility of, external reproduction. The law of life; then, at this level is to feed the *germ-cells*, firstly for regeneration, secondly for generation. In case of deficiency, regeneration must take the first place and generation be suspended. Thus we may learn the origin of the suspension of reproduction and follow it to its later phases of human continence and asceticism generally. Inner reproduction can never be suspended except at the cost of death, the normal origin of which is thus also discerned.

II. REGENERATION IN BIOLOGY

Before passing to the animal and human species, in which sexual differentiation has reached its highest phase and become the norm, we must glance at the intermediate form of reproduction, namely, that which preceded the bi-sexual and followed the non-sexual forms. It has received the mythological name 'hermaphrodite', because it possessed both male and female functions. There still remain a few organisms which exhibit this condition, in which the internal multiplication of germ-cells goes on as above described, but instead of their entire extrusion for external growth, they are only temporarily extruded and passed by intrusion to another part of the body, where they are nurtured until able to begin a life of their own.

The law of growth seems to be that individuals, whether unicellular, multicellular or hermaphrodite, have the potentiality of developing to the stage reached by the parent creature at the time of their extrusion. Thus it is the individual that progresses, each time it gives birth to offspring it is or may be in itself in a higher state of organization than it was before; consequently its offspring will be able to reach the normal point of development attained by its parent. The length of the reproduction period for each species and each individual will differ, but ideally it extends from maturity to approaching decline. Premature or decadent reproduction will secure an inferior offspring according to its dominant conditions. Here, then, we perceive a law for sexual ethic derived from physical conditions. the period when generation is most favourable to the reproduction of the species and to regeneration is full maturity only.

I pass by the history of the differentiation in sex which follows the hermaphrodite, because it is a fact which may be taken for granted. It is necessary to observe, however, a new condition that has made its appearance with the bi-sexual forms. Not only have the 'two halves' of the hermaphrodite become physically separate, but each continues to produce germ-cells independently of the other. The male continues the ancient, fundamental process of internal reproduction by the multiplication of germ-cells (which for external reproduction by extrusion and intrusion are known as *spermatozoa*). the female does likewise, reserving rather than extruding the ova for impregnation by the male germ-cells. In both cases regeneration is primary and absolutely necessary for the individual. Every moment of growth from conception onwards exhibits the increasing process of regeneration. At maturity in the human species generation may take place, but not necessarily for the good of the individual, only for the race. Here, as in the lower forms, if regeneration ceases or is imperfectly performed, disease or death will supervene. Here, too, there is rivalry of interest between the individual and the future race. If there be not superfluity, the use of the germ-cells for generative reproduction will deprive the process of regeneration (internal reproduction) of some of its material. As a matter of fact among civilized human beings sexual intercourse is practised vastly more than is necessary for the production of the next generation and is carried on at the expense of internal reproduction, bringing disease, death and more in its train.

Another and perhaps closer glance may be taken of the human body, using that of the male as an example, though *mutatis mutandis*, the female exhibits similar process.

The central reservoir of germ-cells is the most ancient and fundamental location of biological life. From the first the embryo, daily and hourly, grows by the multiplication of cells nourished by the mother's secretions; here again *feed the germ-cells* is the law of life. As they multiply and differentiate, they assume new forms and functions transitory or permanent as the case may be. The movement of physical birth makes little difference to the process: now through the lips instead of through the *nexus* the infant takes nourishment to feed germ-cells, these in their turn rapidly multiply and pass all over the body to places where they are needed, as they always are, to make good disused tissues. The circulatory system absorbs these cells from their primal seat and disperses them to every part of the body In great groups they take on special duties and form and repair the different organs of the body. They undergo death a thousand times so that life may be preserved in the society of cells to which they belong, all these 'corpses' going to the periphery, and especially to the bones, teeth, skin and hair, hardening in such a way as to give strength and protection to the body Their death is the price of the higher life of the body and all that is dependent upon it. If they did not take nourishment, reproduce, disperse, differentiate and eventually die, the body could not live.

From the germ or sexual cells as already said, come two kinds of life: (1) internal, or regenerative, (2) external, or generative. Regeneration then, as we have called it, is the basis of the life of the body, and it draws its life from the same source as does generation Hence it may be perceived how, in given circumstances, the two processes may be formally opposed to one another and more than formally they may be actually at enmity.

III REGENERATION AND THE UNCONSCIOUS

The process of regeneration is not and cannot be mechanistic in character, but like the primitive fission, is vitalistic. That is to say, it exhibits intelligence and will. To suppose that life separates, differentiates and segregates by a process that is purely mechanistic is inconceivable. True, these fundamental processes are so far removed from our present consciousness as to seem to be uncontrolled by the human or animal will. But a moment's reflection will show that just as the will of the fully developed human being directs his external movements and actions in accordance with the guidance of the intellect — this, indeed, being its function — so the earlier processes of the gradual organization of the body must, within the limits provided by environment, be allowed to be directed by a kind of will guided by a kind of intelligence. This is now known to psychologists as 'the unconscious'. It is a part of our self, disconnected from our normal daily thinking, but intensely awake and alert in regard to its own functions — so much so that it never for a moment subsides into sleep as the consciousness does.

The unconscious, then, is the vital force which superintends the complex processes of regeneration. Its first task is the segmentation of the impregnated ovum, and thereafter, until death, it continues to preserve its appropriate organism by absorbing and despatching the fundamental germ-cells to their respective stations. Though I here may seem to contradict many notable psychologists, I would say that the unconscious is only concerned with the individual and not with the species . therefore, first with regeneration. Only in one sense can the unconscious be said to concern itself with the future generation, to whatsoever state of organization its energy has brought the individual, that the unconscious seeks to conserve. But it cannot do the impossible, it cannot, even with the help of the conscious will, prolong life indefinitely. Therefore it reproduces itself by the impulse of sexual intercourse, in which it may be said the unconscious and the conscious wills unite The gratification, normally, of sexual intercourse may be taken as a sign of there being some purpose to be served beyond that of the individual who eventually pays a price more heavy than he knows. This truth is expressed intuitively in the words of the Hebrew writer who puts a solemn warning into the divine lips. "I will greatly multiply thy sorrow and thy conception, in sorrow thou shalt bring forth children." (Gen. iii. 16)

IV. GENERATION AND DEATH

It is undesirable to load this article with extracts from the writings of scientific specialists, but as the matter here dealt with is so important, and popular ignorance so widespread, I am compelled to make some authoritative quotations. Ray Lankester says:

"It results from the constitution of the protozoon body as a single cell, and its method of multiplication by fission, that death has no place as a natural recurrent phenomenon among these organisms."

Weismann writes: "Natural death occurs only among multicellular organisms, the single-celled forms escape it. There is no end to their development which can be likened to death, nor is the rise of new individuals associated with the death of the old. In the division the two portions are equal: neither is the older nor the younger. Thus there arises an unending series of individuals, each as old as the species itself, each with the power of living on indefinitely, ever dividing, but never dying."

Patrick Geddes writes (in *The Evolution of Sex*, from which the above extracts are taken): "Death, we may thus say, is the price paid for a body, the penalty its attainment and possession sooner or later incurs. Now by a body is meant a complex colony of cells in which there is more or less division of labour." (p. 20)

Again, to quote Weismann's striking words: "The body or *Soma* thus appears to a certain extent as a subsidiary appendage of the true bearers of life—the reproductive cells."

And Ray Lankester has the same idea "Among multicellular animals certain cells are separated from the rest of the constituent units of the body. . . the bodies of the higher animals, which die, may from this point of view be regarded as something temporary and non-essential, destined merely to carry for a time, to nurse and to nourish the more important and deathless fission-products."

But the most striking, and probably most surprising fact among the data before us is the close connection, in higher organisms, between reproduction and death, a subject upon which many scientists write with clarity and certainty. *The nemesis of reproduction is death.* This is patent in many species, where the organism, sometimes the male and sometimes the female, not infrequently dies in continuing the life of the species. Survival of the individual after reproduction is a triumph of life that is not always attained — in some cases never. In his essay on death, Goette has well shown how closely and necessarily bound together are the facts of reproduction and death, which may both be described as katabolic crises. Patrick Geddes writes on this subject (p. 255 *op. cit.*): "The association of death and reproduction is indeed patent enough, but the connection is in popular language usually misstated. Organisms, one hears, have to die, they must therefore reproduce, else the species would come to an end. But such emphasis on posterior utilities is almost always only an afterthought of our invention. The true statement, as far as history furnishes an answer, is not that they reproduce because they have to die, but that they die because they have to reproduce."

And Goette says briefly "It is not death that makes reproduction necessary, but reproduction has death as its inevitable consequence."

After giving a large number of instances Geddes concludes with these remarkable words "In the higher animals the fatality of the reproductive sacrifice has been greatly lessened, yet death may tragically persist, even in human life, as the direct nemesis of love The temporarily exhausting effect of even moderate sexual indulgence is well-known, as well as the increased liability to all forms of disease while the physical energies are thus lowered."

This discussion may be summed up briefly and, I hope, conclusively by saying that in human life the sexual act is essentially katabolic (or a movement towards death) in the male and in parturition of the offspring it is katabolic for the female.

A whole chapter could be written on the effect of undue indulgence on the health of the body. Virility, old age, vitality and immunity from disease are the normal lot of nearly or quite continent persons. A proof of this, if a rather unpleasant one, is derived from the fact that a very large number of diseases in man have been and are cured by the artificial injection of *semen* into debilitated persons.

There may well be a resistance in the mind of the reader to accepting the conclusions offered in the present section of this essay. People will hastily point to the many old and apparently healthy persons who have been parents of large families; they will quote statistics which show that the married live longer than the celibate, and so forth. Neither of these arguments have force in face of the fact that death, scientifically conceived, is not an event which occurs at the end of life but a process which begins — as shown by the authorities I have quoted — with life itself, and continues, moment by moment, to run alongside with life. Anabolic repair and katabolic waste are the parallel forces of life and death. The first leads in the race during youth and early manhood, in middle life they run neck and neck, but in decline the death process gains the lead, and with the last breath, conquers. Everything which leads to this conquest, which hastens it by a day, a year or a decade, is part of the death process. And such, indeed, is sexual intercourse especially when practised to excess.

It is sufficient to say here to those who doubt the authority of my words above that they may do well to consult a most interesting and informative work entitled *The Problem of Age, Growth and Death*, by Charles S. Minot [1908, John Murray], in which the author expounds the physiology of decay and death. Not being a medical book, but a group of popular lectures, specific diseases and sexuality are but lightly discussed. The one fact upon which I rely is that natural death is a *process*, not an isolated event. But the book that I value above all others on the subject of sexuality is *Regeneration, the Gate af Heaven* by Dr. Kenneth Sylvan Guthrie [Boston, the Barta Press], whose title indicates a predominantly spiritual aim, although the physical and ethical aspects are fully discussed, and supported by hosts of scientific and patristic authorities. Strangely enough, however, the author does not emphasize the relation of sex to death, which is the subject of this section of my essay.

V. The Organ of the Mind

The extent of the static opposition between generation and regeneration may be realized when we consider the higher functions of the body, and particularly the physical organ of the mind. The nervous system — cerebro-spinal and sympathetic — are, like all other organs, built up of cells that have once been germ-cells, drawn from the deepest seat of life: in continuous streams they are distributed and differentiated to the ganglia of the systems, and of course, in immense quantities to the brain. Withdrawal of germ-cells from their upward, regenerative course for generative or merely indulgent purposes, deprives the organs of their full replenishing stock of life, to their cost, slowly and ultimately. It is these physical facts which constitute the basis of a personal sexual ethic, counselling moderation if not restraint,—at any rate explaining the origin of restraint, as said above.

I do not hesitate to add to this section one illustration out of several which might be adduced, to show how closely in some philosophical systems continence is believed to minister to mental and spiritual vigour. I allude to the Indian system of *Yoga* The reader may refer to any of the standard translations of Patanjali's *Yoga Sutras* (that by James H. Woods in the Harvard Oriental Series is the best known to me) in order to test the brief statement I now make

It is probably known to those who are familiar with Indian religious and social life that asceticism was and is still practised by the Hindus Originally called *tapas*, it had two aims, one to maintain and increase the powers of the body and the other to transcend the normal powers of the mind. Traditionally one is known as *hathayoga* and is carried to extraordinary degrees of attainment, making bodily perfection an end in itself. The other, known as *rajayoga*, is directed rather towards intellectual and mystical development. Yet the two systems have in common an essential physical ethic, to which I now call attention This is set forth in the classical *sutras* of Patanjali and in many later works derived from this master psychologist of ancient India.

Among the 'hindrances' to the desired attainment, 'passion' is said to be the third (II. 7). Passion is that greed or thirst or desire for either pleasure or the means of attaining it, says the philosopher. Pleasure is to be rejected by the *yogin* because it is intermingled with pain (II. 15). That disposes of the psychological attraction of sexuality, and in later *sutras* we are led to physical considerations.

There are eight aids to *yoga's* end, the first and second are called "Abstentions and Observances" and constitute the preliminary ethic which the *yogin* must observe. It is astonishing that the many babblers on the *yoga* systems either do not know or refrain from saying that the fourth abstention is "Abstinence from incontinence" (II.30), and that "Continence is the control of the hidden organ of generation."

But the consequences of the abstention from incontinence are remarkably rich according to this philosopher, who says (II 38): "As soon as he is grounded in abstinence he acquires energy—that is power. By the acquisition of which he accumulates qualities such as minuteness . . . and when perfected he is endowed with the eight perfections, of which the first is called 'Reasoning' He is able to transfer his thinking to his hearers."

Happy man! Rare attainment! A modern Indian scholar, M N. Dvivedi, has a very significant comment on this *sutra*, with which I will conclude. He says "It is a well-known physiological law that the *semen* has great connection with the intellect, and we might add the spirituality, of man The abstaining from waste of this important element of being gives power, the real occult power such as is desired. No *yoga* is ever reported successful without the observance of this rule as an essential preliminary"

It only remains to be said that in the many commentaries on *yoga* the purpose and process are veiled in quasi-scientific mythology. The 'power' is said to creep silently like a serpent from the lowest *chakram* to the highest: that is, from the tests to the brain.

VI. Personal Sexual Ethic

Ethic in general is derived from facts given in the experience of life whether of individuals or societies or the race. Historically, it has often been formulated by some outstanding personality, and sometimes invested with a divine or semi-divine authority. Moses, the Buddha, Confucius, Socrates, Aristotle, Christ, and great moralists and philosophers who in all countries followed them, all proposed, each in their separate day and country, some criterion by which human conduct might be tried. A general ethical system is dependent, then, upon metaphysics, psychology, physiology and sociology, which together supply the facts, or supposed facts, which speak for themselves. A personal sexual ethic, therefore, for any age or civilization will be drawn from the data which most impress men in their own experience. This personal sexual ethic, like the social sexual ethic, varies from age to age, but it has some elements of stability in it, which are more or less permanent.

In attempting to formulate a personal sexual ethic for these times, one would draw from all known facts and probabilities, especially when these are confirmed by the experience of reliable observers I am not assuming too much when I say that the facts adduced in my sections I to V suggest immediately to the mind of a candid and intelligent reader a number of logical and inevitable conclusions From the point of view of bodily, mental and spiritul welfare, sexual continence would appear to be the irrefutable law deduced from the facts But immediately another law springs up to challenge it—"the law in our members" as the Christian apostle calls it. We are in the presence of an antinomy—law contradicting law The older law is that of Nature, whence we have sexual impulse the newer law is that of intuition, of science, of experience of conviction, of ideal. Obedience to the older law tends to decay and premature death (speaking relatively) the path of the newer law is beset with difficulties so great that one hardly listens seriously to its voice. People cannot get themselves to believe the statement of the case. They begin at once to say But, but, but? It is worthy of remark here that the formulation of the strictest ethic by *yogin*, *bhikkhu* and monk does not, as is so aften believed, rest on mythologic fables or superstitions, but on an intuition of the physiological facts described in this essay

I know of no modern writer who has stated the case for the sexual ethic for the Christian more forcibly or clearly than Leo Tolstoy, the now discredited idealist of what once was Russia. I print it here as an illustration of the old philosopher's views.

102. The instinct of the continuation of the race—the sexual instinct—is innate in man. In the animal condition he

* The reader should remember that Tolstoy's definition of sin has no theological connotation; sin is defined by him as that which constitutes an obstacle to the manifestation of *love*, which in its turn is defined as universal goodwill.

fulfils his destiny by satisfying this instinct, and in so fulfilling it finds welfare.

103. But with the awakening of consciousness, it appears to man that the gratification of this instinct may increase the welfare of his separate being, and he enters into sexual intercourse, not with the object of continuing the race, but to increase his personal welfare. This constitutes the sexual sin. . . .

107. In the first case, when man desires to keep chaste † and to consecrate all his powers to the service of God, sexual sin will consist in any sexual intercourse whatever, even though it has for its object the birth and rearing of children The purest marriage state will be such an innate sin for the man who has chosen the alternative of chastity.

113. The sexual sin, *i.e.*, mistake, for the man who has chosen the service of chastity, consists in this he might have chosen the highest vocation and used all his powers in service of God, and consequently, for the spread of love and towards the attainment of the highest welfare, instead of which he descends to a lower plane of life and deprives himself of his welfare.

114. The sexual sin or mistake for the man who has chosen to continue the race will consist in the fact that, by depriving himself of having children or, at all events, of family relationships, he deprives himself of the highest welfare of sexual life.

115. In addition to this — as with the gratification of all needs — those who try to increase the pleasure of sexual intercourse diminish the natural pleasure in proportion as they addict themselves to lust.

It will be observed that Tolstoy's doctrine is in ethical relativity, the effective absolute is not fixed for man by God or some authoritative teacher, but is chosen by the individual himself. All that is necessary is that he should conform to the law he has accepted.

Such an ethic offers a series of descending prohibitions. To the man who has a conviction in favour of entire continence, and who intelligently controls himself for higher physical and

† The words chaste and chastity are used by the author in their Russian signification which includes complete abstinence from sexual intercourse.

psychic ends, any form of sexual indulgence is disallowed; to the man who has entered into the bond of marriage, sexuality outside it is forbidden. Further, promiscuous or irregular intercourse of the unmarried would nevertheless exclude such a degrading relation as prostitution, while any person engaging in natural act should shun unnatural vices. Finally, to any class of persons indulging at all, over-indulgence would be regarded as an evil, while for the immature and the youthful, indulgence should be postponed. Such is the system of sexual ethic.

I can hardly think that anyone can be found incapable of understanding the nature of this general sexual ethic, and there must be very few who would on serious reflection deny its force. There is a tendency, however, to meet such an ethic by sophistry of various kinds. People suppose that because continence is difficult and undoubtedly rare, its advocacy is invalid. Logically they should say the same of fidelity in marriage — which is in some cases difficult — or restricted indulgence within it, or adherence to the natural practice. If they deny one ideal, they may deny all and permit us to fall into the lowest vices and inordinate lust. Why not? The only reasonable and logical method is to follow the star above us, the star of the ideal that leads us out of one declension after another and enables us to conquer by the power of one law, the power of its antinomy. Thus by the intelligent and volitional practice of this ethic a man may conceivably be raised from the unnatural vices of youth to natural indulgence even if promiscuous; from this he may be drawn to the discipline of married fidelity, and for the sake of himself and his partner, to such restraint as they are able to endure. The same ethic may lead him on to the higher victories of continence, or indeed catch him before he has sunk to the several lower phases of indulgence.

VII. Eros and Agape

The New Testament has much teaching in reference to 'love', and adopts two conceptions, which must be separately examined. The first is that of *eros*, the passive love of life, of the world, of man and woman, of the manifold sensations and emotions that yield us pleasure. This *eros* is not a matter of our wilful choice; we are attracted here and repelled there; we gravitate to life itself, by forces that seem to be greater than ourselves, and to which we, for the most part, respond by appropriate action. Our likes and dislikes, our loves and hates, our affection and disaffection from one system in *eros*. For what does *eros* ask? For welfare: for welfare of that separate personality in which the claims are felt most keenly — namely, for 'myself'. And that welfare is pursued with egoistic motive through every life, every generation, every nation, growing in intensity and remorselessness, until it reaches, as lately, a state of world-war. It passes through innumerable phases, adopts, by the aid of the intellect, all kinds of mechanical and economic devices, and is at the present moment incarnate in the system of modern civilization.

What, then, we may legitimately ask, was the Christian teaching about this *eros*, this love of life? Was it to be despised, neglected, resisted, or stamped out? Or, was it to be given free rein to attain its ends? All the teaching as to *eros* may be summed up in the simple words: "Your Heavenly Father knoweth what thing ye have need of", and "Seek ye first the Kingdom of God and his righteousness, and all these things shall be added unto you". *Eros* is not to be destroyed, but transcended; a higher aim is proposed by Christ which, if attempted with success, will lead to a 'more abundant life' in which a purified *eros* has its share.

It is here we meet with the essential Christian Love called in the New Testament *agape*. We are able to understand at once its distinctive quality as compared with *eros*. *Agape*, unlike *eros*, is an act of personal will. It is 'loving-kindness' that overrides attraction and repulsion, and so can be extended to friend and enemy alike. Christian love emphatically is not, therefore, the weak and sentimental emotion it is so often supposed to be, but is, in its very nature, an effort of the will that rises above all emotion. It is not merely will, but *will qualified by goodness*, and the Christians, in exercising such love accomplish and facilitate for others the aims of their *eros;* like the Heavenly Father, he also "knows what things men have need of". By means of the faculties of imagination and compassion he is prompted to meet their needs, for, as he would that men should do for him, so he strives to do for them: for he knows that *eros* in them, as in him, asks for life. The Christian conception of life, therefore, does not deny the claims of *eros*, but emphasizes the duty of *agape*. Christian ethic is thus a new life direction, a turning round from the way of the world, from the seeking of private welfare, to positive goodwill and universal welfare.

The early Christians were taught, like other people, a 'golden rule', but even though this were intelligible enough they were taught also something still more lofty and metaphysical: men are to imitate God: as He is perfect in loving-kindness, so also must His servants be · "because God is love", *hoti ho · theos agape estin*. (Matt. v, 48; John Ep. I, IV, 8).

VIII. Social Sexual Ethic

Just as society is the extension and co-ordination of the activities of individuals, so a social sexual ethic rises out of a personal one. In other words, society requires additions to and qualifications of the personal ethic, and the chief instance of these is the institution of marriage. A great deal has been written upon the history of marriage by learned scientists, and the data collected are immense. Nothing but the bare conclusion need be cited here in order to enable us to refer to modern expedients that are being offered.

Anciently, and arising out of the facts of the human reproduction, the mother was naturally the more important of the two partners. She was, as she still is, the chief agent of nature's process. Within her and around her are the centres of family growth. Consequently matriarchy, or the rule of the mother, was once widely recognized, and polyandry, the practice of associating several males with the central female, was admitted. There are vestiges of this system still in vogue among the primitive tribes of Asia. Out of it, and partly as a consequence of tribal association, the status of the husband was evolved. One of the several men associated with the mother—the strongest and most attractive defender—was raised to a position of preference. Indeed, the word 'husband' contains the history of the institution down to early Scandinavian times. He was *husbuondi*, the house-dweller, bound, as others were not, to the house. Eventually, the husband became the master of the house, and one of this class the chief or king of the tribe, and just as under the matriarchy the practice of polyandry appeared, so under male rule the practice of polygamy developed.

Psychologically, therefore, if not socially, man is naturally polygamous and woman naturally polyandrous. As a male, the man radiates his desire in many directions always lighting for the time being on the most attractive of the opposite sex. And similarly with the female. But human society, both primitive and modern, could not exist unless some check were placed upon the promiscuous, natural, psychological impulses, which are, in all species and kingdoms below the human, exuberant and prolific. The check invented by society inevitably was marriage, and eventually monogamous marriage. Its only alternative is promiscuity and the utter disruption, at least, of the present form of society. We can, of course, see the contest going on before our eyes. Prostitution, irregular and non-legal unions, adulteries and divorces are the day-to-day evidence that monogamous marriage has not established itself in power over the older and more primitive relationships. Will it ever do so ?

Meanwhile, notice must be given to an expedient that has long been secretly present with us, but has lately shown its face without shame. It is called 'Birth Control', and consists in the use of chemical and mechanical means for preventing conception. Conception, of course, apart from its burden upon the woman, places a restraint for a considerable time upon the man, especially upon the man of good feeling. Birth control or contraception removes all prudential motives for self-restraint and makes it possible for sexual indulgence in marriage to be limited only by the diminution of desire or the advance of age. Apart from this, however, it inevitably has an influence outside the marriage relation. It opens the door for irregular, promiscuous and unfruitful unions, which from the point of view of modern industry, sociology and politics, are full of dangers. I cannot go into these here. It is sufficient to say that by contraception, inordinate sexual indulgence both in and out of marriage is facilitated, and, if I am right in my foregoing physiological arguments, evil must come to both individuals and the race.

IX. Conclusion

Like the seed cast by the sower, this essay will fall into the hands of some who will despise it, of those who from incapacity or sheer idleness will not even understand it. In some of those who for the first time hear of its ideas it will rouse opposition and even anger, but to a few it will appeal as truthful and useful. Yet even they will find doubts and questions rising in their minds. The simplest of them will say to me: "According to your arguments sexual intercourse ought not to take place, the world would then become unpeopled — which is absurd! Therefore you must be wrong." My reply is that I have no such dangerous nostrum to offer. 'Birth Control' is the most potent form of birth prevention and will depopulate the world faster than the attempted practice of continence My purpose is a simple one by offering certain philosophic and scientific truths as a challenge to ignorance and indulgence, I desire to help to purify the sexual life of our time.

Appendix II

CHASTITY AND SENSUALITY*

The subject of sex is a remarkable one, since, though its phenomena concern us so much, both directly and indirectly, and, sooner or later, it occupies the thoughts of all, yet all mankind, as it were, agree to be silent about it, at least the sexes commonly one to another. One of the most interesting of all human facts is veiled more completely than any mystery. It is treated with such secrecy and awe as surely do not go to any religion. I believe that it is unusual even for the most intimate friends to communicate the pleasures and anxieties connected with this fact, much as the external affair of love, its comings and goings are bruited. The Shakers do not exaggerate it so much by their manner of speaking of it as all mankind by their manner of keeping silence about it. Not that men should speak on this or any subject without having anything worthy to say; but it is plain that the education of man has hardly commenced — there is so little genuine intercommunication.

* From *Essays* by Henry David Thoreau.

In a pure society, the subject of marriage would not be so often avoided from shame and not from reverence, winked out of sight, and hinted at only, but treated naturally and simply — perhaps simply avoided, like the kindred mysteries. If it cannot be spoken of for shame, how can it be acted of? But doubtless, there is far more purity, as well as more impurity, than is apparent.

Men commonly couple with their idea of marriage a slight degree at least of sensuality, but every lover the world over believes in its inconceivable purity.

If it is the result of a pure love, there can be nothing sensual in marriage. Chastity is something positive, not negative. It is the virtue of the married especially. All lusts or base pleasures must give place to loftier delights. They who meet as superior beings cannot perform the deeds of inferior ones. The deeds of love are less questionable than any action of an individual can be, for, it being founded on the rarest mutual respect, the parties incessantly stimulate each other to a loftier and purer life, and the act in which they are associated must be pure and noble indeed, for innocence and purity can have no equal. In this relation we deal with one whom we respect more religiously even than we respect our better selves, and we shall necessarily conduct as in the presence of God What presence can be more awful to the lover than the presence of his beloved?

If you seek the warmth even of affection from a similar motive to that from which cats and dogs and slothful persons hug the fire, because your temperature is low through sloth, you are on the downward road, and it is but to plunge yet deeper into sloth. Better the cold affection of the sun, reflected from fields of ice and snow, or his warmth in some still wintry dell. The warmth of celestial love does not relax but nerves and braces its enjoyer. Warm your body by healthful exercise, not by cowering over a stove. Warm your spirit by performing independently noble deeds, not by ignobly seeking the sympathy of your fellows who are no better than yourself. A man's social and spiritual discipline must answer to his corporeal. He must lean on a friend who has a hard breast, as he would lie on a hard bed. He must drink cold water for his only beverage. So he must not hear sweetened and coloured words, but pure and refreshing truths. He must daily bathe in truth cold as spring water, not warmed by the sympathy of friends.

Can love be in ought allied to dissipation? Let us love by refusing, not accepting, one another. Love and lust are far asunder. The one is good, the other bad. When the affectionate sympathize by their higher natures, there is love; but there is danger that they will sympathize by their lower natures, and then there is lust. It is not necessary that this be deliberate, hardly even conscious; but, in the close contact of affection, there is danger that we may stain and pollute one another, for we cannot embrace but with an entire embrace.

We must love our friend so much that she shall be associated with our purest and holiest thoughts alone. When there is impurity we have 'descended to meet', though we know it not.

The *luxury* of affection, — there's the danger. There must be some nerve and heroism in our love, as of a winter morning. In the religion of all nations a purity is hinted at, which, I fear, men never attain to. We may love and not elevate one another. The love that takes us as it finds us degrades us. What watch we must keep over the fairest and purest of our affections, lest there be some taint about them! May we so love as never to have occasion to repent of our love!

There is to be attributed to sensuality the loss to language of how many pregnant symbols? Flowers which, by their infinite hues and fragrance, celebrate the marriage of the plants, are intended, for a symbol of the open and unsuspected beauty of all true marriage, when man's flowering season arrives.

Virginity too is a budding flower, and by an impure marriage the virgin is deflowered. Whoever loves flowers loves virgins and chastity. Love and lust are as far asunder as a flower-garden is from a brothel.

J. Biberg, in the *Amoenitates Botanicoe*, edited by Linnaeus, observes (I translate from the Latin): "The organs of generation, which, in the animal kingdom, are for the most part concealed by nature, as if they were to be ashamed of, in the vegetable kingdom are exposed to the eyes of all; and when the nuptials of plants are celebrated, it is wonderful what delight they afford to the beholder, refreshing the senses with the most agreeable colour and the sweetest odour; and, at the same time, bees and other insects, not to mention the humming-bird, extract honey from their nectaries and gather wax from their effete pollen." Linnaeus himself calls the calyx the *thalamus*, or bridal chamber: and the corolla the *auloeum*, or tapestry of it, and proceeds to explain thus every part of the flower.

Who knows but evil spirits might corrupt the flowers themselves, rob them of their fragrance and their fair hues, and turn their marriage into a secret shame and defilement? Already they are of various qualities, and there is one whose nuptials fill the lowlands in June with the odour of carrion.

The intercourse of the sexes, I have dreamed, is incredibly beautiful, too fair to be remembered. I have had thoughts about it, but they are among the most fleeting and irrecoverable in my experience. It is strange that man will talk of miracles, revelation, inspiration, and the like, as things past, while love remains.

A true marriage will differ in no wise from illumination. In all perception of the truth there is a divine ecstasy, an inexpressible delirium of joy, as when a youth embraces his betrothed virgin. The ultimate delights of a true marriage are one with this.

No wonder that out of such a union, not as end, but as accompaniment, comes the undying race of man. The womb is a most fertile soil.

Some have asked if the stock of man could not be improved, — if they could not be bred as cattle. Let love be purified, and all the rest will follow. A pure love is thus, indeed, the panacea for all the ills of the world.

The only excuse for reproduction is improvement. Nature abhors repetition. Beasts merely propagate their kind; but the offspring of noble men and women will be superior to them selves, as their aspirations are. By their fruits ye shall know them.